The Management of Islamic Activism

SUNY series in Middle East Studies
Shahrough Akhavi, editor

The Management of Islamic Activism

Salafis, the Muslim Brotherhood, and State Power in Jordan

Quintan Wiktorowicz

State University of New York Press

2001

Published by
State University of New York Press

© 2001 State University of New York

For information, address the State University of New York Press,
State University Plaza, Albany, NY 12246

Marketing by Michael Campochiaro
Production by Bernadine Dawes

Library of Congress Cataloging-in-Publication Data

Wiktorowicz, Quintan, 1970–
    The management of Islamic activism : Salafis, the Muslim Brotherhood, and state power in Jordan / Quintan Wiktorowicz.
        p.   cm. — (SUNY series in Middle Eastern studies)
    Includes bibliographical references and index.
    ISBN 0-7914-4835-5 (alk. paper) — ISBN 0-7914-4836-3 (pbk. : alk. paper)
        1. Islam and state—Jordan. 2. Islam and politics—Jordan. 3. Jordan—Politics and government. I. Title. II. Series.

BP63.J6 W55 2001
322' 1'095695—dc21   00-032951

1   2   3   4   5   6   7   8   9   10

For Debra

Contents

Acknowledgments

This book is an ethnographic study of state power and Islamic activism in Jordan. As such, it focuses upon the experiences of both state officials as well as Islamists. Such an endeavor requires building trust with the subjects of research, a process that is not always easy in the Middle East where suspicion of outside scholars can hinder access to the insider's world of politics and social struggle. This is particularly the case for research that deals with Islamic activism. The domestic volatility of the topic often prompts governments to restrict access, while Islamists themselves are frequently reticent to welcome scholars, who could jeopardize their safety and well-being through research.

During my stay in Jordan from 1996 to 1997, I was fortunate to meet a number of individuals who helped overcome such barriers. They not only served as fountains of information, but also provided invaluable contacts that allowed me to expand the ethnographic sample. Introductions from close contacts helped facilitate new meetings and build trust. As a result, I was able to conduct ninety-six interviews with government officials, social movement activists, and Islamists (including moderates as well as those who have engaged in underground activities). This includes interviews with thirty-three Salafis, forty-three volunteers at Islamic Non-Governmental Organizations (NGOs), and ten members of the Muslim Brotherhood. In addition, I visited sixteen NGOs, utilized participant observation to gather data on everyday activities and actions, and collected government and Islamist documents.

Because of the sensitivity of the topic, some of those interviewed will remain anonymous for their safety. This is particularly the case for participants in the Salafi movement, which has suffered from

ix

increased state repression in recent years. Others, especially public figures, are cited and listed in the bibliography. This project would not have been possible without all of their support.

Numerous individuals contributed to this study through support, discussions, and comments, and I am indebted to them for their assistance. Diane Singerman, in particular, has painstakingly provided guidance and encouragement for this research. She has devoted an enormous amount of energy on my behalf and served as a mentor and friend. Chris Stone kindly stepped in for translation work at a moment's notice, while George Marquis helped standardize the transliteration. Najib Hourani patiently listened as I thought through theoretical and conceptual issues and provided his usual insightful commentary. Hamad Dabbas provided contacts at Islamic NGOs and helped me orient the study when I first arrived in Jordan. Mustapha Hamarneh and staff members from the Center for Strategic Studies at the University of Jordan set up interviews and provided essential logistical support. Amer Hadidi served as a research assistant in Jordan and his enthusiasm helped provide momentum for the project. Comments and feedback on various parts of the book were provided by John McCarthy, Ruth Lane, Janine Clark, Denis Sullivan, Debra Cornelius, John Voll, and Diane Singerman. In addition, I benefited from conversations with Vincent Cornell and Charlie Kurzman shortly before the book was completed. All shortcomings are, of course, my own.

I would also like to thank the Binational Jordanian-American Fulbright Commission and the American Center for Oriental Research for their financial and logistical support. Shippensburg University supported trips to conferences where drafts of various chapters of the book were presented. I am also grateful to the staff at SUNY Press, especially my production editor Bernadine E. Dawes, Alan Hewat, Michael A. Rinella, Mike Campochiaro, and Shahrough Akhavi, the editor for the series in Middle East Studies.

Modified sections of the book have appeared in various forms in the *Middle East Journal, Journal of Church and State,* and *Arab Studies Quarterly*. Parts of chapter 1 are from an article titled "Civil Society as Social Control: State Power in Jordan" published by *Comparative Politics* and are reprinted with the journal's permission. Chapter 4 appeared in the *International Journal of Middle East Studies* as "The Salafi Movement in Jordan" and is reprinted with the permission of Cambridge University Press.

List of Tables

Introduction

In April 1989, King Hussein of Jordan initiated a series of reform measures that dramatically altered the political structure of the kingdom. He set forth an agenda of political change to end martial law and ushered in a new period of political liberalization. Various restrictions on political freedoms and civil liberties were repealed, and the most stringent authoritarian measures were curtailed. The role of the security apparatus in the regulation of political activity was reduced as norms of political participation replaced exclusionary practices. In that same year, parliamentary elections were held for the first time since 1966, attracting previously isolated groups and activists from across the political spectrum; and by 1993 twenty political parties had registered with the government. The expansion of formal political participation was accompanied by greater freedom of association and a burgeoning civil society. Jordanians enjoyed new opportunities to form civil society associations and began to act collectively through legal organizations. This process of political liberalization is incomplete and questionable practices persist, but the entire structure of the political system has changed so profoundly that hardly any segment of society remains unaffected.

The Islamic movement in Jordan has undoubtedly benefited enormously from political liberalization measures. In the 1989 parliamentary elections, the movement captured thirty-four of the eighty seats, creating the single largest bloc in the Chamber of Deputies. In 1993, the movement formed the Islamic Action Front Party (IAF), the most powerful political party in the kingdom; and although the IAF won only twenty-two seats in the 1993 elections, it remained a formidable political actor.

In civil society, Islamic groups have taken advantage of new opportunities to form a myriad of formal, grassroots organizations. These Islamic Non-Governmental Organizations (NGOs) provide basic goods and services to communities in a manner Islamists deem consistent with the teachings of the faith. Various organizations, such as medical clinics, hospitals, charitable societies, cultural associations, and schools, have been created to demonstrate how Islam can be applied to everyday life. Slogans such as "Islam is the solution" reflect a belief that these organizations are effective in solving pressing social needs without violating Islamic principles. In the process, Islamic organizations serve as institutions for the production, articulation, and dissemination of religious values, connecting the movement to the community of the faithful through daily interactions. The proliferation of these grassroots societies and the creation of the IAF are attempts to institutionalize the Islamic movement through legal, formal organizations.

Despite political liberalization and the proliferation of Islamic organizations, an alternative pattern of Islamist activism in Jordan rejects civic organization and formal institutionalization. Rather than mobilizing through civil society organizations, many Islamists instead operate through informal social networks. These networks connect like-minded Islamists to one another through a complex web of personal relationships, small group interactions, meetings in private homes, and religious ritual. They are informal in the sense that they are outside the juridical control of the state. Networks form an organizational grid that connects these Islamists to one another as they promote their message of religious change.

These divergent organizational patterns raise a series of important questions that serve as the foundation of this book. Why do Islamic groups use informal networks rather than formal organizations? What kinds of Islamic groups are most likely to mobilize through associational activities in civil society after the advent of democratization? And how do movement networks develop, grow, and serve social movement functions?

In answering these specific questions, this study attempts to contribute to broader debates about the organization of social and political activism. Social movement theory has long viewed formal organizations as mechanisms of collective empowerment. Social movement organizations (SMOs) provide institutional resources for collective action and protest, linking movement members through organizational structure. As stable crucibles for the movement message, SMOs are seen as vital for the institutionalization of mature collective action. Other less formal patterns of mobilization are often characterized as ephemeral or transitory.

Given this perspective, the divergence in Islamist mobilization patterns in Jordan seems puzzling. If the new organizational space provided by political liberalization represents an opportunity for movement empowerment, why do some Islamic groups use informal social networks that seem less stable or structured?

This book argues that the efficacy of formal organizations depends upon the particular political context in which they operate. Formal organizations are regulated by a system of law, whether produced by a democratic regime or an authoritarian ruler, and as a result are subject to exogenous regulative state institutions and practices that condition social movement activities. Regulations, permit requirements, tax codes, repression, and a host of other state instruments define the limits for organizational projects, programs, and objectives. In liberal democracies, such as those in Western societies, these limits do not typically outweigh the benefits of collective action through formal organizations. Formality and the stability it provides, however, are not always assets. In less open political systems, SMOs are vulnerable to state repression and manipulation and may actually harm the movement rather than foster success. It is therefore necessary to elucidate the particular context of movement activities to explain concomitant patterns of organization.[1]

In Jordan, formal organization is more a mechanism of state control than an instrument of collective empowerment. Despite political liberalization, the Jordanian state utilizes an array of administrative techniques to limit the scope and content of civil society organizations. While the most overt forms of repression have been removed, authoritarian tendencies are embedded in bureaucratic processes, procedures, and regulations, which are used to shape the content of social interactions in civil society. Selective administrative practices ensure that civil society organizations are not mobilized to challenge the regime or the political system. Moderate groups, which do not threaten state control, are encouraged to organize while more critical groups find organizational space limited or closed. Authoritarian practices are thus projected through the manipulation of the bureaucracy to support state interests and priorities, a process I term "the management of collective action." The scope of organization has expanded in Jordan, but the content of organizational activities is apolitical and passive in the face of state power.

To escape this form of state control, Islamic groups that challenge the regime retreat to personal networks based upon individuals with shared beliefs and do not rely upon organizations to achieve goals. Because SMOs are subject to the administrative and regulative control of the state, which limits the content of collective action, critical Islamic groups mobilize through informal social networks. These networks are embedded in everyday interactions, practices, and relationships and are more impervious to the surveillance and control of the state. Informal social networks delink individuals from the system of state control, and activists in these networks believe they have more liberty to pursue social movement goals. In effect, networks represent an "exit" from the system of opportunities created by political liberalization.[2] This rejection of formal organizations and the use of informal social networks are borne from a pragmatic assessment of the tactical efficacy of formal organizations. It is a strategic choice informed by the realities of continued state power.

THE MUSLIM BROTHERHOOD AND THE SALAFIS

In Jordan, the divergent effects of state regulative practices on patterns of Islamist activism are apparent when comparing two of the largest Islamic groups in the kingdom—the Muslim Brotherhood and the Salafis. The Muslim Brotherhood is an Islamic reform movement founded in Egypt in 1928 by Hassan al-Banna.[3] Although it initially began as a movement for the reform of individual and social morality, its broader political significance grew to challenge secular leadership in Muslim societies. Its strategy of change was to facilitate a more Muslim society through grassroots programs in education, charity, and social activities. Over time, branches of the Muslim Brotherhood were founded in other Arab countries, including Saudi Arabia, the Sudan, Kuwait, and Jordan. Although the various Brotherhood branches are connected through shared symbolic and ideological linkages, historical experiences differ and there is administrative independence.

Founded in 1945, the Jordanian Brotherhood has historically enjoyed an amicable relationship with the regime. It has never attempted to overthrow the ruling Hashemite family, espoused violence, or operated underground. Its criticisms of government policy are always leveled at the policies themselves, rather than the structure of the political system or regime legitimacy. As a result, the regime has manipulated the state apparatus to favor the formal organization of the Brotherhood through a variety of Islamic NGOs in civil society. These organizations do not challenge the raison d'être of the state or threaten to mobilize mass-based social protest against the regime. Instead, they are devoted to promoting social and religious change through charity and cultural activities.

The Brotherhood has grown to become the single most formally organized social movement in the kingdom, which provides it with a familiar public face. This high profile has led to successful campaigns in professional associations and electoral politics at the national and local level. Because of its success, numerous studies examine the role of the Brotherhood and the IAF, the de facto political wing of the Brotherhood, in the new democracy, using it as a case study to explore the relationship between Islam/Islamic movements and democracy.[4] The result is that research to date has focused almost exclusively upon the Brotherhood,[5] implying that it is representative of the broader Islamic movement in Jordan and leading many scholars, the Jordanian press, and policy makers to use the terms "Islamic movement" and "Muslim Brotherhood" interchangeably.

Despite its importance in society and politics, the Brotherhood is not the single manifestation of Islamic activism in the kingdom; and it is important to examine these other groups to gain a complete understanding. This is especially important given that the Brotherhood is formally organized and does not adequately represent the use of informal social networks among Islamists.

The Salafis constitute another important Islamic group in Jordan, and their use of informal social networks sharply contrasts with the organization of the Muslim Brothers.[6] The Salafis believe that over centuries of practice errant Muslims have introduced religious innovations and distortions, which corrupt the pure message of the Prophet Mohammed. To rectify this condition, the movement advocates a strict return to the fundamentals of the religion as outlined in the Qur'an, Sunna (actions and sayings of the Prophet), and the religious understanding of the first three generations of Muslims. Decisions in every aspect of life must be based upon these sources;

and in instances where particular actions or beliefs were not specifically sanctioned or practiced by the Prophet, they are rejected as un-Islamic. The Salafis are thus attempting to institute religious behavior and practices that capture the purity of Islam, as understood by practitioners during the initial phases of its development. While the Brotherhood is the most politically active Islamic group, Salafi leaders dominate the '*ulama* (religious scholars) of Jordan. They are the sheikhs of religious knowledge and attract the vast majority of students of Islamic learning to traditional Salafi lessons and study circles. This movement has grown substantially since the 1970s and is now ubiquitous in every major city in the kingdom.

Despite the new organizational opportunities presented by political liberalization, the Salafis mobilize through informal social networks rather than formal organizations. The strict Salafi interpretation of Islam and the emergence of several violent Salafi groups in the 1990s challenge regime power. As a result, the regime has limited the organizational opportunities of the movement. Salafis have instead opted to utilize networks of personal relationships for social and political activism. These networks are predicated upon the ideological orientation of the movement, common religious experiences, and personal relationships. Rather than propagating Salafi ideology through grassroots organizations, such as those operated by the Brotherhood, the movement utilizes social networks as institutional resources for activism. Through a variety of interactional contexts, such as lessons in private homes, study groups, and other religious activities, the Salafis communicate, recruit, educate, and facilitate the movement's goal of transforming society and individual religious beliefs.

ORGANIZATIONS, INFORMAL NETWORKS, AND COLLECTIVE ACTION

Very few studies link research on Islamic collective action to broader social movement theory. Those that do tend to focus on the Iranian revolution rather than the more prevalent Sunni Islamic movements that characterize most of the Muslim world.[7] As a result, Islamic movements have remained outside the plethora of theoretical developments in social movement theory, implicitly essentializing Islamic activism as somehow "different" from other forms of collective action. But the rich tradition of social movement research offers theoretical leverage over many of the issues related to Islamic collective action and can be used as an effective tool for enhancing our understanding of Islamic movements. In particular, it helps shift Islamic movement research away from a common focus on ideology to issues of organization. At the same time, the study of Islamic activism provides a new testing ground to challenge social movement theory, thus possibly generating insights for broader debates on social movements.[8]

According to social movement theory, in particular its resource mobilization variant, movements require resources and organization of some kind to mobilize sustained collective action.[9] Though structural strains, relative deprivation, ideology, or the emergence of new political issues may engender grievances, resources and organization are necessary to channel these grievances into directed activism. Social movements are not irrational outbursts of spontaneous opposition; they are structured through mechanisms of mobilization, which provide strategic resources for sustained collective action. As a result, collective action is often patterned, directed, and organized like other forms of institutionalized political activism.

For many social movement theorists, the most important resource for mobilization is the formal social movement organization (SMO). Formal organization is viewed as an effective instrument for empowering politically excluded collectivities because it coordinates and focuses activities, thereby collectivizing what would otherwise remain individualized grievances and concerns. Empirical research supports arguments that organization decreases the cost of participation,[10] facilitates the mobilization of aggrieved groups,[11] and provides the necessary infrastructure to sustain collective action.[12] William Gamson's seminal study of collective action, for example, concludes that formal, centralized, bureaucratic organizations are the most effective mechanism for realizing social movement success because of a clear division of labor, efficient decision-making structures, and a high degree of "combat readiness."[13] In contrast, he argues, other organizational patterns, such as decentralization, non-bureaucratic organization, or factionalism are less likely to succeed.[14] For many social movement theorists, formal organizations with professional staffs and career movement "entrepreneurs" help institutionalize movements and provide enduring collective action stability. Because of the importance of SMOs in social movement theory, movements are frequently conceptualized as interorganizational networks operating within a broader "multiorganizational field" of allies and opponents.[15] Less formal institutions, such as networks, are often viewed as transitory stages in a social movement's development, which inevitably give way to more formal structures.[16]

Perhaps the staunchest critics of this focus, Frances Fox Piven and Richard A. Cloward have questioned the organizational efficacy of SMOs.[17] They argue that "The strategic usefulness of this organizational form, its effectiveness as a vehicle for influence, has been treated as axiomatic."[18] A focus on SMOs tends to equate movements with formal organizations, thus diverting attention away from informal forms of collective action. This prevents us from asking important questions about less formally institutionalized movements, which while less visible are nonetheless important for society and politics.

The formal SMO is not the only pattern of organization available for movement mobilization,[19] and a number of recent studies point to the use of informal social networks in sustained collective action.[20] Stephen Buechler describes this pattern of organization as a "social movement community," comprised of "informal networks of politicized participants who are active in promoting the goals of a social movement outside the boundaries of formal organization."[21] In instances where overt protest and activism are absent, social movements may instead mobilize through social movement communities "with fluid boundaries, flexible leadership structures, and malleable divisions of labor."[22] This is particularly the case for many new social movements, which reject the hierarchy and rigidity of formal organization. Instead, these movements mobilize through "networks of shared meaning," which link individuals through a common understanding about how society should be organized and governed.[23]

The use of informal social networks in collective action is most often seen in less open political systems where overt protest and formal organizations risk harsh regime reprisals and activism is more subtle.[24] Open and visible organizations represent public challenges to domination and are therefore targeted by political authorities and the state. Because formal organizations typically have a location, membership lists, and documents, they are vulnerable to repression. Under such circumstances, movements often instead mobilize through informal social networks, which are more impervious to state control because they embed collective action in everyday interactions.[25] In his analysis of the 1989 "revolution" in Eastern Europe, for example, Steven Pfaff finds that in "societies in which the state virtually eliminates an open public sphere and organization independent of regime control, informal ties are of critical importance. Tightly knit networks nurture collective identities and solidarity, provide informal organization and contacts, and supply information otherwise unavailable to individuals."[26] Similar patterns of organization were found in China among students and pro-democracy supporters. These activists used social networks, campus study groups, student unions, dormitory networks, and informal communications, such as protest notices, all of which facilitated protest.[27]

In the Middle East, informal networks are an indelible component of the social matrix and are frequently used in collective action. Tribes, patron-client ties, religion, norms of reciprocity, and *wasta* (a Jordanian colloquialism for "social connections") undergird the organizational structure of society and can be utilized to mobilize collectivities.[28] Diane Singerman's rich ethnographic study of Cairene urban quarters demonstrates how communities use social networks to perpetuate the family unit, obtain employment, acquire goods and services, and influence politics.[29] These networks permeate civil society and the state and tie individuals together through a complex web of social relationships that sustain and support collectivities. Similarly, Asef Bayat shows how seemingly apolitical groups in Iran, such as squatters, the unemployed, and street vendors, use informal networks in survival strategies. Individuals from these groups share public space and develop "passive networks" that can be activated for collective action.[30] And Guilain Denoeux points to the potential volatility of informal networks and their role in urban unrest in the Middle East. Especially where formal organizations are limited, informal networks can be used for political purposes by social movements and communities.[31]

The study of informal networks in less open political systems implies the centrality of political context for understanding the organization of collective action. Western polities enjoy a range of civil liberties and political freedoms that provide social space for collective action and render formal organization possible and effective. Various legal rights and practices allow movements to openly pursue goals through SMOs; and while repression does still occur, there is enough space to operate through formal organizations. This political openness is often lacking in other political systems. Many

Middle Eastern countries, for example, have experienced movement toward democracy, but continue to employ authoritarian practices that threaten the viability of SMOs. These organizations provide visible signals of opposition which regimes often target for repression. Under such conditions, social networks may allow a social movement to survive.

THE POLITICAL CONTEXT OF ISLAMIC ACTIVISM IN JORDAN

Social movements are not unfettered agents of change operating in a vacuum; they are embedded in a social and political milieu that provides opportunities and constraints for collective action.[32] In addition to grievances and resource availability, exogenous factors both limit and enable social movement activities and organization. Strategic decisions about tactics, action, and movement organizing are informed by the reality of political context. Research has demonstrated that the state represents an important component of this context and structures many of the opportunities available for collective action.[33] Though there has been some movement toward democracy in Jordan, persistent repressive tendencies continue to inform the political context of Islamic activism and concomitant patterns of organization. These tendencies reflect the regime's persistent historical concern over stability and social control.

The current context of political liberalization in Jordan has historical precedent.[34] The country flirted with liberalization and democratization shortly following King Hussein's ascension to the throne in 1953 when the king expanded political freedoms and civil liberties. Political parties were formed, political prisoners released, and restrictions on the freedom of the press and association were repealed. The liberalization measures culminated in a parliamentary election in 1956, which brought an Arab nationalist government to power. The kingdom had experienced its first taste of democracy and political freedom.

This experiment, however, was short-lived and came to an abrupt end when Arab nationalists began to challenge royal sovereignty. Supported by external allies such as Nasser in Egypt, the pitch of the nationalists' rhetoric exceedingly infringed upon the prerogatives of the king and his sovereignty over the kingdom. The nationalists believed that Jordan would eventually have to be integrated into other

Arab states to successfully combat Israel. While King Hussein supported mutual cooperation among Arab states, he viewed it as an equal partnership, rather than full integration, and was not prepared to tolerate an erosion of his power and control. An attempted coup, an assassination attempt, and national strikes led by nationalist sympathizers prompted the king to impose martial law in 1957. Though martial law was lifted in November 1958, it was reestablished during the 1967 war with Israel. Glimpses of political liberalization emerged during the ensuing period, but the regime's concern with maintaining royal sovereignty and social control superseded any democratic inclinations the king may have had.

This concern for stability was reinforced over the years by a growing Palestinian presence, which threatened the power of the throne. Following various confrontations between Israel and Arabs, waves of Palestinian refugees flooded Jordan. The Palestinians used the kingdom as a launching point for attacks against Israel and as a site for military organizing. In the 1960s, Palestinian groups, especially the Palestinian Liberation Organization (PLO), asserted their organizational power in Jordan, claiming sovereignty over certain geographical areas and constituency. The PLO, in effect, created a "state within a state" that increasingly rivaled the institutions of the Jordanian state. In Irbid, Palestinian groups eventually proclaimed a "people's government," further testing King Hussein's patience. Following this proclamation and a series of Palestinian hijackings, the king brutally cracked down on the growing Palestinian presence. The ensuing 1970–71 civil war led to the deaths of 3,400 Palestinians and the expulsion of the PLO from Jordanian territory.[35] Because of these and other political challenges, the regime in Jordan has always been, at least in part, motivated by a survival imperative; and the transition to democracy in 1989 reflects this logic.

Democratization in Jordan represents a "survival strategy" by a semi-rentier state.[36] Rentier or semi-rentier states derive substantial revenues from exogenous sources rather than domestic production or taxation.[37] In Jordan, "rent" historically derived from workers' remittances and subsidies provided by the British, United States, and other Arab countries. Reliance upon rent weakens a regime's accountability to society since it can function without extracting substantial revenues from domestic sources. In other words, "no taxation, no representation."[38] Instead, the rentier social contract is one in which the state provides goods and services to society (such as subsidies on basic commodities) without imposing economic burdens, while society provides state officials with a degree of autonomy in decision making and policy. Legitimacy rests upon the ability to enhance quality of life rather than democratic principles. The state thus reduces "formal politics to the issue of distribution, and participation to the realm of consumption."[39]

While the rentier social contract perpetuates nondemocratic political structures and practices, it is also vulnerable to external factors that undermine sources of rent. The decline in oil-related revenues during the 1980s undermined the logic of the social contract in many Middle Eastern countries, and the subsequent financial crisis served as an important catalyst for democratization and political liberalization. In Jordan, high levels of debt, inflation, and the return of expatriate Jordanian workers from the Gulf strained the financial capabilities of the state. The kingdom was forced to capitulate to an International Monetary Fund (IMF) structural adjustment package that included harsh austerity measures and a reduction in public employment, thus weakening regime legitimacy.

Without avenues of political participation, those affected by the changes were unable to voice their concerns through formal political institutions and instead carried their grievances into the streets. After fuel prices increased, a series of riots erupted in several southern towns and shattered the control of marital law. For the regime, what was most disconcerting was not simply the protest itself, but rather who protested. The southern towns are populated by Jordanian tribes loyal to the royal family and serve as the backbone of regime support. The fact that traditional regime supporters, and not marginalized opposition groups, were responsible for the riots signaled that political change was necessary.

While the riots themselves were not a protest for greater political participation, the regime decided to initiate political liberalization measures to assuage the situation. Malik Mufi's interviews with decision makers responsible for the process of political liberalization in Jordan show that incumbent elites "calculated that some liberalization measure would serve as a useful safety valve once the inevitable austerity measures began to bite."[40] As a result, a decision was made to hold elections and implement political liberalization reforms. Democratization thus served as a means for reinforcing ties to the king's traditional constituency of support by providing political space for the frustrations of groups adversely affected by the economic austerity measures.[41]

The transition was driven by the need to maintain stability and social control, not by a benevolent desire for enhanced political participation. It was part of a "survival strategy" in the face of economic crisis.[42] Economic reforms were necessary, but carried consequences for stability; and political reforms were seen as a way of placating disaffected groups. Daniel Brumberg refers to this as a "democratic bargain"—"an arrangement by which democratic reforms are used as a device to obtain economic reform."[43] It was a tactical strategy to enhance regime survival.

As a result, the regime has carefully crafted and coordinated democratization from above to promote democratic reforms without fully relinquishing power. The transition in Jordan was a "defensive democratization," a strategy designed to maintain regime control through preemptive reform.[44] As a result, in controlling the pace and scope of political change in the kingdom, the regime has retained particular authoritarian practices to prevent the mobilization of political activism that could undermine its power.

The post-1989 system of social control, inherited by King Abdullah II following his ascension to the throne in February 1999 after King Hussein's death, predominantly relies upon legal codes and procedures to regulate collective action. Permit requirements, bureaucratic processes, and the law represent state-enforced rules for social movement activism. These are subtle and less visible than overt repression, but they are omnipresent in constraining collective action. In contrast to the direct policing policies that dominated the social control of collective action during the martial law period, these techniques constitute a pervasive and routine system for the "management of collective action," which channels movements in particular directions by setting boundaries for permissible activities. It is a relatively invisible process of regulation used to control social movements.

John McCarthy and his colleagues imply this management process in their study of state channeling in the United States.[45] They point to a hidden process in the United States whereby the state offers a "tangle of incentives" that narrows the shape, form, tactics, and goals of social movements. In particular, the provision of tax-exempt status and its accompanying restrictions on social movement actions channel movement organizations into nondisruptive forms of activism. Internal Revenue Service regulations impose a range of conditions for acceptance, such as abstention from partisan politics and minimal political activity. Because of the various benefits associated with tax-exempt status, many social movement organizations willingly comply with these regulations, thus channeling movements into particular forms. In a competitive social movement environment with scarce resources, tax exemption entices movements to conform to an array of regulations.

In addition to the tangle of incentives, there is also what I call a "web of disincentives," which discourages particular forms of activism. Various administrative mechanisms and requirements may discourage social movements from engaging in particular interactions or activities. Cumbersome and expensive demonstration requirements, for example, may dissuade social movements from engaging in public protest marches. These disincentives channel movements by erecting a host of barriers to collective action.

The precise balance of social control mechanisms often depends upon the degree of political freedom in a particular political context. Repressive states tend to favor coercive force, even if only as a deterrent to collective action, while democratic states more frequently rely upon management strategies, even while periodically mobilizing instruments of repression.

In Jordan, the state utilizes a symbiotic combination of repressive and administrative techniques of social control in the regulation of collective action. Following political liberalization in 1989, the use of draconian instruments of coercion was gradually eclipsed by management strategies in regulative practices. The decline of repression, however, does not represent an abrogation of state control. On the contrary, the Jordanian state has shifted the balance of social control to effective bureaucratic regulations, processes, and procedures, which are used to constrain the scope and content of social movement activities. In particular, the state "manages" collective action through the manipulation of the bureaucracy to encourage the organization of supportive social groups while preventing more critical groups from operating effectively through formal organizations. At the same time, repression is still used (though less frequently) to channel collective action into formal organizations where the regime can assert control through indirect administrative techniques. As a result, while political liberalization offers new opportunities for the organization of social movements, the management of collective action in Jordan ensures that the content of activities in these organizations remains apolitical, passive, and supportive of state interests. Though these practices existed during the marital law period, the state now relies upon them more exclusively.

The regime is particularly concerned with managing Islamic activism, since this constitutes the most serious potential challenge to regime power and legitimacy. This concern is reflected in the regime's painstaking use of the administrative apparatus to control access to Islamic institutions in the kingdom. It carefully uses the bureaucracy to limit which Islamic voices can use the mosques and other important religious institutions in society. Moderate Islamists who avoid controversial political statements and support the legitimacy of the regime receive permission to give sermons, lessons, and religious rulings through public Islamic space. More critical voices, which challenge the Islamic legitimacy of the regime, are prevented from mobilizing through these institutions. At the same time, the regime sponsors its own organizations, religious activities, and Islamic personalities to articulate an interpretation of Islam that supports regime and state power. The Salafis and other critical Islamists are routinely excluded from religious space, thereby blocking their participation in prominent religious institutions that could otherwise be used to reach a broader audience.

In addition to controlling public religious space, the regime attempts to use the management of collective action to squelch critical Islamist opposition. Moderate groups, such as the Muslim Brotherhood, receive special treatment in forming SMOs at the grassroots level. This has allowed the movement to construct a vast network of formal organizations that reaches into virtually every area of social concern. The more radical Salafis, on the other hand, have endured numerous obstacles to formal organization; and in the end most Salafis have decided that SMOs are ineffective for achieving movement goals.

Given this particular political context and state regulative practices, the divergent patterns of Islamic activism in Jordan are readily intelligible. Locked out of effective participation in formal organizations and Islamic institutions, the Salafis must find alternative institutional resources to mobilize and operate. In the Middle East, the Salafis have turned to the informal social networks that form the natural matrix of society. They have not invented a new method of mobilization; the movement has adopted an indigenous structure of activism that Salafis believe allows greater freedom to pursue objectives. The Brotherhood, on its part, has experienced organizational opportunities and tacitly accepts the limitations to its grassroots activities. Each group's strategic choice about institutional resources for mobilization is informed by the realities of political context.

THE STRUCTURE OF THE BOOK

Because this book is a study of the impact of political context on patterns of Islamic collective action, it is comprised of two main topics. First, the book outlines the political context by examining how the state utilizes bureaucratic processes and management strategies to shape and limit social movements and Islamic activism. Chapter 1 details the management of collective action to explain the state social control mechanisms that circumscribe formal organizations. Though overt repression still exists, this chapter explains the more subtle use of legal regulations and bureaucratic oversight that is a more ubiquitous manifestation of state power in post-1989 Jordan.

The political context of Islamic activism, in particular, is shaped not only by these administrative constraints, but also by the regime's overall concern with controlling interpretations of Islam. Chapter 2 examines the regime's interest in shaping and monopolizing Islamic discourse. It mobilizes resources to extend its control over religious space and prevent alternative interpretations of Islam that could undermine regime legitimacy. This interest in limiting radical Islamic discourse combines with the management of collective action to delineate the overall political context for Islamic groups.

The second topic is the impact of state power and context on patterns of Islamic activism and constitutes the remainder of the book. Chapter 3 examines formal Islamic organizations in civil society. Moderate Islamic groups have successfully expanded their presence through formal institutions, but they do not challenge regime legitimacy or its interest in controlling Islamic discourse. While the number of Islamic NGOs has expanded, they are limited by the realities of state management strategies and as a result are depoliticized. A case study of the Muslim Brotherhood's organizational experience explores the relationship between Islamist support for the regime and organizational growth in civil society.

Chapter 4 demonstrates the limits of organizational opportunities for more radical Islamist groups, such as the Salafi movement, and examines alternatives for mobilization. The Salafis articulate a critical interpretation of Islam with an emphasis on social justice and proper Islamic practices that challenges the regime's own religious discourse and legitimacy. In addition, a number of more violent Salafi groups have emerged since the 1990s, leading the regime to limit organizational opportunities for Salafis, despite any movement toward democracy. The Salafis have, in turn, activated informal social networks as an alternative institutional resource through which to carry out social movement functions and goals. The chapter highlights the structure and role of these networks as Salafis attempt to evade state power and the management of Islamic activism.

The book concludes by calling for a more nuanced conceptualization of social movements that incorporates informally structured collective action into mainstream theory. Informal movements, such as the Salafis, necessitate a deeper understanding of the structure of collective action and require that we not only recognize informal mechanisms of activism, but explain the choice of informality as well.

CHAPTER 1

The Management of
Collective Action

The power to control collective action and formal organizations does not simply derive from raw, coercive force or repression. The modern state is armed with more effective and insidious techniques of control, though these can be utilized in conjunction with alternative methods of physical social restrictions. In Jordan, control derives in part from state disciplinary technologies and tactics, which facilitate its ability to manage the population. As Michel Foucault argues, disciplinary power derives not from the use of visible coercion and commands, but from its ability to partition space into surveillable units, which can be regulated and administrated.[1] Discipline orders individuals in spatial settings to maximize the ability of the state or those in power to maintain constant surveillance through observation. By dictating when and where individuals are present and even their relations with one another, the state enhances its social control.[2]

A key element of disciplinary power is that it creates order and predictability, thus enabling the state to institute technologies for surveillance. Disorder and chaos are difficult to monitor and regulate efficiently. Ordered spatial arrangements, on the other hand, permit modern instruments to observe, measure, count, and control the objects of surveillance. Disciplinary power enhances the social control capacity of the modern state by creating a system of objectification, classification, and management that can track and monitor changes in large collectivities. Populations are broken down into administratable units and categories where social control mechanisms are applied.

Management and surveillance necessitate that the objects of control are constantly within view of the social control apparatus:

> Disciplinary power . . . imposes on those whom it subjects a principle of compulsory visibility. In discipline, it is the subjects who have to be seen. Their visibility assures the hold of power that is exercised over them. It is the fact of being constantly seen, of being always to be seen, that maintains the disciplined individual in his subjection.[3]

The penultimate disciplinary technology of surveillance is Jeremy Bentham's panopticon with its penetrating and constant gaze. Initially designed for prisons, it facilitates observation by producing constant and omnipresent surveillance. It is a disciplinary "apparatus of observation" that renders its objects constantly visible.[4]

The Jordanian state wields disciplinary power through its use of the administrative apparatus and regulation. To maintain constant surveillance, the state has developed a series of administrative and bureaucratic techniques to observe, register, record, and monitor all forms of collective action in the kingdom. This system produces documentation, a written record, files, notations, and data, all designed to more effectively regulate social interactions and behavior. It provides the state with instruments to record the minutiae of detail in collective action and renders all aspects visible and subject to the surveillance of the state. The disciplinary gaze of the modern bureaucracy replaces the disciplinary gaze of the panopticon. The state has created the means for "domestic colonization," reflecting its "desire for the elimination of unsurveillable, uncontrollable space."[5]

All forms of group work and collective action in Jordan must be registered at an appropriate ministry, which is charged with reporting, inspecting, observing, and counting collective activities within its administrative purview. Group work is ordered, categorized, and regulated by functionally differentiated government agencies and branches to produce efficient control through a division of labor— the Ministry of Interior regulates political parties, unions, and professional associations; the Ministry of Culture regulates cultural voluntary organizations; and the Ministry of Social Development regulates charitable organizations. Each government ministry controls all activities within its respective area of responsibility, and organizations are not permitted to engage in activities that cross into the purview of multiple ministries. Collective action and group work is thus partitioned and segmented into administrative units based upon the logic of bureaucratic control. It does not reflect natural divisions of social activity, but rather the imperative of administrative efficiency.

Through the management of collective action, the regime continues to project authoritarian power through less visible bureaucratic practices intended to limit the scope of participation and activity in civil society. While the Jordanian state maintains an appearance of political liberty and democracy, freedom is curtailed by continued authoritarian tendencies in the regulation of collective action. Beneath the fanfare of elections and enhanced political participation exists an array of less democratic practices intended to support regime power. This system of control is not hegemonic, nor is it complete; but it is pervasive and constitutes an important part of the political context of Islamic activism.

POLITICAL LIBERALIZATION AND ORGANIZATIONAL GROWTH

Prior to political liberalization in 1989, social movement organization was severely circumscribed by restrictive measures. Any group political activity was harshly repressed by the *mukhabarat*, the army, and public security.[6] Opportunities for social movements to operate in this environment were limited at best, and more often engendered violent state reprisals. Rather than exclusively targeting the state, most movements instead competed with one another in professional association elections. Arab nationalists, communists, Ba'thists, Palestinians, and Islamists embedded their movements in association institutions, utilizing this social space as a surrogate arena for political activism. The state tolerated this activity to some extent, cracking down when it believed possible threats to state power and martial law could emerge. Expansions beyond these fairly limited circumstances most often incurred pernicious responses by the regime.

The use of repressive mechanisms during this period was ubiquitous and social movements were a favorite target because the regime feared they might lead to revolutionary tendencies and undermine the system of control achieved by martial law. To maintain social control, the *mukhabarat* utilized torture, intimidation, and surveillance to limit collective action.[7] It funded an extensive network of informants, which was used in conjunction with more traditional police surveillance techniques to monitor possible "troublemakers." In addition, *mukhabarat* agents regularly threatened to remove individuals from their positions of employment and possessed the coercive power to successfully carry out these threats if necessary. This included control over "certificates of good behavior," which are required for various employment opportunities. Prior to 1989, the regime often withheld these certificates to place pressure on political activists.

For the most part, torture was utilized not as a mechanism of punishment, but as an instrument for information gathering and prevention. It was not atypical that a political activist was brought in for "questioning" without a single question being raised. Other times, interrogators asked general questions like "What are you up to? We know you are up to something," without any specific accusations. These periods of detention were usually accompanied by severe beatings. One Islamic activist showed me the permanent knee injury he suffered during questioning in the mid-1980s, reflecting only one of a series of similar accounts by other Islamic activists. Of the various Islamists interviewed, especially outside the Muslim Brotherhood, the vast majority had been detained and tortured at various points. The two most cited reasons for detention were engaging in collective action of various kinds and spreading ideas deemed threatening to national security.[8]

The point of security strategies was not only to gather information, but also to instill a sense of fear and distrust. With the prospects of informants revealing information, threats to job security, intimidation, and physical harm, people were understandably hesitant to participate in social movement activism beyond the boundaries delineated by the regime. While many activists attempted to operate through friendship networks and everyday interactions, organized work was infrequent. Formal organizations were simply out of the question for most movements since civic association in general was forbidden and tightly controlled.[9]

The one notable exception was the relative freedom to organize in charity work. The number of charitable organizations steadily expanded during the years of martial law, but this growth was more a sign of economic necessity than political freedom. Charitable NGOs reduced the financial burden on state-run social welfare programs by providing a society-generated alternative. The scope of charitable NGO work was carefully constricted and limited to socioeconomic development and charity. Other voluntary. organizations, such as cultural societies, were negligible during this period. In 1988 before the transition toward democracy, there were 422 charitable organizations, but only 39 cultural societies (see tables 1.1 and 1.2).

Following political liberalization in 1989, various social groups took advantage of the new freedoms of association and organizational opportunities to form a variety of formal organizations. From 1989 to 1994, the number of indigenous NGOs grew by 67 percent, as compared to growth during the preceding 1985–89 period of only 24 percent (table 1.3). The rate of postliberalization growth among cultural organizations was substantially higher than that of charitable societies. In the five years following the transition, 114 new cultural organizations were registered, representing a 271 percent increase. This expansion dwarfs the more modest 47 percent growth rate of charitable NGOs during the same period (see tables 1.1 and 1.2). While charitable work was common prior to political liberalization because of socioeconomic need, cultural activities enjoyed greater organizational opportunities only after 1989.

Table 1.1. Growth of Jordanian Charitable NGOs

Year	Number of NGOs	Change per Year (%)
1985	364	–
1986	393	8.0
1987	412	4.8
1988	422	2.4
1989	433	2.6
1990	480	10.9
1991	527	9.8
1992	559	6.1
1993	602	7.7
1994	638	6.0
1995	655	2.7

Source: General Union of Voluntary Societies, *Executive Council Report* (Amman: GUVS, 1996), 58.

Table 1.2. Growth of Cultural NGOs

Year	Number of NGOs	Change per Year (%)
1985	25	—
1986	30	20.0
1987	34	13.3
1988	39	14.7
1989	42	10.5
1990	48	14.3
1991	59	22.9
1992	101	71.2
1993	137	35.6
1994	156	13.9

Source: Calculated using information from the Ministry of Culture, *Annual Report* (Amman: Hashemite Kingdom of Jordan, 1994).

Table 1.3. Overall Growth of Jordanian NGOs

Year	Number of NGOs	Change per Year (%)
1985	391	—
1986	425	8.7
1987	448	5.4
1988	463	3.4
1989	477	3.0
1990	530	11.1
1991	588	9.8
1992	662	6.1
1993	741	7.7
1994	796	6.0

Source: Calculated using information from Ministry of Culture, *Annual Report*; and Ministry of Social Development, *Annual Report* (Amman: Hashemite Kingdom of Jordan, 1995).

Note: Includes all cultural societies, charitable organizations, the General Union of Voluntary Societies, and the Council for Islamic Organizations and Societies. This does not include non-Jordanian NGOs operating in Jordan.

Table 1.4. Number of Beneficiaries According
to Charitable Service as of Late 1995

Service	Number of Beneficiaries	
Kindergartens	20,139	
Nurseries	412	
Disabled	4,212	
Children's homes	1,603	
Care for the elderly	110	
Children's clubs	6,075	
Vocational training*	6,373	
Schools	16,422	
Adult education	211	
Libraries	765	
Student loans and aid	1,221	
Health services	331,322	
Financial and in-kind	44,359	
Credit funds	110	families
Productive projects	69	organizations
Projects with USAID	73	organizations

Source: General Union of Voluntary Societies, *Profiles, Programs, Projects* (Amman: GUVS, 1996), 4.
*Vocational training consists of programs for women in sewing, tricot, handicrafts, cosmetics, and flower arrangement.

While data for the number of volunteers and beneficiaries in cultural work are not available, there is detailed information for charitable organizations that provides a partial picture of the extent of NGO activities (see table 1.4). There are approximately 70,000 volunteers in charitable organizations in Jordan,[10] reaching more than 434,446 beneficiaries as of the end of 1995, about one-eighth of the entire population.[11] The number of beneficiaries does not include more general community benefits that are diffused throughout society. Such data demonstrate the relevance and extent of NGO activity in Jordan, especially given that they do not include the reach of cultural organizations, which have proliferated rapidly since 1991.

The overall growth of NGOs in the country has accelerated since political liberalization, reflecting the profound shift in organizational opportunities. While there is certainly greater socioeconomic need since economic austerity measures were imposed, this does not account for the pace of change, especially in the area of culture. Rather, various groups now experience more freedom to register and participate in formal organizations to affect society.

THE CONDITIONALITY OF PARTICIPATION

While social movement groups ostensibly enjoy the freedom to form NGOs since political liberalization, the state manipulates the application of the law and administrative practices to guarantee that formal organizations are not utilized to challenge the state or government policies. In order to organize in civil society, an interested group must meet three primary conditions. First, organizational activities must be limited to a particular set of activities registered by the state. This limitation is designed to enhance the state's regulative capacity. Second, voluntary organizations cannot engage in any "political" activities, as defined by the state. The NGO community is thus depoliticized. And third, assertive and critical opposition through NGOs is prohibited. The state directly interferes with NGO leadership structures to prevent and remove members it deems threatening to state interests. All of these conditions are enforced through selective regulative practices and the manipulation of the law.

The legal basis for NGOs was established in 1936 with Law 33. Subsequent revisions were made in 1956, 1965, and finally in 1966. The Law of Societies and Social Organizations, Law 33 of 1966, is the current law applied to voluntary organizations in the kingdom.[12] Although initially intended for charitable organizations, the law is currently applied to cultural societies as well since they do not have an independent legal basis. It covers all voluntary societies and organizations comprised of at least seven individuals who have organized "to provide social services without any intention of financial gains or any other personal gains, including political gains." This includes organizations devoted to charity, culture, science and training, and sports activities.[13]

To form an organization, a minimum of seven individuals, at least twenty-one years old, must first draft an internal law that clearly stipulates the goals, objectives, and activities of the prospective organization. The application must include the names, ages, occupations, and addresses of all founding members. It must also describe the conditions for membership and contributions, the selection process for the administrative committee, how finances are administered, and the structure of the general assembly meetings.[14] The minister of social development, with input from both the governor of the district where the NGO would be registered and the General Union of Voluntary Societies (GUVS), approves applications for charitable activities. There is no cultural union, so cultural societies are approved by the Ministry of Culture without union coordination. The respective ministry has full discretion to reject or accept applications. Most critical groups are rejected at this point and prevented from forming an NGO. If approved, the internal law of the society serves as a rigid guideline for permissible activities at the society; and the government must approve any changes.

NGOs apply to a specific ministry for permission to operate and their activities are therefore confined to that ministry's purview of regulation. Thus, if an organization is applying to the Ministry of Culture, it must demonstrate that its activities will only be in the field of culture. If applying to the Ministry of Social Development, the organization must show that it will only engage in charity or socioeconomic development activities. Organized work in civil society is thus channeled into separate administrative units where the respective bureaucratic agency is charged with overseeing a particular category of activities. In practice, these categories are not absolutely discrete and some overlap occurs, especially in charitable organizations, which may provide some cultural activities as well. But this is more an exception to organizational patterns than the rule, and the majority of organizational activities must remain within the jurisdiction of the ministry with which the NGO is registered.

The internal law further narrows the range of activities to a specific subset within the broader field of interest. Within the field of charity, for example, a society might receive permission to open a center for the disabled, but not to form an orphanage. Or an organization might receive permission to provide job training for women, but not to offer programs for the deaf. The state can strike specific activities from the proposed list. One of the most successful Islamic charitable societies in Zarqa is permitted to provide a variety of services, but it is not legally allowed to engage in marriage-related activities, such as matching prospective marriage partners or providing financial assistance to young couples to lessen the financial burden of a wedding. The ministry official who reviewed the application simply drew a line through that portion of the proposal and then issued a permit.[15] Such discretionary power allows the state to shape the specifics of organizational activity in the kingdom.

Law 33 provides the state with legal standing to regulate the minutiae of organizational activities and institutes mechanisms for surveillance that help sustain the administrative divisions and prevent the use of NGOs for oppositional purposes. The most important requirement is that organizations must maintain a detailed record of all activities, which is submitted in an annual report to the state. This record includes information on finances, correspondence, board meetings, fixed assets, revenues and disbursements, and working members.[16] In addition, the law provides the state with sweeping opportunities to interfere in the affairs of any organization through inspections: "[T]he general manager or any employee in the department is entitled to visit any society, committee or union to examine its financial records to ensure that its money is spent in the manner for which it was established according to the law."[17] The law emphasizes the surveillance of finances to ensure that money is not used for unregistered activities, which are not monitored by the state. Ministry officials also attend elections to the administrative boards and must approve the results.[18]

All of these requirements arm the state with the legal basis for dissolution should an organization wander beyond the confines of the internal law or fail to provide the state with the information that renders surveillance possible. Most dissolutions occur because the organization does not fulfill its specified goals, engages in activities for which it is not registered, fails to meet regularly, or does not provide the administrative agency with relevant records, especially financial records.[19] The most frequent cause of dissolution is prompted by an NGO's failure to provide relevant information and detailed reports—in other words, failure to provide the information necessary for surveillance and discipline. Without records of organizational activity, it is difficult for the state to observe collective action and sustain surveillance; and any failure to provide such information threatens the disciplinary power of the state. Between 1995 and 1996, twenty-nine charitable societies were closed,[20] and in January 1997 alone, the Ministry of Social Development canceled five other organizations.[21] The Ministry of Culture has also suspended numerous cultural organizations. Despite political liberalization, the state retains its right to maintain disciplinary power and is willing to cancel any organization that does not comply with the instruments of surveillance and regulative control.

In many instances, the state stops short of canceling a society and instead reorganizes the leadership and organizational structure.[22] The regulating ministry has the right to dissolve the administrative committee of any society and replace it with a temporary one until new elections are held.[23] Usually, the dissolution of the administrative committee occurs if there is insufficient attendance at board meetings or if there has been a violation of the internal law. In one case, the Ministry of Social Development removed the administrative board members of the Jericho Society in Amman because there were continual disagreements and disputes among the board members. The ministry reasoned that the society was unable to achieve its goals because of this disarray and dissolved the administrative board. A temporary committee was appointed for six months during which time it went through all of the society's records and assets and reorganized the entire NGO. After the reorganization, new elections were held and the society continued its work.[24] This demonstrates the discretionary power and leeway the state has to interfere in the internal affairs of NGOs.

In its quest to control organizational space and prevent the emergence of an organized opposition through civil society, the state strictly prohibits any transgression into the political sphere. Organized political activities of any kind are only permitted through political parties, which were formally legalized by The Political Party Law, Law 32 of 1992. This law stipulates that "The use of the premises, instrumentalities, and assets of associations, charitable organizations and clubs for the benefit of any partisan organization, shall be prohibited."[25] This separation between NGO activities and politics is also reflected in Law 33 of 1966, which prohibits the use of NGOs for political gains.[26] Events, lectures, and activities are regulated so that they maintain an unambiguously apolitical content; and work that wanders into the political realm is repressed and constrained.

Government officials argue that new political freedoms provide opportunities to organize in politics through political parties and that any political activities should be confined to this space.[27] The productivity and utility of political parties, however, are questionable. In the 1989 elections, political parties were still banned. In

1993, parties ran a relatively unsuccessful campaign, and the majority of those elected to the Chamber of Deputies ran as members of a particular clan or tribe. Even strong party candidates, such as IAF leaders, still relied heavily upon tribal support. In 1997, the major opposition parties boycotted the elections to protest government corruption, peace with Israel, and the electoral law. The remaining parties did not fare well (only five fielded candidates), and once again tribal candidates dominated the electoral process. In a survey of 176 randomly selected candidates published by *al-ʿArab al-Yaum*, only 15 percent of the candidates indicated a political party affiliation.[28] As a result, forty-three of the eighty members of the 1997–2001 parliament were tribal representatives.[29]

In reality, political parties hold little relevance for people, even in politics. In a survey in 1995 by the Center for Strategic Studies at the University of Jordan, only 46.2 percent of those surveyed had even heard of the IAF, at the time the single largest political party bloc in Parliament. Fewer than 25 percent were aware of any other party and awareness quickly diminished with smaller political parties (see table 1.5). This level of awareness is certainly related to the novelty of political parties and their rapid proliferation since the Political Party Law was enacted, but it is also due to the fact that

Table 1.5. Level of Awareness of Political Parties

Party Name	Percent of Respondents Aware of Party
Islamic Action Front Party	42.6
Pledge Party	20.7
Arab Socialist Baʻth Party	16.8
Communist Party	15.1
People's Democratic Party	9.6
Reawakening Party	8.3
Progressive Democratic Party	7.6
Popular Unity Party	5.6
Arab Baʻth Progressive Party	5.0
Democratic Socialist Party	5.0

Source: Center for Strategic Studies, University of Jordan, *Democracy in Jordan* (Amman: Center for Strategic Studies, 1995), 32.

Note: Parties below 5 percent awareness level are not included. There were thirteen parties in this category.

political parties, even the largest ones, have little impact in society thus far. Despite this relative insignificance, however, the state only permits organized political activities through political parties, which are regulated at the Ministry of the Interior. Political content in other venues of organizational work is suppressed.[30]

The state utilizes both the law and repressive measures to ensure that the integrity of the separation between politics and all other forms of organized work is upheld, and there are numerous examples of state intervention designed to reinforce this division. Since political liberalization began, cultural societies in particular have increasingly felt the weight of state repression. Many grassroots organizers in the cultural arena claim that issues such as democracy, human rights, and political freedom are cultural issues. These NGOs therefore attempt to incorporate political themes into organizational activities, only to face reprisals from the state as it seeks to protect administrative distinctions. For example, women from the Center for Women's Studies, a cultural society, were brought in by the *mukhabarat* for questioning because they had discussed the role of women in elections at the society. This is a cultural issue (the role of women in society) with political import (elections). The *mukhabarat* charged that they were not licensed to engage in political activities, including discussions about electoral strategy.[31] In another incident in January 1997, the Ministry of Culture canceled the Karak Cultural Forum after Layth Shubaylat criticized the government in a lecture at the organization.[32] Members of the society intended to establish another organization but the ministry demanded that they first form a new administrative committee. The members refused and a new organization was never formed.[33]

Following the closing of the Karak Cultural Forum, Ahmad al-Quddah, then minister of culture, issued a directive that banned any cultural meetings from taking place anywhere in the kingdom without prior approval from the administrator charged with overseeing cultural activities in the respective governate. This was generally viewed as a direct reaction to the speech by Shubaylat and engendered virulent opposition from cultural societies throughout Jordan. Members of the Jordanian Writers Association believed the directive was aimed at their society after it hosted a cultural week entitled "debate of choices," which focused on the political, economic, cultural, and creative issues facing the country.[34] Though the directive was eventually rescinded, other lectures about issues such as the temporary press law, economics, and the peace treaty were canceled; and there is continuous interference in the freedom of assembly to prevent NGOs from discussing political issues.[35]

In the following September, the subsequent minister of culture, Qasim Abu Ein, sent a directive to cultural societies warning them to refrain from political activities.[36] There was an ensuing confrontation between the minister of culture and the Jordanian Writers Association over the "political nature" of some of the association's work. The minister claimed that the organization was involved in political activities and that it was hosting illegal organizations (i.e., unregistered political parties). The association president, Fakhri Kawar, responded that "any cultural activity will one way or another include politics in it," and asserted the association's right to "conduct political activities because they are part of culture." The minister sent a letter of complaint to the minister of the interior stating that the organization was involved in political work. He sent another letter to the Jordanian Writers Association warning that the ministry would close the organization if it persisted in any "political, tribal or sectarian activity."[37]

In addition to these legal tactics, discretionary state power is used to control the leadership and general membership of NGOs. Although it is not explicitly stated in Law 33, all volunteers as well as administrative board members must first be approved by the "security department,"[38] a euphemism for the *mukhabarat* and public security at the Ministry of the Interior.[39] These agencies are charged with the responsibility of preventing collective action that threatens the security of the state, national unity, or the Hashemite regime. This input in registration decisions represents the veto power of the security apparatus. Through this power, the state enjoys absolute control over the composition of volunteers in NGO activities and is able to shape and mold the makeup of participants in the voluntary sector. The state uses this power to exclude particular individuals, deemed threatening to the regime, from participating in voluntary activities.

These bureaucratic and extralegal instruments provide the state with broad control over formal NGOs. Social movements that oppose the regime or articulate serious political opposition are limited in formal organizations by the realities of state regulative practices. The regime attempts to utilize these practices to prevent the politicization of grassroots voluntary organizations; and by controlling elections, the composition of the membership, and the leadership in NGOs, the state limits formally organized opposition.

CORPORATISM AND SELF-DISCIPLINE:
THE GENERAL UNION OF VOLUNTARY SOCIETIES

While controlling the composition and content of NGOs in civil society through disciplinary power, upheld by repression, the state has also implemented self-disciplining mechanisms within the NGO community itself, thereby reducing the cost of control for the state. The General Union of Voluntary Societies (GUVS) is the corporatist creation of the state, formed to regulate and control all charitable activities in the kingdom.[40] Comprised of charitable NGOs and volunteers from these organizations, the GUVS enforces self-discipline and self-regulation in the community. It utilizes its own disciplinary tactics to regulate and manage NGO activities that fall under the purview of the Ministry of Social Development and monitors the details of organizational activity.

In accordance with Law 33 of 1956, governate level unions were formed in 1956 and the GUVS was formed in 1959. According to the law, the GUVS was chartered to function as the umbrella organization for all governate unions and charitable NGOs in the kingdom. As the number of NGOs and governate unions expanded over the years, the GUVS became an increasingly important tool for managing voluntary activities. As an instrument of corporatism, it is an organizational link between grassroots organizations and the state. It is registered at the Ministry of Social Development like any other organization and is subject to the same rules and regulations. In practice, however, it is inextricably linked to the administrative apparatus through its regulative and oversight functions. Decisions about whether to register new societies or expand an organization's activities is a joint decision between the GUVS and the ministry. Though this serves as a form of corporatist participation whereby the interests of the NGOs are represented through the GUVS, in the end the ministry retains the final decision and has rejected GUVS recommendations. In addition, the ministry is represented at all executive council meetings of the GUVS; and although this representative does not enjoy veto power, the ministry can eventually reject any decisions that the government opposes. The GUVS is so intimately

connected to the state apparatus, that one Islamist organizer referred to it as the "Ministry of Associations."

The subservience of the GUVS to the ministry is a point of frustration for many in the GUVS itself. In an outline of the GUVS, one
publication complains that,

> GUVS needs more independence to enhance its role as a partner
> in social development with public and private sectors. Although it
> is a non-governmental organization, it remains closely linked to
> the Ministry of Social Development and its rules and regulations.
> The more independence GUVS has, the more capable it will [be
> in] making decisions in line with national development plans and
> avoiding any sort of tension which may arise from [the] constant
> instructions that the voluntary sector receives [from the ministry]
> regarding its tasks, giving no flexibility to volunteers.[41]

The partnership between the GUVS and the ministry is one in which
the GUVS serves the interests of the state. Though it has some input in decisions, it acts as an instrument of state control.

To maximize control over NGOs in Jordan, the GUVS structure is hierarchical, characteristic of most corporatist entities where
decisions are limited to peak representative associations (see table
1.6). At the bottom of the organizational pyramid are the grassroots
NGOs. All charitable organizations are required to register with the
Ministry of Social Development, the governate union, and the GUVS.
Union membership is mandatory. These NGOs are tied to the GUVS
through an intermediary level of governate unions, which represent
the interests of the local NGOs at the national level through a general assembly and the executive committee at the GUVS. The number of representatives sent to the general assembly is determined by
a specific formula. Each governate has at least three representatives
and receives an additional seat at the Assembly for every 25 NGOs
registered in its district. For example, the Amman Voluntary Union
has 237 organizations in its district and sends thirteen representatives, while the Jericho Voluntary Union, with only 14 societies,
sends three. No governate union may send more than fifteen representatives. The general assembly currently consists of sixty-one members. The assembly, in turn, elects an executive council, which makes
all binding decisions and runs the GUVS. The council includes the
president, vice president, treasurer, and secretary of the GUVS, and

Table 1.6. General Union of Voluntary Societies,
Corporatist Structure

Executive Council
General Assembly

Number of Union Representatives in General Assembly
According to Governate

Amman	Irbid	Zarqa	Balqa	Ma'an	Kerak
13	9	5	6	5	4

Mafraq	Tafileh	Madaba	Ajloun	Jerash	Aqaba
4	3	3	3	3	3

Number of Voluntary Societies
in Each Governate Union

Amman	Irbid	Zarqa	Balqa	Ma'an	Kerak
237	114	49	50	45	38

Mafraq	Tafileh	Madaba	Ajloun	Jerash	Aqaba
37	17	20	16	14	17

Source: General Union of Voluntary Societies, *Profiles,* 2.

is currently comprised of eighteen people. All governate unions must be represented by at least one executive committee member.[42]

Aside from its input in the regulation and administration of charitable NGO activities, the GUVS enhances the disciplinary power of the state through statistical analysis and data collection. It has access to all NGO records and reports; and it uses these to monitor, track, and analyze NGO activities in the kingdom. The GUVS gathers data on various dimensions of organizational work, which are compiled in an annual report. It also monitors voluntary activities through the affiliated Voluntary Center-Jordan (VCJ), which was established in 1989 and reactivated in 1995,[43] and the Social Data Bank at the GUVS. This not only enhances the state's ability to coordinate all NGO activities in the kingdom, but also serves as a mechanism of control and discipline. It permits the surveillance of both aggregate trends and the minutiae of NGO detail, and the state can regulate the NGO community according to the conclusions it draws from the data.

The power of the GUVS derives not only from this surveillance and its regulative capacity, but from its financial role in the NGO community as well. It provides approximately 30 percent of all charitable NGO investment in the country, most of which is raised through donations and the National Charitable Lottery run by the GUVS.[44] The latter source raises JD1.5 million a year (approximately $2.14 million).[45] As the representative of charitable NGO work in Jordan, the GUVS is also one of the primary recipients of international aid. For example, the GUVS received a $350,000 five-year grant (1988–93) from USAID (United States Agency for International Development).[46] NGOs must also financially contribute to the GUVS, though this is a nominal fee. Organizations with more than fifty members are required to contribute JD100 ($144) a year while those with fewer than fifty members contribute JD50 ($72).[47] The GUVS uses all of these financial resources to invest in its own charity programs and to assist individual NGOs.

Though the GUVS only oversees organizational activities registered at the Ministry of Social Development, it is an important example of state corporatist strategies designed to monitor and regulate NGO activities. It was initiated by the state and serves the interests of bureaucratic control. Cultural organizations have become more prevalent only since 1991–92 when the number of organizations increased from 59 to 101. As a result, they are still regulated directly by the Ministry of Culture.

SOCIAL CONTROL AND ALTERNATIVE FORMS OF COLLECTIVE ACTION

At the same time as the regime utilizes the bureaucratic apparatus to maintain control over NGOs, it attempts to limit other collective action alternatives that operate outside the reach of administrative power. In order to subject social movements and other groups to bureaucratic control and discipline, the Jordanian state must ensure that collective action is performed within surveillable, state-delineated space. Movements that operate in the shadows of society outside the panopticon gaze of the bureaucracy are unpredictable, and thus potentially threatening to regime power. The most serious challenge to a system of control based upon predictability and visibility is group work that does not conform to the logic of the system and instead remains outside state surveillance. As a result, the state attempts to limit the possibility of collective action in the niches of society by requiring that all group work be performed in the open through space that is within reach of administrative practices. This section examines how the state prevents two alternatives to NGO work—protest demonstrations and unregistered group activities. In both cases, it represses collective action in order to discourage activism outside the structure of formal organizations.

Demonstrations

The most disruptive form of collective action in Jordan, aside from violent acts, is public protest demonstrations. Despite enhanced freedoms since political liberalization, civil dissent through overt demonstrations remains limited. Large gatherings of aggrieved publics are not easily controlled by the state, except with the use of repression, which carries its own costs (particularly where state rhetoric proclaims freedom of expression and democracy). Not only do such events threaten stability and control, but also their visibility often publicly articulates opposition to government policies. The regime has therefore taken measures to prevent demonstrations and to reduce the message and effect of those that are permitted.

The first barrier to demonstrations is that protest organizers must receive permission from the district governor, permission that is rarely forthcoming. Even high profile, moderate opposition figures, such as members of the IAF, encounter difficulties; and state opposition arises regardless of whether the proposed demonstration targets an external agent, such as the United States, or the government itself. According to Abdul Latif Arabiyyat, the current president of the IAF, Islamic activists are routinely told that they cannot demonstrate because "the situation is too dangerous" for protest activities.[48] Security forces use this ambiguous explanation, in conjunction with national security interests and the need for national unity, to consistently deny permission. For example, following the bread riots in 1996, which resulted from subsidy reductions, the government refused to grant the IAF permission to hold a "hungry million march" to protest the subsidy policies.[49] In the wake of the riots, the regime was not willing to risk more uncontrolled collective action should the protest dissipate into unpredictable forms.

In another well-publicized incident in 1997, opposition groups led by Fou'ad Dabour, the secretary general of the Progressive Ba'th Party, applied for permission to hold a rally in Irbid to protest a U.S. military buildup (in anticipation of a strike against Iraq), but were blocked by the regime. The governor of the district wanted to review the speeches before granting permission. Included in the list of speakers were outspoken oppositional figures such as Layth Shubaylat, Toujan Faisal, and Khalil Haddadin.[50] Given such controversial personalities, the governor was concerned about the content of the speeches. The security forces went so far as to prevent Layth Shubaylat from entering Irbid and he was forced to return to Amman.[51] Eventually, a rally was permitted in Amman, scaled down from the original proposal, which would have included a much broader demonstration. It was confined to the Professional Associations Building where it was carefully monitored and controlled by security forces and the police.[52] The regime occasionally permits such rallies if they are held indoors, but in most instances there are no facilities available to accommodate large numbers of people, in effect preventing protest. In addition, demonstrations that are held indoors lose their effectiveness in impacting bystanders, especially prospective supporters, because they are less visible. The potential "contagion of conflict" is thus limited.[53]

In the weeks building up to a possible U.S. strike against Iraq in February 1998, the regime went even further by prohibiting demonstrations altogether. In response to a request from opposition groups to hold a rally in downtown Amman in support of Iraq, Nathir Rashid, the minister of the interior, issued a statement that the government "will not allow any marches under any slogan and for any reason anywhere in the Kingdom at these critical circumstances and this crucial stage which the country is passing through."[54] The minister argued that the measures were designed to prevent "any attempt by those harboring ill-intentions against this country from infiltrating our ranks."[55] This concern most likely derives from the government's belief that external Ba'thist infiltrators were responsible for the 1996 riots, an assessment that remains unsubstantiated.

Defying the order issued by the Ministry of the Interior, supporters of the IAF and other opposition groups attempted to launch a demonstration from King Hussein mosque following Friday prayers. Thousands of people gathered to protest the U.S. military buildup, but were met by hundreds of antiriot police armed with guns, batons, tear gas, a police helicopter, and dogs. Police beat back the protesters and eventually entered the mosque to arrest sixty people, including leaders of the Muslim Brotherhood, a move that engendered harsh criticism from opposition leaders. The IAF issued a statement condemning the forcible invasion of the mosque's sanctity as "unprecedented," stating, "Throughout our history, no government dared to attack the prayers in the mosque and to beat them in the pulpit of the mosque."[56] The government claimed that it feared a "fifth column" of infiltrators that might destabilize the country and charged that protesters were ready to throw bombs at police.[57]

Shortly after this clash, the state again asserted its right to use force to control and contain demonstrations. According to the government, Layth Shubaylat urged inhabitants of Ma'an to demonstrate in support of Iraq after the Friday prayers on 20 February 1998.[58] Several hundred protesters began demonstrating but were stopped by police. In the ensuing confrontation, violence erupted and the police fired tear gas from the rooftops of government buildings. As the chaos mounted, a shot was fired, killing an innocent bystander.[59] News of the incident spread throughout the city and rioting erupted. The following day, two thousand mourners demonstrated in the streets, carrying the shrouded body of the bystander killed in the earlier clash. Police fired tear gas and the procession devolved into a riot as protesters burned a Housing Bank office, an Education Ministry building, and electrical utilities. Weapons were visible in the crowd and fighting broke out while the crowd chanted pro-Iraq slogans. The army was called in to restore order and a curfew was imposed. The army conducted a house-to-house search for weapons, confiscating pieces of artillery and guns. King Hussein told a group of soldiers that "Everyone who tries to stir trouble and riots in this country is contributing to the implementation of conspiracies."[60] The curfew was held for a week and security forces detained forty-seven people for questioning. In total, more than twenty people were injured in the protests and confrontation.[61] The effect of the ban on demonstrations and the state's forceful reaction to attempted protests reflect the regime's concern with controlling collective action, even at the expense of civil liberties and democratic principles.[62]

Unregistered Collective Action

In addition to preventing and limiting the unruliness and disorder of public collective action, the state also represses less volatile
forms of group work that nevertheless operate outside state-delineated space in civil society. Collective action that falls outside the
regulative capacity of the administrative apparatus is unacceptable
to state disciplinary schemes and constitutes a threat to "social order." All such social interactions are considered illegal and are subject to repressive measures. State officials base this policy on the Law
of Public Meetings (Law 60 of 1953), a regulative holdover from
martial law. The law stipulates that individuals must obtain permission to hold public meetings, defined as "any meeting called to discuss political affairs."[63] In practice, it is a prohibition of any group
activities, outside formal organizations, which are unregistered and
therefore not regulated by the bureaucracy.[64]

The term "public affairs" is an ambiguous concept that provides
the state with broad discretion and latitude. In Jordan, politics are
the topic of conversation in a variety of settings, including coffee
shops, taxis, and private homes. Even at NGOs, conversation invari-
ably wanders to political subjects such as the peace process, government policies, public corruption, and human rights. In effect, any
social gathering constitutes an opportunity to "talk politics"; and
depending upon how state officials interpret such interactions, any
number of meetings could be deemed "political." This directly affects Islamists, who routinely complain that they are detained and
questioned by the *mukhabarat* for allegedly holding a public meeting. In reality, these meetings are typically religiously oriented, but
inevitably open political issues such as Jerusalem, peace with Israel,
and how to make the current system more Islamic.

The requirements for public meetings or gatherings are stringent and explicit. The authorities must be notified at least forty-
eight hours in advance,[65] though in practice much greater notice is
often required. This notification must be signed by at least fifty "well-
known individuals," and include information such as the location
and objectives of the meeting. "Well-known individuals" usually
means personalities that are not objectionable to the regime, even if
they are in the opposition. For many such meetings, it is almost
impossible to gather fifty public personalities for the notification,
especially since some meetings include as few as ten individuals. The

notification must be submitted to the governor of the district for permission,[66] and the district manager or a delegated administrator attends the meeting.[67] The governor has broad powers to disperse any permitted gathering, with violence if deemed necessary. Article 6 of the Law of Public Meetings states: "In case there is an incident of security disorder or issues discussed were not in the original intent of the meeting, the area leader [governor] can call for the cancellation of the meeting, using force if necessary and the people causing the disorder can be indicted and sentenced."[68] The law continues to state that any individual who organizes a meeting without prior consent is liable and subject to jail.[69] Any meeting held illegally is subject to force.[70]

The law is rarely enforced to its extreme. In most instances, the group engaged in illegal meetings or activities is issued a warning by either the Ministry of the Interior, charged with preventing unregistered group activities, or the *mukhabarat*, who enjoy wide-ranging authority to repress any actions deemed threatening to the security of the country. Groups that do not threaten the regime are often allowed to continue operating without a permit, though the threat of state action is always present. These groups are typically pro-regime and non-threatening. For example, in Amman an informal women's group regularly meets once a month to discuss topics of interest, usually politics. At each meeting, a speaker is invited to present a lecture and answer questions. The subject of the discussion includes any number of political interests, ranging from elections to the Islamic movement. When asked whether the group was registered, the organizer responded that they had not received permission, but that a government official told her the *mukhabarat* were already aware of their activities and were not concerned.[71] The women involved in this group are a collection of Western women living in Jordan and educated, Westernized Jordanians. Some of the members are connected to prominent, pro-regime supporters through marriage, and the group is not oppositional.

A more politically oriented and critical women's group, however, faced greater state opposition to its activities. In 1996, the unregistered Coalition for Jordanian Women met to discuss possibilities for female quotas in the 1997 parliamentary elections. Women are underrepresented in parliament and there have been numerous proposals to create quotas to enhance their political stature. Because Jordan is a conservative, tribal society, female quota proposals have faced serious resistance. The Coalition for Jordanian Women was highly visible in the media, meeting with members of parliament to discuss the issue. Security groups complained that the group was unregistered and therefore technically illegal. Eventually, five of its members were brought in for questioning by the *mukhabarat*. Though the *mukhabarat* did not prevent the group from meeting, they maintained close surveillance, which prompted the group to limit its activities and the scope of its work.[72]

While channeling group work into a specific, controlled space, the state also delegitimizes alternative forms of collective action. Ministry officials at various regulative offices argue that if a particular group's activities are not violent or a direct threat to the regime, they should have no qualms about creating a formal organization rather than operating in the shadows of society. From this perspective, if a group has nothing to hide, it should operate in the open. Of course, such an argument presupposes real freedom of association. Regardless, the state points to the opportunities for organization in state-delineated social space to delegitimize groups that act outside this framework.

CONCLUSION

Doug McAdam has argued that the "pace of insurgency" reflects the ability of a social movement to engage in "tactical innovation."[73] Because movements typically lack institutional access or political power, they must develop innovative protest techniques to offset this relative powerlessness. However, movement opponents can counter these innovations in the medium to long term through "tactical adaption" in which they learn to offset the new techniques of protest.[74] The Jordanian state has tried to eliminate the ability of social movements to innovate by requiring that all collective action conform to a particular format that can be controlled. It has institutionalized the relationship between the state and social activism through administrative structures, thereby rendering collective action predictable. Innovation is precluded and the political leverage that derives from disruptive protest activities is limited.

The system of control that underlies the disciplinary power of the state and maintains this predictability in the post-1989 period does not include new legislative weapons. On the contrary, most of the laws that demand vulnerability to surveillance have been in place since the 1950s and 1960s. But since political liberalization in 1989, the regime has relied more exclusively upon these administrative techniques rather than brutal repression since it is constrained by both its own democratic discourse as well as popular political expectations. But while the regime maintains an appearance of political freedom by supporting elections and other democratic institutions, it manipulates rules and continues authoritarian practices to reify its own power. Farsoun and Fort describe such a political system as "an electoral regime embedded in an authoritarian state."[75] The regime manipulates democratic institutions and processes to remain in power, creating a "façade democracy."[76]

This system of control is not hegemonic or unitary. There is continuous ebb and flow in the level of actual regime control. Various professional associations, for example, continue to contest state control and engage in political activities. The long tradition of political contestation and participation through professional associations that existed during the martial law period is difficult to uproot, even if members of the regime have quietly suggested reforms.[77] In addition, the clash between the regime and the cultural societies demonstrates that civil society leaders have not unconditionally accepted the limits imposed by the state and are actively challenging the boundaries of the political. But this dialectical interaction has thus far favored the regime, which has successfully imposed its own vision of democracy. The system of control may not be complete, but it is pervasive and substantially affects prospects for social movements that seek to organize through NGOs.

CHAPTER 2

State Power and the Regulation of Islam

For the Islamic movement, organizational opportunities and the application of regulative practices are determined by state interest in controlling Islamic discourse and interpretations. As in other Middle East countries, regime legitimacy in Jordan is based in part upon Islamic credentials. As a result, the regime sponsors its own interpretation of Islam and attempts to prevent the projection of alternative views. The Jordanian state's regulation of Islamic activism is therefore inextricably linked to broader issues of religious control in the kingdom, and authoritarian tendencies are apparent in the religious sphere.

Like other religions, Islam is subject to interpretation, and various actors compete to assert their own particular variant in what Dale Eickelman and James Piscatori term "Muslim politics"—"the competition and contest over both the interpretation of symbols and the control of the institutions, both formal and informal, that produce and sustain them."[1] Muslim politics involve attempts to monopolize "sacred authority"—the right to interpret Islam and religious symbols on behalf of the community.[2] Each participant in the struggle over religious meaning presents an alternative interpretation to legitimate a right to sacred authority. In this struggle, ideas do not act alone. They are produced, articulated, and disseminated through institutions such as the mosque, religious lessons, the Friday sermon, and grassroots organizations. In Muslim politics, the parties to the symbolic contest mobilize institutions to promote particular understandings of the political and social role of Islam. The struggle

45

over meaning is thus not simply a struggle over ideas and interpretations, but also a contest to control the institutions that are capable of effectively propagating religious meaning.

In the regulation of religion, the Jordanian regime attempts to produce a depoliticized and unthreatening interpretation of Islam to reify its legitimacy and power; and in this effort, it regulates the minutiae of religious activity in the kingdom by controlling Islamic institutions and rituals. Alternative understandings are subtly excluded from public religious space through administrative practices and repression. The mosque, which was once an instrument of social activism, has become a mouthpiece for the state. The careful and coordinated effort by the regime to mobilize religious institutions for its own interests highlights the importance it places on the regulation of religion and emphasizes the relevance of Islamic discourse for the management of collective action.

Islamic Legitimacy and State Power

State interest in controlling Islamic discourse derives from concerns about legitimacy. Throughout the Middle East, regimes have been afflicted by a "crisis of legitimacy." As a result, they have experimented with a variety of legitimating ideologies, including socialism, nationalism, pan-Arabism, and Islam.[3] Islam, in particular, has been used by every regime in the region to justify its right to rule. Skeptics often argue that this recourse to religion is a superficial façade, a veneer of religiosity intended to legitimate secular policies or authoritarian rule, but it implies the importance of Islamic appearances for governance. Charles Tripp argues that Islam has been mobilized by states in the Middle East primarily for two reasons linked to legitimation:

> First, Islamic themes and symbols have been used to shore up patrimonial, authoritarian systems of rule, supposedly lending them a coloration that augments their authority among predominantly Muslim members of the associated societies. Second, Islam, variously interpreted, has been used by these regimes to give a distinctive character to the identity of the state in order to correspond to the notion that the state represents and speaks for a distinct ethical community.[4]

This instrumental use of Islam was especially pervasive during the period surrounding decolonization in the region. Around the turn of the nineteenth century, the Middle East suffered from various forms of colonization by Western powers. In North Africa, the French not only asserted control over territory, but also implemented a policy of cultural imperialism to replace indigenous practices with "superior" French culture. As a result, leaders in the movements for independence used Islam to assert a unique Arab culture and to mobilize communities under a common framework of identity.[5] Following independence, Islam was incorporated into the process of state development to claim legitimacy for the new regimes and policies. Most of these countries were dominated by socialist agendas, and leaders used particular interpretations of Islam to equate the socialist emphasis on socioeconomic equality with Islamic notions of justice.[6] Jean-Claude Vatin has referred to this as a kind of "political spirituality" in which "religion is used by the state, and by the political elite, who tend to rely on the sacred sources (texts and traditions) in order to obtain the consensus necessary for secular undertakings."[7] In other countries not afflicted by colonialism, such as Saudi Arabia, regimes successfully used *ijtihad* (independent reasoning), selected legal opinions, administrative discretion, and sovereign prerogatives to adapt Islam to the demands of modernization and economic development.[8] Regardless of whether one believes these different states or ruling regimes are Islamic, those in power believe it is necessary to incorporate Islam into legitimation strategies.

In their attempt to use Islam to justify state power and policies, regimes have enacted numerous measures to control the institutions and personalities in society responsible for articulating and disseminating Islam. Mosques, religious institutes of higher education, the *ʿulama, fatwas* (religious legal rulings), and various religious practices have all increasingly fallen within the purview of the state. Islamic institutions have become bureaucratized and linked to the state through the "nationalization of the religious sphere."[9] Religious functionaries are now dependent upon states for their salaries and positions, and religious institutions have become proponents of the state's interpretation of Islam. Serious divergence from state religious policy can lead to a dismissal or serious reprimands, and this creates pressure to articulate the state's version of Islam. Robert Bianchi argues that various reorganizations and reforms in religious institutions in

Egypt have created a "quasi-monopoly in religious censorship and interpretation" that is controlled by the state.[10] Referring to the Saudi Arabian context, James Piscatori writes that "the *ʿulama* have had to depend on the government for their salaries and positions; they have become agents of the state. And because their methods of selection and education have been regularized, they have become bureaucratized."[11] Fouad Ajami notes that al-Azhar University, the Islamic university in Cairo, functions to provide "religious interpretation in the service of the custodians of power."[12] According to many of the Islamists interviewed in this study, religious scholars affiliated with these Islamic institutions are, in essence, "sheikhs of authority."

Regimes have recently tried to tighten control over religious institutions to combat the rise of Islamic movements, many of which challenge the state's interpretation of Islam and its attempted project of religious hegemony. As Vatin notes, "Islam is the language of power and resistance to power,"[13] and Islamic movements use a religious framework to critique incumbent regimes. Because regimes have relied to some extent on Islam for legitimacy, they are vulnerable to charges that they are not really Islamic in practice. In this manner, Islamic movement critiques are based upon criteria the regime has claimed for itself. States have reacted to the new challenge by "rising to the defense of respect for the places of worship and appropriating the production and diffusion of religious discourse."[14] They have tightened state control over religious institutions such as mosques and openly deride more "radical" Islamic understandings. The struggle over Islamic meaning has grown more volatile as Islamic movements and states lock into a battle for hegemony over religious interpretation and sacred authority.

Jordan is not immune to this struggle, and the regime has enacted a series of measures and strategies to control the interpretation of Islam. Like other states in the Middle East, the Jordanian state has usurped the independence of religious institutions and appropriated them to support state control. Islamic institutions are incorporated into the state apparatus to enhance the state's regulative capacity vis-à-vis religious discourse. The interpretation of Islam represented through these institutions and practices reflects regime interests in the struggle over meaning and its ability to effectively regulate public religious fora.

RELIGIOUS LEGITIMACY IN JORDAN

In Jordan, the regime's legitimacy is to a large extent predicated upon its historical relationship with Islam. First, the Hashemites of Jordan (the ruling family) are from the Qurayshi tribe, the same tribe as the Prophet Mohammed. King Abdullah II, who ascended the throne after King Hussein's death in February 1999, is the forty-third generation of direct descent from the Prophet through the male line of the Prophet's grandson, al-Hassan. As a result, the royal family claims a genealogical link to the messenger of God and derives legitimacy based upon this relationship. In the Muslim world, this genealogical link to the Prophet, who represents the Muslim exemplar, carries substantial weight in creating an aura of religious legitimacy.

Second, the Hashemites ruled Mecca from 1201 to 1925. King Abdullah's great-great-grandfather, Sharif Hussein, was the keeper and guardian of the holiest city in Islam until the Wahhabis of Saudi Arabia gained control of the Hijaz in 1926. Prior to World War I, the Hashemites also controlled Medina, the second holiest city in Islam.

Third, the Hashemites' past and present role in protecting al-Aqsa Mosque and the Dome of the Rock in Jerusalem, the site of the Prophet's miraculous night journey and ascension to heaven, links the royal family to the third holiest city in Islam.[15] Despite the Israeli occupation of Jerusalem since 1967, Jordan has continued to provide financial support and oversight for Islamic monuments in the city. In addition, Sharif Hussein is buried in Jerusalem and King Abdullah I (the current king's great-grandfather and founder of the kingdom), was shot and killed at al-Aqsa mosque in 1951. A member of the Hashemites was thus "martyred" at the third holiest site in Islam.

Fourth, the regime claims responsibility for ensuring the application of Islamic principles of jurisprudence in the kingdom. At present, this application is nominal, but the regime consistently invokes *shari'a* (Islamic law) principles to support various policies and actions. In the Jordanian legal system, the application of the *shari'a* is currently limited to personal status issues (marriage, divorce, child custody, and inheritance), but the regime still finds it necessary to at least use Islamic values as a rhetorical device to legitimate decisions in other issue areas.

And finally, the ruling family is responsible for renovating and maintaining Islamic sites in Jordan, especially sites commemorating the Prophet's companions. This support includes not only state initiatives, but also personal donations and programs run by the Hashemite family.

The Hashemites consistently draw upon this special relationship with Islam, especially the Qurayshi and Jerusalem linkages, to perpetuate Islamic legitimacy and control. On television and in the print media one can find numerous statements by the late King Hussein in which he blatantly and directly refers to his Islamic heritage and the role of his family in Islamic history. In one such context, he utilized this linkage in a 1993 speech about his decision to issue a royal decree amending the election law.[16] He stated that, "I call upon you all to realize that the Arab Hashemite Hussein, who has been honored by the Almighty Allah to be a descendent of the Prophet Mohammed bin Abdullah, peace be upon him, is above all worldly titles and positions."[17]

In another example, during an address to the nation in 1993 that touched upon the sensitive issue of Jerusalem, King Hussein unhesitatingly reemphasized his own special relationship to the city:

> We Hashemites have borne a special historic honor through our distinctive connection with Jerusalem. For it is the site where Allah took his Prophet for a journey by night. And the site is the resting-place of Hussein I. The soil of Al Aqsa Mosque has been moistened by the blood of my martyred grandfather, founder of the Kingdom Abdullah bin al-Hussein.[18]

Public statements such as these are common, especially during periods of unrest in the kingdom or when pockets of resistance emerge.

In Jordan, the Islamic sources of legitimacy are of particular importance because of the challenge posed by other ideological groups, both inside and outside the kingdom. Over the years, Arab nationalists, Nasserists, Ba'thists, communists, Islamists, and Palestinian groups have challenged the sovereignty of the state and the prerogatives of the ruling family. Vulnerability to these challenges is due to the history of state formation in Jordan. The kingdom was carved from British mandate territory following the defeat of the Ottoman

Empire in World War I. In exchange for Hashemite support against the Ottomans, the British gave Abdullah I the Transjordan territory, what is now contemporary Jordan. At the time of its "creation" as a political entity, Jordan was dominated by a multitude of independent tribes with little or no loyalty to their new ruler. The Jordanian state was an artificial entity imposed upon tribes by an external force, the British, which armed King Abdullah I with the military capacity to quell tribal independence.[19] Hashemite power was thus initially supported by a British military and administrative presence. Even after independence, the British supported the regime through subsidies for political and economic development. As a result, both national identity and the legitimacy of the state were weak and susceptible to attacks by ideological challenges. King Hussein, during his long reign, therefore relied to some extent on his Islamic sources of legitimacy to stave off attacks from challenges to his right to rule.

Because of the importance of religion in society and for the royal family's power, there is ample attention given to the regulation and control of Islam in the kingdom. The symbolic meaning of Islam is important for regime legitimation, and the state carefully supervises the institutions capable of disseminating this meaning in a manner that reifies regime interests. By regulating the institutions charged with propagating understandings of Islam and Islamic symbols, the regime prevents oppositional elements from using public religious space to mobilize dissent.

THE MOSQUE

The mosque represents the central institution for religious practice in Muslim societies, providing a religio-spatial structure for ritual and community interaction. The role of the mosque in neighborhoods and communities is multifunctional and complex, at once religious, social, cultural, and political. Beginning with the Prophet's mosque-house in Medina and the founding of the first Muslim community, mosques have been involved in all facets of community life. Through the mosque, Muslims pray, congregate for the *khutba* (Friday sermon), collect and distribute *zakat* (religiously obligated charity), listen to religious lessons, and receive *fatwas*. It has served as a forum for political discussions and decisions, often fusing religious and political symbols to mobilize collectivities. The mosque is involved in life cycle and social issues, such as marriage, death, and the resolution of local disputes, and serves as a center for communication. The call to prayer structures the temporal pace of community activity, which often spatially revolves around the mosque. As an institution, the mosque ties communities together through its various roles in everyday life.[20]

The multifunctionality of the mosque, its communal dimensions, and its centrality in neighborhoods not only serve the needs of the community, but also create a potential institution for revolutionary action. In North Africa, nationalist movements used the mosques in the struggle for independence, organizing and linking religious symbols to anticolonial discourse in order to broaden the movement's appeal. Various Islamic groups disseminate ideology through the *khutba*, lessons, and informal interactions, and utilize the mosque as a site for movement recruitment. In Egypt, private mosques have served as recruitment grounds for violent Islamic groups, such as Islamic Jihad and the Gamiyya Islamiyya, prompting the state to tighten its control of mosques throughout the country. In Algeria, the mosque became an arena for state opposition, providing a forum for excluded oppositional figures and various Islamic groups.

The mosque also provides a social site for the mobilization of collective action. Many instances of open defiance and protest originate at mosques following the Friday sermon. Not only are large numbers of prospective demonstrators already gathered, but also the *khutba* can be used to inspire and motivate individuals and groups to participate. In Amman, the King Hussein mosque, nestled downtown in the *suq* (marketplace), is regularly used as a launching point for protests. Following the bread riots in 1996, which erupted over subsidy reductions, and again after the second uprising in the West Bank later that year, demonstrations were organized outside the mosque after the Friday prayers. Mobilization and recruitment at mosques are difficult to regulate because regimes cannot prevent people from praying. In addition, demonstrations are often unannounced, agitated once people are already gathered.[21]

The potential of mosques as social sites for collective action has prompted various regimes to incorporate mosques and mosque-related activities into the state bureaucracy through the Ministry of Awqaf and Religious Affairs, or equivalent administrative apparatus.[22] Throughout the Muslim world, there has traditionally been a distinction between "official" mosques and independent or "private" mosques, sometimes known as "free" mosques because they are not operated by the state.[23] The former are funded by the state, which controls all related activities, and disseminate a highly depoliticized version of Islam designed to remain passive in the face of state power. The private mosques, in contrast, are built with private donations, often from a single, wealthy individual. Until recently, the patron or benefactor of the private mosque usually decided the affairs of the mosque and this "free" space provided room for an alternative Islamic discourse. Because of the rising challenge posed by Islamic groups working through independent mosques, states have attempted to erode the private mosque's independence, most directly by proclaiming it a public mosque and therefore under state management. In Egypt, for example, Law 157 of 1960 authorized the Ministry of Awqaf to take control of the supervision of all mosques by the year 1970. A 1964 report detailing a survey of mosques and mosque-related personnel explicitly stated that the purpose of the survey was to help bring all private mosques within the control of the ministry.[24] The difficulty of this task is reflected by the fact that the Egyptian government has to this day been unable to incorporate all mosques into the state. In 1997, the Minister of Islamic Affairs, Mahmoud Hamdi Zaqaouq, expressed the regime's intention to take control of the remaining 30,000 private mosques (out of a total of 55,000). More importantly, the stated reason for this reinvigorated effort to control mosques is that it will help prevent the dissemination of "unorthodox" Islamic views that are critical of the regime.[25]

In Jordan, all mosques are controlled by the government, regardless of whether they are state or privately funded.[26] In contrast to Egypt, in a small country such as Jordan it is easier for the government to take control of the mosques. While the total number of mosques in Egypt is currently estimated at 55,000, in Jordan it is only 2,245, reflecting its much smaller population.[27] Although the number of mosques in the kingdom has grown (see table 2.1), the expansion is matched by the extension of government control into this traditional institution of religious space. There is no "independent" or "free" space in Jordanian mosques.[28]

The regulative control of mosques as physical structures is in itself less significant than control over the kinds of social interactions and practices that are permissible within this space. The effect of the

Table 2.1. Growth of Mosques

Year	Number of Mosques	Change per Year (%)
1950	420	–
1955	461	9.8
1960	563	22.1
1965	747	32.8
1970	901	20.6
1975	1,062	17.9
1980	1,456	37.1
1985	1,988	36.5
1990	2,021	1.7
1995	2,218	9.8
1996	2,245	1.2

Source: Ministry of Awqaf, *Annual Report,* 191.

control over mosques thus manifests itself through the limitations imposed upon those who operate within its context. Most importantly, it means that the state controls who can speak and work through mosques, thus directly determining who has "sacred authority" through arguably the most important institution in religious space. This control, in turn, produces a docile version of Islam that reifies regime power and prevents critical elements from utilizing this space to disseminate an alternative interpretation of meaning.

IMAMS, PREACHERS, AND THE *KHUTBA*

Religious knowledge and understanding is acquired through a mediated process of interpretation. Even the most erudite Islamic scholar learns from others, both past and present, and is affected by personal experiences and aptitude. Interpretations are disseminated through books, cassettes, videos, television, radio, religious lessons, sermons, personal interactions, etc. These instruments represent the means for obtaining religious understanding. While some groups and individuals turn directly to the sources of the religion, the Qur'an and Sunna, even they rely upon other scholars and past religious knowledge. Dependence on others for interpreting Islam is often exacerbated by illiteracy because of the inability to refer directly to religious texts. In recent years, however, increasing literacy rates have replaced this absolute dependence with a relative dependency on those who are considered more knowledgeable about Islam. Two of the most powerful institutions for shaping and disseminating interpretations of Islam are the imam and the preacher.

An imam is the leader of the congregational prayers, but contemporary usage in Jordan more often narrowly refers to the individual in charge of the mosque. This person is, in theory, someone who is knowledgeable about Islam and capable of leading ritualistic practices. The imam is typically familiar with the community and can therefore mediate disputes and care to the specific religious needs of the congregation, though this is not always the case and in some instances a community outsider is appointed due to necessity. Because the imam is charged with overseeing the mosque and its activities, it is important to the regime that the individual does not foment dissension or opposition. The selection and training process is therefore tightly controlled and monitored by the Ministry of Awqaf.[29]

Imams are considered civil servants and are hired under the civil servant laws as government employees. They are supposed to have a baccalaureate in *shari'a*, but frequently community college degrees are accepted because of the low level of candidate quality. Many of the imams receive their education at the Ministry of Awqaf's two year College of Islamic Sciences or the four year Da'wa and Basics of Religion College.[30] There is an interview process at the Civil Servants Department, in conjunction with the Ministry of Awqaf, and candidates are treated like other civil servant applicants. Selective hiring practices tend to produce moderate, apolitical imams.[31] After being hired, all imams must continue to attend classes at the Center for the Rehabilitation of Imams, which holds seminars on various contemporary issues, such as drug use, water conservation, traffic accidents, and the environment. The imams are paid civil servant wages—JD200 ($286) a month (an average income in Jordan)— and are provided housing at the mosque. In several instances, other benefits accrue as a result of the position of the imam. Richard Antoun, for example, found that the imam he studied received additional money from his role as a marriage official and pilgrimage guide.[32] Mohammed Abu Shaqra, a prominent imam in Amman and Prince Hassan's religious advisor, is reported to drive a government-provided car. Other funds are disseminated through donations for missionary work, either from individuals or governments such as Saudi Arabia.[33] The main roles of the imam are to act as a mediator within the community, work with the local *zakat* committee, teach Qur'anic reading, and deliver the *khutba*.

The director of preaching and guidance at the Ministry of Awqaf labeled this last function "the most important role for the imam."[34] The *khutba* is the weekly religious sermon held every Friday at the noon prayers. In the sermon, preachers are supposed to discuss issues of concern to the community from an Islamic perspective, including local disputes, current events, and broader theological issues. The *minbar* (pulpit) is used as an instrument for addressing the community, and the *khutba* is a corporate experience whereby individual Muslims reinvigorate collective ties through their mutual participation as audience. Even individuals who do not pray during the week often attend the Friday sermon, a weekly religious ritual that reconnects Muslims to their obligations and duties as part of the *umma* (Muslim community).[35] As a "cultural broker," the preacher interprets and applies Islam to rapidly changing conditions in the modern world, mediating between the great traditions of Islam and local practices and events.[36] The *khutba* has recently been revitalized as a form of political communication, channeling ideology through religious speech and ritual.[37] Particularly where the press and publications are curtailed or constrained, the *khutba* becomes an important medium of expression, at once religious and political, purveying a message wrapped in religious symbolism. All of these factors mean that the *khutba* can have a powerful influence on communities, often invigorating faith, mobilizing activism, and tightening the ties that bind individuals together into a community.[38]

The ambiguous role of the preacher, at once religious, political, and social, poses a challenge for states concerned with Islamic legitimacy.[39] Preachers are obligated to discuss injustice and wrongdoing and may threaten the state's Islamic façade if criticism is leveled at state action and policy. The audience—the community—looks to the preacher for guidance in interpreting the world through an Islamic framework. Where preachers attack the state or its agenda as un-Islamic, they can affect broader opposition throughout the community. The oratory skills of many oppositional preachers, with the rise and fall of intonation combined with powerful religious analogies, can inspire Muslims to achieve great goals; and regimes fear that the mobilizing potential of the *khutba* could inspire challenges to the state or its functionaries.

Because of the potential role of the preacher in political communication and opposition to the state, regimes have increasingly curtailed the independence of the *khutba* and harnessed it for their own purposes. Throughout the Muslim world, preachers have come increasingly under the auspices of the various state ministries charged with overseeing the mosque and its activities. The freedom of the "free" preacher, operating outside state control, is rapidly shrinking as the state extends the administrative apparatus into the realm of the *khutba*, shaping its message to prevent any mobilizing effect. By incorporating preachers into the administrative structure and providing standardized training, the state has in effect created a professional preacher class.[40] Where the state has not directly incorporated all preachers into the bureaucracy, various requirements are promulgated to limit any oppositional content in the *khutba*.[41]

In Jordan, control over preachers and the content of the *khutba* has expanded. In the 1960s, the local *qadi* (religious judge) and the Department of Religious Endowments supervised the preacher.[42] In 1964, the Department of Religious Endowments began sending out newsletters that suggested topics for the sermon, though evidence indicates that some preachers did not always adopt these suggestions and retained some measure of independence. The department also required that all preachers retain a written copy of the sermons, though again it is not clear whether this was strictly enforced or followed.[43] This practice continued after the establishment of the Ministry of Awqaf in 1966. During the 1970s, the ministry began sending preachers a monthly journal with complete sermons that could be used verbatim.[44] As the Ministry of Awqaf developed from the late 1960s onward, functional differentiation within the ministry progressed and departments were set up to regulate the minutia of religious activity, including the *khutba*.

Preaching now falls under the purview of the Department of Preaching and Guidance at the Ministry of Awqaf, which regulates not only imams, but also nongovernment preachers who are brought from outside the administrative apparatus. The growth of mosques has surpassed the government's capability to staff them with qualified imams and preachers. There is a deficit of 1,037 imams and preachers for the some 2,245 mosques in the country, leaving 46 percent of the mosques unstaffed by an imam or preacher from the

Table 2.2. Number of Government
Imams and Preachers

Governate	Imams and Preachers
Amman	245
Jerusalem	82
Zarqa	147
Madaba	30
Balqa	78
Irbid	122
Kura	38
Ramtha	29
Mafraq	110
Ajlun	35
Jerash	47
Kerak	90
Tafeelah	44
Ma'an	58
Aqaba	26
Northern Jordan Valley	27
Total	1208

Source: Ministry of Awqaf, *Annual Report,* 208.

government (see tables 2.1 and 2.2).[45] Though there are other government officials at the local branch of the Ministry of Awqaf charged with overseeing these mosques, the important functions of the imam and the preacher remain unfulfilled in a substantial number of instances. As a result of this deficit, outside preachers are frequently brought in to deliver the *khutba.* In addition, although one of the primary functions of the imam is to give the *khutba,* officials at the ministry recognize that not all imams are qualified.[46] As the director of the department notes, "preaching is a gift from God," and not all imams have this gift, though they may be qualified for other activities at the mosque.[47] In such instances, an outside preacher may be used. The imam does not have a choice in the selection of an external speaker and the preacher need not necessarily work for the government. For example, at the mosque near the University of Jordan, professors from the Shari'a College at the university are frequently asked to deliver a *khutba.* Professors, religious judges, teachers, and anyone who is qualified can be brought in to give a sermon. The director estimates that about 60 percent of all preachers are government imams while 40 percent are brought from outside. His estimate indicates that not all mosques hold a *khutba*, since 40 percent would not fill the unstaffed mosques and replace unqualified imams. Typically, individual preachers request to give a sermon, though the ministry does advertise if it needs to fill positions. The preachers are paid a nominal sum for their services, but it is a symbolic reward, not a financial incentive.

The fact that there are a substantial number of non-ministry preachers does not indicate that the government has loosened its control of the *khutba*; on the contrary, the selection process and regulative techniques are utilized to ensure that the *khutba* remains supportive of the regime and uncritical. First, the ministry often dictates the subject of the *khutba*. About once every two or three months, the ministry requires that imams and preachers speak on a certain subject, typically the topic of the latest seminar at the Center for the Rehabilitation of Imams or an issue of pressing concern.[48] Second, in the selection process, the government brings in "balanced thinkers," everyday speak in Jordan for those who are not critical of the government or its policies. The ministry consciously avoids controversial or oppositional figures that may espouse "radical" ideologies. Third, the ministry rotates outside preachers from mosque to mosque. While the director in charge of these appointments claims that the rotation is done so that the congregation does not tire of listening to the same preacher every week, it has the more controlling effect of reducing the opportunity for nongovernment preachers to cultivate a loyal following through the mosques. In other countries, specific private mosques are known for particular opposition figures, but in Jordan the fact that all the mosques are government controlled means that the regime decides which preachers can develop a following through the *khutba*. Imams who are qualified to deliver the *khutba* remain at the same mosque, thus creating opportunities for government employed preachers to develop a clientele through the Friday sermon. As a result, those who are less likely to be critical of the state and its policies have a greater chance of fostering a loyal constituency through the mosque.

The final, and most important, mechanism of control for preachers, both government as well as nongovernment, is a set of informal rules known as "red lines." A great deal of politics in Jordan has always been characterized by a certain degree of informality (the informal rights and prerogatives of various tribes or the royal family's personalistic politics, for example). There is a set of unwritten, but well-recognized, rules governing the political system and social interactions, negotiated and understood by participants in the political and social game. These informal rules, or red lines, represent the limits to behavior and action tolerated by the regime, and crossing these lines incurs reprisals. They are not explicit, only hesitantly discussed, and extremely effective. While the government requests that preachers discuss issues of concern to the community, this rhetorical openness bows to the weight of informal red lines, which in reality guide content.

The most significant red line is that "preachers cannot go against state policy" or else they will be prevented from speaking.[49] Officials at the Ministry of Awqaf argue that this is the "spirit" of the Law of Preaching, Guidance, and Teaching in Mosques, which states: "The preacher shall be committed to wisdom and proper preaching and shall not attack, accuse, or instigate and go beyond the guidelines of the Islamic *da'wa*."[50] Since one of the roles of the Department of Preaching and Guidance is the "supervision of clearing the atmosphere in mosques from disagreements and conflicts,"[51] officials interpret the limits of preaching as a prohibition of criticism directed against the state. Several ministry officials referred to mosques as "government agencies," reiterating the state's control and denying their status as community and social institutions. As a consequence, the informal policy is to prevent any actions that might be harmful to the government and its Islamic legitimacy, a source of legitimacy that would be affected by any attacks from the *minbar*.

The government's enforcement of the red lines derives from several practices. First, the Department of Preaching and Guidance receives and reviews the names of prospective preachers before the Friday sermon and can deny permission to any candidate without specifying a reason. This is used to systematically prevent oppositional figures from using the *khutba* as a medium of opposition. Individuals who preach despite being barred from doing so are punished according to the law, which states: "If a preacher insists on speaking publicly upon written notification of prevention, he shall be punished by imprisonment for a period of one week to one month or fined a sum of JD20–100."[52] In reality, the punishment is often harsher and can mean referral to the *mukhabarat* or the Ministry of the Interior.

A second technique is to ban and punish preachers who receive permission to speak but cross the red line by criticizing state policy. While the director of preaching and guidance recognizes that imams and preachers do disagree with state policies, he argues that they must find an acceptable way of presenting this criticism or face repercussions. When they pass the limits of acceptability they are first warned. If they continue, they are banned for a period of two or three months. More outspoken or influential figures are banned for longer periods of time. Though this latter ban is not in strict accordance with the law, ministry officials admit that there are cases where preachers are blacklisted from delivering the *khutba* for long periods of time.

The practice of banning certain preachers has become more common since the signing of the peace treaty with Israel in 1994, a move opposed by most religious figures in the country. This issue, more than any other, has been a source of contention between the ministry and preachers. Prior to the signing of the peace treaty, preachers openly decried Israel, often actively encouraged to do so by the government. Once the peace process was underway, regardless of widespread grassroots opposition, preachers were prevented from criticizing the treaty. 'Ali Hasan al-Halabi, an influential Salafi sheikh who is known to attract large audiences, has been prevented from delivering sermons since 1994 when he first criticized the regime's decision to make peace with Israel. The ministry further restricted his activities by preventing him from delivering weekly lessons at the mosque, which were at times attended by more than three hundred people.[53]

Even the Muslim Brotherhood has been affected by this control. A famous case in point is Abdul Munem Abu Zant, a member of the Brotherhood and an Islamic Action Front Party parliamentarian from 1989 to 1997. In 1994, Abu Zant was at the center of controversy because he defied government orders preventing him from speaking in mosques. Despite the prohibition, he delivered a *khutba* condemning the peace treaty. Following his speech, Abu Zant claimed that police assaulted him. While police argue that he was attacked by supporters of the official imam, Sami al-Najjar, who had been prevented from delivering his own sermon by Abu Zant and his followers,[54] most imams and preachers accept Abu Zant's version of the story. They point to his treatment as part of an unannounced government policy to remove all opposition from the mosques. Abu Zant subsequently went on a tirade in parliament, charging that preachers appointed by the ministry were imploring God to be merciful to the Israelis whom he referred to as "the killers of all God's emissaries and prophets." In an ugly incident that led to personal insults in parliament, he was denied a request for the names of all appointed preachers and the dates of their sermons.[55] He was later detained because he criticized a south Amman court that at the time was trying twenty-four people accused of disrupting the peace during demonstrations against the signing of the peace accords.

In September 1999, Abu Zant was again at the center of controversy. He is close to Hamas and in his sermons supports their activities. Because the regime began to crack down on Hamas in August of that summer, the Amman governor, Qaftan Majali, placed Zant under administrative arrest detention for refusing to sign a pledge not to deliver pro-Hamas sermons. He was arrested at three different times during a single week for refusing to comply with the governor's demands.[56]

Since the peace treaty, the regime has also attempted to remove critical imams from their government positions. Salah Khaldi, who for ten years was the imam at the central mosque in Sweileh, a neighborhood in West Amman, was removed from his position in the mid-1990s, widely recognized in the Islamist community as a move to crack down on imams opposed to the peace process. He is known to be an outspoken critic of the government's policies, especially toward Israel. In Sweileh, there is little tribal influence because of the predominance of the Islamic movement, which emphasizes religion, rather than tribe, as an overarching identity. This has created a situation where, as the current imam at the mosque states, "whoever controls the mosque, controls the community."[57] The regime decided it could not afford to have a government critic controlling the community. The government also tried to fire another imam who delivered a *khutba* arguing that Shimon Peres is more dangerous than other Israeli leaders. Since Peres is considered a friend of the Jordanian regime, or at least a potential ally, such charges were unacceptable. The *mukhabarat* ransacked his library and the Ministry of Awqaf took measures to fire him from his position. He was able to retain his post only after using significant *wasta*.

This censorship and control, however, does not always prevent preachers from disseminating their message in a subtler format. Critical imams that I interviewed referred to "loopholes" and "ways to get around" the rules.[58] One preacher commented, "There are limits to what I can do, but there are ways around these limits so that I can bring a message without incriminating myself. The Qur'an is the best instrument of change so I explain change by going back to the Qur'an." Critiques are masked in direct quotes from the Qur'an and *hadiths* (reported sayings and traditions of the Prophet Mohammed), presented as hidden analogies to current circumstances and conditions. By quoting the Qur'an and *hadiths*, preachers can insulate themselves from direct reprisals because sermons are wrapped in the word of God, something the regime simply cannot afford to contradict or punish. Without naming people or events specifically, the preacher can creatively use religious symbols and analogies to discuss topics such as Jerusalem or the peace process. As one imam described it, "Through the various *ayas* [verses of the Qur'an], the preacher can say exactly what he wants to say." The meaning and significance of the *ayas* change with circumstances so that the same reference can mean different things at different historical moments.

But this technique requires a particular skill. Not every preacher is capable of effectively disseminating a message and subtly discussing a topic without referring to it by name. As one preacher noted, "many imams cannot do this except directly," and these imams often find themselves facing reprisals. The preacher must be careful not to be too obvious and must be prepared to defend the sermon on religious grounds with alternative interpretations that mask the true intent. One imam cautioned, "Every Friday preacher can use interpretations of the Qur'an to bring through thoughts and ideas without saying something specifically, but he should know exactly what he is saying." The implication is that he should be able to present a reasonable and innocuous interpretation of the *khutba* should the government ever question him.

The use of hidden analogies and continued opposition by some preachers and imams indicate that the regime does not enjoy complete hegemony over the mosque and its religious space. Its control, however, is substantial and significantly limits how this space can be effectively utilized. Preachers admit that their subtle, embedded messages are not always understood and that even if they are, it is only by a small number of people. The state also retains the right to remove imams or prevent specific individuals from delivering the *khutba*. Permission is contingent upon government approval of content, and this approval is only forthcoming for "balanced" thinkers who do not openly criticize or oppose the regime or state policy. The mobilizing potential of the *khutba* is thus diminished, and it has become a reflection of state control rather than social concerns or community interests.

ZAKAT

According to Islamic principles, Muslims with the financial capability are required to provide approximately 2.5 percent of their annual income for *zakat*, frequently translated as religiously obligated charity. It is one of the five pillars of Islamic obligation and is therefore a ritualistic duty, though in contemporary practice it is often institutionalized in secular tax codes and is considered voluntary. Although it is a religious duty, not all Muslims give *zakat* and most governments do not force individuals to do so. As one Ministry of Awqaf official expressed, giving *zakat* is "between them [Muslims] and their God." *Zakat* is a mechanism that emphasizes the material and financial responsibility of Muslims to one another as members of the *umma*. It thereby fulfills both an economic function, by providing for the less fortunate, and a religio-psychological function, by giving donors a sense of religious purity.[59]

Because of both the religious and socioeconomic dimensions of *zakat*, it is potentially a powerful institution for mobilizing support for particular Islamic groups or movements. Control over the mechanisms of collecting and distributing *zakat* can provide a source of patronage-based power. By selectively distributing *zakat* to supporters, a movement or group can develop a strong clientele and following. It is an institution within religious space that provides an opportunity to disseminate an ideological message and muster support for mobilization or a cause. The Islamic charitable societies run by radical Islamic groups such as Hamas and Hizballah, and the loyalty these organizations engender among recipients, is evidence of the possible political usage of religious charitable institutions such as *zakat*. In Jordan, for example, the Muslim Brotherhood attempted to utilize the *zakat* committee in the Widat Palestinian refugee camp to garner support. There were so many complaints of "unbalanced" and selective practices that the Ministry of Awqaf finally demanded that the Muslim Brotherhood members of the committee resign and a new committee was established.

The Jordanian state has consolidated *zakat* under the auspices of Sanduq al-Zakat in the Ministry of Awqaf. According to the Law of Zakat Committees, "It is not allowed for any person/persons to collect *zakat* and disburse it except through the *zakat* committees officially formed in accordance with these regulations and through official receipts, and the committee member must show an identification card proving he is part of a licensed committee."[60] These committees are pseudo-governmental institutions, tightly linked to Sanduq al-Zakat, which oversees all their activities. The director of the Widat camp *zakat* committee called the *zakat* committees "a cover for government control."[61] Though formed and staffed by private citizens, they must obtain approval from Sanduq al-Zakat; and once created this department controls them. In effect, they operate as a private branch of the state and constitute the only permissible institutions for dealing with *zakat*.

Table 2.3. Number of *Zakat* Committees by Governate

Governate	Committees
Amman	59
Zarqa	11
Aqaba	1
Ma'an	3
Madaba	2
Jerash	9
Karak	0
Northern Jordan Valley	7
Balqa	8
Mafraq	5
Ajlun	8
Irbid	20
Kura	11
Ramtha	1
Tafeelah	2
Total	158

Source: Sanduq al-Zakat, "Report" (in Arabic) (Amman: Hashemite Kingdom of Jordan, 1995).

Through 158 *zakat* committees, mostly neighborhood-based, the state extends its ability to control and penetrate religious space. These committees are charged with assessing community needs and collecting and distributing donations. Each committee is comprised of between seven and fifteen members with renewable memberships every two years, as stipulated by law. The most important instrument of the committee is a subcommittee comprised of social welfare experts or individuals familiar with the community who engage in fieldwork to ascertain which families and individuals need *zakat* assistance. While some members of the committee have higher degrees, the most important qualification is familiarity with the families in the area so that an accurate appraisal can be made. The committee uses a questionnaire to study the community where it is located, visiting homes to ask questions and make visual assessments. The committee considers factors such as the number of family members, living conditions, whether children are in school, whether the family rents or owns its home, and income. Files are kept at the *zakat* committee headquarters, which houses all relevant information, filed according to family identification card number. The files are updated and reevaluated every six months to take into account changing circumstances, such as new employment or an illness in the family.

Money and other donations for *zakat* are primarily collected from three sources. The first is individual domestic donations. In Jordan, according to local understandings of the *shariʿa*, anyone who makes the equivalent of JD600 ($857) or more a year should donate at least 2.5 percent of their annual income.[62] This obligation is not an official legal requirement, but rather a religious interpretation of Islamic duties. The second source is businesses and merchants. Businesses that give *zakat* typically donate 2.5 percent of annual profits while merchants prefer to provide services and basic goods such as food, clothing, and other essential commodities. There are no data available to determine what percent of businesses and merchants actually donate *zakat*. The third source is donations from outside the country. This kind of *zakat* is typically donated through Sanduq al-Zakat rather than the local *zakat* committees, although former residents may prefer to give back to their neighborhood and therefore donate directly to the local branch. Most *zakat* donations are given during the month of Ramadan, when the committees and Sanduq al-Zakat receive about 60–70 percent of all annual donations.

Table 2.4. Number of Families Receiving
Recurring *Zakat* Financial Support

Year	Number of Families
1989	4,105
1990	5,919
1991	10,622
1992	11,257
1993	12,253
1994	12,750
1995	13,170

Source: Sanduq al-Zakat, "Report."

The committees reach a number of families. In the Widat refugee camp, for example, the committee provides monthly payments of approximately JD50 ($72) to six hundred families. In the Baqa'a camp, the local committee reaches about 650 families. The largest committee is the Islamic Committee for the Palestinian People, which donates around three-quarters of a million dinars (over $1 million) a year to families in the West Bank and Gaza Strip, demonstrating Jordan's continued commitment to the Occupied Territories. Most of the *zakat* committees are significantly smaller than these, but the aggregate number of families receiving recurring *zakat* support expanded by more than 300 percent from 1989 to 1995, reflecting its growing importance (see table 2.4). Overall, the *zakat* committees spend around $7.1 million and affect more than sixty thousand people.[63]

In addition to financial support, some committees also provide social services. In the Widat Camp, for example, the committee runs a medical clinic, staffed by nine specialists. There is a medical center, a dental lab, and a medical lab. The families that receive monthly payments can use the clinic free of charge. Other individuals and families that are not well off, but either have not qualified for financial assistance or are on a waiting list, receive discounts to visit the clinics.[64] The discount is generally half of the normal cost, or JD3 ($4.25) per visit. With the money from this second group and from others who pay full price, the committee supports free services for the needy and pays doctors a salary that is commensurate with those at private and government hospitals. Some committees charge everyone half price in the belief that they will attract more patients and thus remain competitive with other clinics and hospitals. A recent ruling by the Ministry of Health prohibits these clinics from charging low prices for everyone, but it still occurs and is not carefully monitored by the government. Approximately three thousand to five thousand people, or over one hundred a day, utilize the medical facilities at the Widat camp committee. Other social service activities include scholarships to attend university and occupational training for women in areas such as sewing, embroidery, and plant arrangement.

Table 2.5 Amount of *Zakat* Distributed
through Sanduq al-Zakat

Year	Amount (JD)	Year	Amount (JD)
1978	5,780	1987	276,016
1979	11,111	1988	902,793
1980	20,013	1989	877,715
1981	29,022	1990	626,622
1982	74,036	1991	788,515
1983	176,519	1992	1,079,925
1984	183,775	1993	1,277,562
1985	228,660	1994	1,771,643

Source: Sanduq al-Zakat, "Report."

Zakat activities also operate through Sanduq al-Zakat. This department of the Ministry of Awqaf receives donations directly from individuals who do not live in poor areas, do not know any needy families, or prefer to give to a central agency capable of distributing the donation to the neediest families in the country. In addition, individuals seeking assistance may petition the Ministry of Awqaf directly for *zakat*. Frequently, they approach an employee they know (or to whom they are referred by friends or family) and describe their particular circumstances or needs. At the discretion of the employee, the request is then passed upward through the bureaucracy, often directly to the minister of awqaf, who personally examines each case and determines whether to recommend that Sanduq al-Zakat provide assistance. In one instance, a women came to the ministry and asked the assistant to the secretary general for money to pay for medical treatment for what she called "poor blood." Her face was a sickly jaundiced color and she had been ill for some time, but was unable to pay for treatment. The ministry employee asked her to write down her condition and the request, and the paper was sent on to the minister who reviewed it and recommended that Sanduq al-Zakat provide financial assistance. Other individuals come to the ministry to request assistance on behalf of a family that may be too proud to ask for help directly. In instances where the request is for ongoing assistance, Sanduq al-Zakat operates like the local *zakat* committees and sends a team into the field to assess the living conditions and need. To assure its ability to distribute *zakat* at a broader national level, the department collects 10 percent of donations given to local *zakat* committees. This means that the Ministry of Awqaf, to a certain extent, centralizes donations. Approximately one-third of all *zakat* donations are given through Sanduq al-Zakat, while the rest are donated through local *zakat* committees.[65]

Sanduq al-Zakat and the Ministry of Awqaf carefully monitor the institution of *zakat* through both administrative and regulative mechanisms. Since all *zakat* activity must be registered with the ministry and operate through the local *zakat* committees, as a practice it is centralized in the state apparatus. Annual reports must be submitted to Sanduq al-Zakat and financial records are carefully audited. In addition, two to three surprise inspections are performed to ascertain where the money is being directed and whether it is reaching needy families. Committees are also required to maintain a record of weekly meetings. While this oversight is ostensibly designed to prohibit the abuse of *zakat* for personal gain, its effect is to prevent alternative centers of power, such as Islamic movements, from utilizing this religious and institutional space.

Of course, this does not mean that other avenues for *zakat* are not created. As with the subtle use of the *khutba*, there are other less visible, informal means for *zakat*. One of the most prominent is the "informal *zakat* committees"—ad hoc committees created when circumstances necessitate immediate charitable action. These are usually created during community disasters or when there is dire need. The authorities typically know about the ad hoc committees; and while not formally acknowledged as legal, the state nonetheless tolerates their existence so long as they do not engage in any activities that might mobilize or organize people beyond the specific charitable act. Individuals who frequent the neighborhood mosque and are concerned about providing charity for their community typically form more permanent informal committees. Through regular interactions during prayer and other mosque-related events, these individuals get to know one another and form a kind of "family" unit. While some members of this unit may be members of Islamic groups, they are more often just concerned residents of the neighborhood. Since most are from the area, they know the needs of the community around the mosque and may create an informal committee to address these needs. They collect *zakat* informally, without receipts, accounting books, or the permission of the state, thus operating independently of the Ministry of Awqaf. Abdullah El Khatib, the president of the GUVS, estimates that the amount of *zakat* distributed through informal mechanisms could equal the amount channeled through Sanduq al-Zakat and local *zakat* committees.[66] Still other Islamic charitable activities are not formally known as *zakat*, but because their work operates through donations, the distribution of services, and support for the needy, they work in the "spirit of *zakat*" and are part of *zakat* activity, though not formally.[67]

The state's involvement in *zakat* provides some measure of Islamic legitimacy. By sponsoring *zakat* committees and the collection and distribution of *zakat*, the state helps and encourages individuals to fulfill an Islamic obligation. At the same time, by centralizing and limiting *zakat* activity to institutions controlled and supported by the state, the regime ensures that its use for political or ideological purposes remains limited at best. It constrains *zakat* within the context of ritual, preventing it from becoming a tool for the mobilization of political activism.

ISLAMIC LAW AND THE *FATWA*

States control the application of Islamic law and jurisprudence. Regardless of the religious fervor of Muslims and the pressure of Islamic movements, the state, in the end, structures legal institutions. Since the postindependence era began in the Middle East at the turn of the twentieth century, the application of Islamic rules and norms has been increasingly eroded by the dominance of secular codes. In many cases, the emasculation of Islamic legal norms by secularism has resulted in a bifurcation in the legal system between Islamic courts, limited to personal status issues such as marriage, divorce, and inheritance, and secular courts responsible for all other issues. Though this bifurcation is not a clean distinction and issues do overlap, the general trend has been to segment the institutions of law; and the application of Islam in rulings has diminished in modern legal systems.[68] In areas where it is applied, it is controlled by the state.

In almost all instances throughout the Muslim world, including Jordan, the *qadi*, or Islamic judge, is appointed by the state. States do not, as a principle, appoint judges who espouse "radical" interpretations or may oppose state policies. *Qadis* are generally quite conservative in their understanding of Islam, though this is certainly not universally the case. As Richard Antoun argues, the *qadi* is another "cultural broker," interpreting Islam in local contexts and disseminating a particular Islamic perspective through legal rulings and decisions.[69] As an instrument of the state, the *qadi* ensures the reproduction of a nonthreatening interpretation of Islam by the legal system. It is extremely rare that a *qadi* issues a decision that jeopardizes the regime's Islamic legitimacy or important matters of state.

But the *qadi* is not the only cultural broker in the area of law and a more important institution in Islamic jurisprudence is the *mufti*, or Islamic legal expert, who issues *fatwas*. A *fatwa* is a jurisprudential opinion based on Islamic law. As a religious ruling, it is generally produced by a *mufti* according to the four schools of jurisprudence or a combination thereof.[70] Though not legally binding, particularly where secular legal codes tend to prevail, it does have a significant impact on Muslims and their view of contemporary issues. Even *qadis* will consult with *muftis* on aspects of Islamic law. A *fatwa* produced by a prominent *mufti* has great influence on Muslims' understandings of the norms and rules that guide behavior.

The use of the *fatwa* is increasingly controlled by the modern state in the Muslim world and has become an instrument to justify state actions and policies. Throughout the Middle East, states have moved to control the institutions and individuals that issue *fatwas* to harness them for policy purposes. In Saudi Arabia, for example, the state routinely uses *fatwas* to justify its decisions and actions. The government appoints members of the Council of the Grand 'Ulama, which issues *fatwas*, and as employees of the state, this group is financially and structurally dependent. Before engaging in controversial action, the Saudi regime is careful to procure a *fatwa* in favor of its actions. Prior to the use of force to extract the Islamic group

that occupied the Ka'ba on 20 November 1979, the regime ob-
tained a *fatwa* legitimating the use of force at the holiest site in
Islam.[71] Another prominent example came after Western forces were
stationed in Saudi Arabia prior to the Gulf War, a circumstance that
many Islamic scholars condemned as un-Islamic. In this case, the
fatwa came after the fact, on the heels of burgeoning Muslim criticism over the presence of Western troops in the heart of the Muslim
holy land. The council endorsed the king's decision and the *mufti*
of Saudi Arabia, 'Abd al-'Aziz Bin Baz, issued a *fatwa* condoning
the use of outside force.[72] Perhaps the most famous case, at least one
that sticks in the minds of many Islamic activists, is the declarations
produced by the various religious institutions controlled by the Egyptian state, including the Fatwa Committee and the *mufti* of Egypt,
in support of the Camp David Accords.[73]

In Jordan, there is a Council of Ifta' charged with issuing *fatwas*
and appointing *muftis*. The Council is comprised of the chief of the
Islamic courts, the general *mufti*, the dean of the School of Shari'a
at the University of Jordan, the *mufti* of the armed forces, the manager of the Fatwa Department at the Ministry of Awqaf, and six
Islamic scholars appointed by the council of ministers for a period of
three years. The Council of Ifta' meets once a month and regularly
issues *fatwas* through the *mufti* of Jordan. The most blatant use of
the *fatwa* by the state, and one that drew sharp criticism from Islamist circles, was related to the 1997 parliamentary elections. The
Muslim Brotherhood, the professional associations, independent
opposition figures, and opposition parties decided to boycott the
elections because of continued government repression, the treaty
with Israel, and other factors. There was widespread concern that
the boycott would produce a low voter turnout and jeopardize the
consolidation of democracy in the country. The *mufti* of Jordan,
Saad Hijawi, issued a *fatwa* that cited the principle of *maslaha
mursalah*, or public interest, claiming that this principle required
Muslims to vote since it was in the best interest of the country.[74]
The Muslim Brotherhood and the boycotting opposition bloc viewed
this as an attempt to validate the elections at a time when support
for the government was waning.[75]

Scholars outside the state complex do issue *fatwas*, but the existence of a state-sponsored institution indicates that the room for
independent *fatwas* is growing smaller. In addition, most Muslims
do not generally recognize the *fatwas* that are issued by alternative

individuals in Jordan. For example, the late Mohammed Nasir al-Din al-Bani (d. 1999), one of the great Salafi scholars who worked in Jordan, while well respected for his work on the authentication of *hadith*, was not considered a reputable source of *fatwas*. Even his former students criticized his *fatwas* as "uninformed" by modern circumstances, a criticism that often turned to embarrassment, since they respect him in all other areas of Islamic scholarship.[76] The alternative *fatwas* that do have more of an impact are those issued by prominent sheikhs outside Jordan, particularly scholars from Saudi Arabia. But these individuals are frequently tied to the Saudi state and are more conservative than perhaps they would be if they had complete independence. As a result, the state has successfully usurped the *fatwa* and institutions of Islamic jurisprudence for its own purposes, and their utility as instruments for Islamic activism has diminished.

RAMADAN AND THE EFFECT OF STATE CONTROL

Perhaps at no other time during the year is the religious potential of Muslims greater and the state's control of public religious space more apparent than during the month of Ramadan. Ramadan is held during the ninth month of the Muslim lunar calendar year to commemorate the first revelation of the Qur'an. During this month, Muslims fast from sunrise to sunset. They not only refrain from eating and drinking during the day, but sexual activity is prohibited and they must not allow anything to pass their lips, including cigarettes and gum. It is a time for Muslims to become aware of their bodily needs and the suffering of others in order to reflect on God as creator and provider. The month highlights the ethical and moral responsibility of individuals toward their fellow Muslims. During this period, religious practices such as *zakat*, prayer, religious lessons, and Qur'anic recitation reach their peak. It is a collective experience that brings Muslims and communities together through shared religious practice. Beyond merely ritual practices such as fasting and prayer, Muslims try to better understand their religion and many seek out experts to provide explanations about points of religion. Ramadan heightens religious awareness as Muslims strive for goodness and piety.[77]

During Ramadan, everything, including social, political, and economic activity, revolves around the rituals of Ramadan and the fast.

Many Muslims wake early to have a dinner before sunrise to carry them through the day. During the day, people go about their everyday activities, but once the sun begins to set, people, cabs, and activity disappear and the streets empty. Unlike in Cairo and other Arab capitals where the celebration after Muslims break the fast is carried into the streets, public space in Amman remains barren, abandoned in favor of private interactions.

Every night, Muslims hold *iftar* dinners to break the fast with family and friends.[78] Because of the celebratory nature of these dinners, the food consumption in Jordan actually increases during Ramadan, despite the fast. One young Muslim described *iftar* dinners as "Christmas every night." Dinners are held by different branches of the family and provide opportunities for relatives to grow closer through a common religious experience. Even non-Muslims and non-practicing Muslims are swept up in the spirit of Ramadan. Some Christian families hold *iftar* dinners and Muslims who do not practice their religion throughout the year do so during Ramadan. One Westernized and secular Muslim, with whom I became friends, did not pray or attend the *khutba* throughout the year, yet fasted diligently during Ramadan. This is because Ramadan is part of the cultural heritage of the country, for Muslims and non-Muslims alike. The entire society takes part and everyone is affected by the tempo of the month.

This religious fervor is a potential resource for mobilization by Islamic movements. Muslims are typically more sensitive to their religion and its demands during Ramadan. One Islamic activist stated that "they [Muslims] are ready to believe and do almost anything." The religious energy of Muslims reaches an apex and is ready to be tapped. Many informants argued that during this month the potential of ordinary Muslims becomes extraordinary and Islamic movements have their widest opportunities. If this Ramadan energy were channeled into political activism, it could become a powerful engine for recruitment and mobilization.

But the regime's control of religious space and public displays of Islam ensures that this energy is channeled into nondisruptive forms. The *khutba*, lessons, and prayer are still performed predominantly in mosques, which remain tightly controlled by the regime. In fact, during Ramadan, surveillance and control are increased. Ministry of Awqaf officials prohibit the unauthorized collection of money at mosques; and because of surveillance, Islamists are often caught illegally collecting donations. In one instance, the president of an Islamic cultural society, who was collecting donations for his organization, was brought to the minister of awqaf himself and forced to sign a document stating that he and the other members would never again engage in such activities. The next step would be more severe and might include arrests and worse.[79]

What might be called a "discourse of Ramadan"—the expressed interpretation of Ramadan through both speech and ritual—is controlled by the regime, which channels it into ritualism and concern with the hereafter. The Friday sermons are more widely attended, but the *khutba* remains nonpolitical and focuses on ritualistic acts and individual obligations of piety. Most of the sermons are ceremonial, about fasting, praying, and giving *zakat*. Issues of personal salvation and the hereafter tend to predominate, and less emphasis is given to society as a whole or to social consciousness tied to political issues. Images of damnation and the need to ask God for forgiveness prevail over social activism. The discourse through the mosque tends to focus on what one Islamist termed "superstitions" and the "legendary qualities" of Ramadan. He called the preachers during this period "harbingers of doomsday," alluding to their emphasis on individual salvation. During Ramadan, the state sponsors Islam as individual ritual rather than as a framework for social activism.

Critical Islamists lament this channeled perspective and argue that the religious energy of Ramadan is wasted on ritualism when it should be used to raise greater concern for equality and justice. While activists believe that these ritualistic acts are important components of Islam, they view them as only one, and not necessarily the most important, aspect of Muslim responsibility. Other dimensions include social justice, activism, and confronting oppression and religious ignorance. For such Muslims, it is not simply a time for individuals to be "better Muslims," an act that for many only lasts through Ramadan. It is a time to revolt, whether physically or spiritually. It is a time to move beyond the ritualism of the state's discourse of Ramadan and an opportunity to tap into the religious fervor to promote great changes. It is a time to shake the system. As one critical Islamist put it, the state and state-controlled religious institutions "do not take the real meaning or look for injustice and wrongdoing. That is why its potential energy is wasted. Ramadan has lost its meaning and there is only ritual left."

During Ramadan, the regime combines its control of religious institutions and practice with its use of the modern media to affect a wider audience. Religious programming increases dramatically during this period, but the content remains the same—uncontroversial, focused on ritual, and designed to represent the Islamic nature of the state and the regime. For example, every evening the *iftar* dinner held by the royal family is televised. Numerous prominent politicians and community leaders are present and wade through the long greeting line to pay homage to their Islamic sponsors. Critical Islamists scoff at this "spectacle," arguing that such displays do not erase the injustices perpetrated by the regime in Jordan and others throughout the Muslim world. But for the majority of citizens, this public display of state leaders engaged in the rituals of Islam reinforces their belief that the state is fulfilling some Islamic obligations. Of course, there is hardly anyone who would argue that the Jordanian state is a "pure" Islamic state or that it strictly adheres to all Islamic rules, but these public "spectacles" show that the state is concerned with Islam and that leaders consider it an important aspect of legitimation.

Other Islamic programs are also more frequent. Educational religious programs, hosted by state officials or state-sanctioned religious leaders, are provided large blocs of time and promote the discourse of the state. Some oppositional figures, such as Ishaq Farhan of the Muslim Brotherhood and IAF, do participate in programs such as "Islam in a Changing World." But these figures are moderates within the movement and the programs never dare discuss controversial topics such as the peace process, instead concentrating either on rituals or Western misperceptions of Islam. The result is that the state is able to utilize its control over the media, especially its monopoly over television, to project its rather benign discourse of Ramadan. During this month, there is a quicker and more concentrated flow of religious practice and adherence, but this flow is constrained within the conduits of state structures and religious space.

State Islamic Organizations

While controlling religious institutions, the state also directly sponsors its own Islamic organizations to further propagate its particular variant of Islam. Through Islamic Cultural Centers, run by the Ministry of Awqaf, and a few NGOs sponsored by the royal family, the regime articulates a ritualistic and nonconfrontational interpretation of Islam. This provides the regime with points of interaction with neighborhoods and society that can be used to further regime interests.

The Ministry of Awqaf runs twenty-six Islamic Cultural Centers throughout the kingdom, thirteen for women and thirteen for men. The stated aim of each center is "to strengthen contact with citizens and to encourage participation in its activities in support of the role of mosques in guidance and education."[80] These centers are evenly distributed throughout the country, but most are located in urban centers (see table 2.6). Only the Islamic Center at King Abdullah Mosque in Amman is physically located in a mosque; the rest are situated in separate buildings, though close to a community mosque.

Activities at Islamic Cultural Centers fall into three categories: charitable, occupational, and cultural. In the area of charity, centers frequently hold "charity bazaars" to raise money for the poor. At these markets, poor families sell items produced at home, such as clothing and food. In 1995, twelve charity bazaars were held. A permanent market was formed at the King Abdullah Islamic Center in 1996 and provides space for seven vendors devoted to charitable activities, including the Save the Children Fund, the Young Muslim Women's Association, and the Society of Employment. These organizations sell basic arts and crafts, mostly made by poor women, to raise money for their respective causes and poor families. Additional charity is raised through the sale of handcrafted "charity plates," donations from local merchants, and charity boxes located at all Islamic Centers.

In order to improve the socioeconomic status of women, some Islamic Centers offer occupational training for vocational skills. This training is available only to women and focuses on skills traditionally viewed in Jordanian society as part of female occupations, such as flower arrangement, typing, and sewing (table 2.7). There is a small, symbolic JD2 fee for the courses, and the classes are generally one month to a year in length. In 1995, there were a total of 2,988 female graduates from these training classes.[81]

In the area of culture, the Islamic Centers offer a variety of courses and seminars on subjects related to Islam. In 1995, they held four courses throughout the year and eight special summer courses to train Muslims in the rules for reading the Qur'an. Other subjects addressed in cultural programs include family rule in Islam, the Bader

Table 2.6. Geographic Distribution of
State Islamic Cultural Centers

Governate	Male Centers	Female Centers	Total
Amman	1	4	5
Zarqa	1	2	3
Madaba	1	–	1
Balqa	–	1	1
Irbid	3	1	4
al-Qurah	1	–	1
Mafraq	2	1	3
Jerash	1	–	1
Kerak	1	2	3
Tafeelah	1	–	1
Ma'an	–	1	1
Aqaba	1	1	1
Total	13	13	26

Source: Ministry of Awqaf, *Annual Report*, 44.

Table 2.7. Training at State Islamic Centers
for Women in 1995

Course Name	No. per Year	Duration	No. of Graduates
Knitting	3	4 months	386
Sewing	6	6 months	670
Typing	3	4 months	448
Qur'anic reading	1	1 year	968
Artificial flowers	3	4 months	332
Cloth drawing	4	2 months	122
Bamboo	3	4 months	37
Good ethics	6	2 months	9
Turkish knitting	6	2 months	16
Arabic for non-Arabs	3	4 months	none

Source: Ministry of Awqaf, *Annual Report*, 109.

and Mecca wars, and faith and science. There is also a "cultural season" held for several days, which addresses specific topics of social concern from an Islamic perspective. Interestingly, the subjects of these cultural seasons tend to focus on issues of discipline and social control, such as crime and drug use. In 1995, the Islamic Centers also issued thirteen bulletins on various Islamic subjects, held three Islamic book exhibits, printed ten thousand copies of prayer rules, printed five thousand copies of the rules for fasting and *zakat*, organized contests in Qur'anic memorization, issued twenty bulletins for men on religious issues, held *iftar* dinners, and organized trips to Islamic sites.

Daily Islamic lessons are also given at the centers. The subjects vary from day to day, but include such things as the role of women in raising children, Islamic manners, and ritualistic practices. Occasionally, volunteers at the centers visit schools to provide similar Islamic lessons. Individuals who want to give lessons, at either the centers or schools, must first pass a qualification exam. More importantly, they cannot have a political party affiliation. The director of Islamic centers argued that the lectures and seminars should reflect the views of the Ministry of Awqaf and not a political party perspective.[82] Since many of the most effective and prominent Islamists work through the IAF, the Muslim Brotherhood, or illegal underground parties, this in effect prevents qualified Islamic activists from participating in state-sponsored grassroots organizations and restricts the centers' possible usage by politically oriented groups. The ministry consciously tries not to use members of the Brotherhood, but because many Muslim Brothers are employees at the ministry and highly qualified to teach Islamic subjects, it is often difficult to avoid. The ministry does, however, closely monitor the lessons to prevent the employees from presenting "a particular perspective."

Though there is no formal monitoring process, oversight occurs through three instruments of surveillance. First, supervisors from the centers attend the lessons or lectures and note any deviations from the ministry's position or perspective. Second, ministry officials ask members of the congregation at the local mosque to inform them if people are "speaking in a certain way" during the activities (i.e., in a manner not sanctioned by the state or its interpretation of Islam). Third, informants take it upon themselves to report any breach in ministry policy. Despite these instruments and the ministry's attempts to prevent alternative interpretations of Islam, occasionally

controversial figures do utilize these lessons and lectures as a plat-
form. In one instance, the ministry appointed an individual to give
lessons and later realized that he was a member of Hizb al-Tahrir
(The Liberation Party), a militant Islamic group that seeks to rein-
state the caliphate, by force if necessary.[83] Hizb al-Tahrir rejects the
sovereignty of the Hashemite regime and the Jordanian constitu-
tion.[84] Members of the group unsuccessfully attempted to seize power
in 1960, and Hizb al-Tahrir is widely recognized as responsible for
numerous assassination attempts against the late King Hussein. This
particular individual used the opportunity to present the ideas of his
movement and was prevented from speaking again by the Ministry
of Awqaf.

In addition to propagating the state's interpretation of Islam
through activities and lessons, the displays at the King Abdullah Islamic Center, by far the largest and best-known state Islamic Center, celebrate the role of the royal family in Islamic history. This
center exudes a particular discourse of Islamic legitimacy through
presentation and display. There is a permanent exhibition that describes the Hashemites role in rebuilding and renovating Islamic
monuments. The most important of these displays is one that emphasizes the Hashemites' formal and informal relationship to Jerusalem and al-Aqsa mosque. Brass plaques prominently advertise King
Hussein's $10 million personal donation for renovations at al-Aqsa
Mosque and the Dome of the Rock, which were damaged by fire in
1969. Other displays describe the Hashemite's role in restoring Islamic shrines throughout the kingdom, including a description of
one renovation that alone cost $4 million. Still other exhibits at the
center emphasize the regime's historical relationship to Islam, explaining its Islamic heritage and genealogical link to the Prophet.
Pictures depict the Hashemites performing the *hajj*, *'umra*, and
zakat.[85] A small museum at the center celebrates the regime's involvement in Islam and its role in the construction of the Jordanian
state. Pictures of King Abdullah I in Palestine and London, his
Qur'an, a photocopy of a letter sent by the Prophet Mohammed to
Hercules describing Islam, and historic pictures of Abdullah I proclaiming independence from Britain all visually detail the role of the
Hashemite family in Islamic and Jordanian history. Other pictures
show King Hussein when he was young and provide details about
his great-grandfather, Sharif Hussein. These presentations juxtapose
Islamic symbols with the royal family, thus emphasizing the Islamic

legitimacy of the regime through visual presentation. The interweaving of Islamic, national, and Hashemite symbolism projects a particular mixture of legitimacy that reinforces the power of the regime. In conjunction with the apolitical and state-sponsored Islamic perspective pervading activities at these centers, the regime projects a variant of Islam that emphasizes its own right to rule.

In addition to the Islamic Centers, which are the most prominent examples of state-sponsored Islamic organizations, there are also three Islamic NGOs led by members of the royal family. The first two organizations are run by Prince Hassan and reflect his belief in "a centrist and moderate Islam that can bridge our fears and provide a clear programme of action."[86] The Royal Institute for Inter-Faith Studies, registered at the Ministry of Culture in 1994, promotes interfaith dialogue and understanding through publications, lectures, and conferences. It publishes two high quality, though small, periodicals—*Inter-Faith Quarterly* (in English) and *al-Nashra* (in Arabic). His other Islamic organization is the Royal Academy for Islamic Civilization Research al-Albeit Foundation, founded in 1980 to address a wide variety of Islamic issues. The third organization is the Young Muslim Women Association, which is run by Princess Sarvat al-Hassan, Prince Hassan's daughter.[87] These organizations are registered with the state as private societies. Obviously, none of these organizations challenge the regime since they are, in effect, the NGO arm of the Hashemite family.[88]

The state cultural centers and Hashemite NGOs link the regime and state to grassroots beneficiaries and serve as instruments to promote the state's view and interpretation of Islam. They address issues of ritual or general social concerns such as drugs, the environment, interfaith dialogue, and charity. While regulating the flow of religious discourse and practice, the regime utilizes Islamic organizations in civil society to project its own Islamic meaning.

CONCLUSION

Through its regulation of the mosque and concomitant activities, the regime has blocked critical Islamist voices from participating in public discourse through central Islamic institutions. For many radical groups, this is an affront to the religion itself. In interviews, many argued that regime control of the mosque, in effect, prevents Muslims from freely worshipping Allah, an unacceptable fate that deserves resistance. To date, however, this resistance has been unsuccessful. Traditional religious institutions have been usurped by the state and their revolutionary potential continues to be seriously circumscribed.

The regime's control of religious space combines with its administrative capacity in civil society to inform the organizational opportunities of Islamic groups. Because of its concern with Islamic legitimacy, the regime uses its social control to determine which Islamists can participate in public discourse and collective action through SMOs. The political context of Islamic activism is thus structured by the regime's manipulation of bureaucratic processes, rules, and procedures in its attempt to maintain power and legitimacy after moving toward democracy.

CHAPTER 3

Islamic Social Movement Organizations
and the Muslim Brotherhood

Throughout the Muslim world, Islamic movements have mobilized through an assortment of Islamic NGOs, including Islamic hospitals, medical clinics, schools, orphanages, training centers, charity centers, and cultural societies.[1] Termed "social" or "moderate" Islam, these organizations reflect a growing functional synthesis between socioeconomic need and religious values. As the dominant type of SMO in the kingdom and an important point of contact between communities and the Islamic movement, these organizations offer Islamists potential vehicles for the production and dissemination of an Islamic discourse that could challenge state power.

Despite this potential, however, the particular political context in Jordan means that only moderate Islamic groups can effectively utilize NGOs. Informed by a concern with controlling religious discourse, the regime uses administration, repression, and legal mechanisms to create a web of disincentives for more critical Islamic groups, which as a result find formal organizations constraining in the struggle over sacred authority. Moderate Islamists with a strong relationship to the regime, on the other hand, are allowed to act through formal organizations, so long as they limit their activities in accordance with the conditions of participation and do not challenge the state's Islamic discourse. The Muslim Brotherhood is a case in point. The Brotherhood has always supported the prerogatives of the crown. While the movement may be critical of specific government policies and call for greater Islamic fervor, it supports the current system, democracy, and Hashemite rule. The regime has, in turn, granted special favors to the Muslim Brotherhood and has allowed it to form organizations.

83

The Islamic NGO Community: An Overview

Islamic NGOs provide basic goods and services to communities in a manner Islamists deem consistent with the values of Islam. In doing so, they function as points of contact between Islamists and neighborhoods where religious values are promoted while volunteers provide goods and services to beneficiaries. Islamic activists hope that in providing needed programs, projects, and services they will spread the Islamic message and foster a more religious society.

Table 3.1. Growth of Islamic NGOs

Year	Number of Organizations
1984	28
1985	29
1986	30
1987	30
1988	30
1989	30
1990	33
1991	42
1992	43
1993	46
1994	48
1995	49

Source: Calculated using information from General Union of Voluntary Societies, *Directory of Charitable Societies* (Amman: GUVS, 1995); and Ministry of Culture, handwritten list of Islamic cultural societies provided by the Ministry (n.d.).

The pattern of Islamic NGO growth parallels the overall growth of the NGO community in Jordan. The greatest expansion occurred following political liberalization in 1989 as a result of greater organizational opportunities. While the growth rate of Islamic NGOs in the 1985–89 period preceding liberalization was only 3.3 percent, between 1989 and 1994 the number of Islamic NGOs grew by 60 percent. In the five years following political liberalization, the number of Islamic charitable organizations, in particular, expanded from twenty-six in 1989 to thirty-eight in 1994, representing a 50 percent increase (as opposed to the more modest 4 percent growth rate during the 1985–89 period). The number of Islamic cultural organizations is much lower. Prior to 1989, there were only three Islamic cultural organizations. This number expanded to a total of nine by 1996.

While the expansion of Islamic organizational activity since 1989 is substantial, it does not represent a unique Islamic phenomenon; rather, it is part of the overall expansion of organizational activities in the kingdom. As a percent of NGOs in the country, the number of Islamic NGOs has remained constant or actually declined. Islamic NGOs as a percent of all NGOs decreased slightly from 7.4 percent in 1985 to 6 percent in 1994. Islamic charitable NGOs as a percent of all charitable NGOs in both 1985 and 1995 was 6 percent, while Islamic cultural societies as a percent of all cultural organizations dropped from 10 percent in 1986 to 5.8 percent in 1994. After liberalization began, there were certainly more organizational opportunities for Islamic groups, but this opportunity must be taken in its broader context. The expansion of the Islamic NGO community was part of the larger wave of civil society growth.

The activities at most Islamic NGOs in Jordan do not differ substantially from those of secular and non-Islamic voluntary organizations. As with the general NGO community, Islamic NGOs limit their activities and do not engage in political work. They focus on providing basic goods and services to communities in order to promote Muslim values and do not seek a radical transformation of the political system. The priority is the services themselves, not a specific Islamic message or a political agenda.[2] Religiosity thus becomes the residual effect of doing good deeds for the community. Members spend more time discussing the effectiveness of projects in terms of their socioeconomic impact instead of religious effect. What differentiates Islamic NGOs from their secular counterparts is, for the most part, not the particular Islamic nature of their activities, but volunteers' belief that they are promoting Islam through their work.[3] It is an insider belief in the mission, more than the activities themselves, that distinguishes them.

Islamic NGOs in Jordan differ from similar organizations in other Arab countries in that they are not directly affiliated with a mosque. In Egypt, for example, many Islamic NGOs are physically attached to a neighborhood mosque and enjoy a special relationship in which the mosque raises funds while the NGO provides services to the community.[4] In Jordan, because all mosques are controlled by the state, there is no formal NGO-mosque relationship. Some Islamic NGOs are informally affiliated with a local mosque through charitable work, often located nearby or adjacent to the mosque, but explicit financial or material relationships are rare. The nature of the relationship is more symbolic and derives from the religious nature of the NGO's work.

Most Islamic NGOs are located in Palestinian areas. Over the years following various confrontations between Israel and Arabs, Palestinian refugees flooded Jordan. In the name of national unity and to prevent conflict between East Bank Jordanians (the original inhabitants of Jordan) and Jordanians of Palestinian decent, the government has refused to release demographic information from the most recent census, which would include information about the distribution of Palestinians and East Bankers in the kingdom.[5] However, unofficial estimates indicate that Palestinians represent somewhere between 40 and 60 percent of the population. The numbers vary, often depending upon the political objectives of those making the estimates, but a member of a Norwegian demographic research team informally reported that the number hovers around 50 percent.[6] The majority of Palestinians are located in the northern governates and in urban centers, while the south and rural areas are dominated by Transjordanians (East Bankers). There are also several Palestinian refugee camps surrounding Amman, which are run by the United Nations Relief and Work Agency (UNRWA). These camps are in reality more like small cities with permanent structures and communities.[7]

Table 3.2 details the geographic distribution of Islamic NGOs. They are predominantly located in governates with high Palestinian populations, such as Amman and Zarqa. Though some are located in lower-class neighborhoods, most are in middle-class areas. In contrast to the general charitable NGO community, which is evenly disbursed in rural and urban communities, most Islamic NGOs are located in urban centers, especially in the cities of Amman and Zarqa. An overwhelming number are located in the Amman governate, which has the largest Palestinian population in the country, and virtually all of those located in this governate are located specifically in the city of Amman itself. Like most cultural societies in Jordan, the Islamic cultural NGOs are urban-based (all nine societies are located in Amman).

Perhaps not surprisingly, given the geographic distribution of

Table 3.2. Geographic Distribution of Islamic NGOs

Governate	Number of NGOs
Amman	34
Zarqa	7
Irbid	4
Balqa	2
Mafraq	1
Aqaba	1

Source: Calculated from GUVS, *Directory,* and information from the Ministry of Culture.

Islamic NGOs, most Islamic NGO informants in this study are of Palestinian decent. A few are Transjordanian and Syrian, but the overwhelming majority, around 90 percent, are Palestinian. This provides further evidence for those who claim that the Islamic movement in Jordan is dominated by Palestinians.[8] Determining the exact ethnic composition of the Islamic NGO community, however, is difficult for two reasons. First, members of the Islamic movement downplay the role of ethnicity because of their belief in the transcendent nature of religious identity. Second, members attempt to portray the movement as a broadly based religious resurgence that incorporates (or can incorporate) all segments of society. As a result, volunteers and members of the movement were unwilling to divulge demographic estimates (it is unlikely that they maintain such statistics in any event). Regardless, this research and other evidence indicate that the movement is mostly Palestinian-based at present. As a result, many of the Islamic NGO volunteers are avidly involved in organizations concerned with Palestinian issues. A number of those interviewed belong to the Islamic Conference on Jerusalem, Bait al-Maqdes, headed by Kamel al-Sharif, a former minister of awqaf. Even those who do not formally belong to such organizations still attend lectures, seminars, and conferences related to Palestinian issues.

Islamic NGOs are also male-dominated. There are three Islamic organizations run entirely by women, all of which focus on services and activities for women only. The remaining Islamic NGOs are almost entirely comprised of males. This is particularly the case in leadership positions. In a sample of thirty-one Islamic NGOs, women serve on the administrative board at only five societies.[9] When the three female Islamic NGOs are dropped from this sample, only two of the remaining organizations have women in leadership positions. Of the 248 board members in the sample, 34 (14 percent) are women. If the female Islamic NGOs are again dropped from the sample, only 2 of the remaining 216 board members are women. Aside from the specifically women-based Islamic NGOs, there are no female presidents.

This fits the general pattern at the working member level as well. In my visits to various Islamic NGOs, there were few female members, even at general meetings. Women are frequently the beneficiaries, especially at charitable societies, but few are Islamic NGO volunteers. Even where women are beneficiaries, many organizations enforce gender segregation by providing different services for men and women. In addition, some charitable organizations provide special vocational training for women to enhance occupational skills such as sewing, embroidery, typing, and flower arrangement. Other services, such as medical assistance, are provided to both men and women without strict separation.

The dominance of men in Islamic NGOs reflects two factors. First, the Islamic movement itself is male-dominated. There are women involved, but they are often part of separate "women's auxiliaries" or branches. They are rarely part of the leadership structure. For example, there are no women in the Muslim Brotherhood. In addition, there were no women in the preparatory committee of the IAF, and only 11 of the 353 founding members were women.[10] In 1992, there were no women in the 120-member IAF *shura* council (the general assembly), and only one woman was elected for the subsequent council.[11] Various interviews with Islamists outside the Muslim Brotherhood indicate a similar pattern of gender participation. Some movements are specifically women-based, but these are smaller and less frequent.[12]

Second, the absence of women in Islamic NGOs reflects Islamist values of gender segregation, which separates men and women and typically places women in less public roles. For Islamists, the family is the primary responsibility of women. This requires that women focus on child rearing and maintaining the household. Islamists interviewed during this project argued that women were free to engage in activities outside the household if their primary responsibilities were fulfilled. In practice, this is rarely possible and women are therefore subjugated to the private sphere. It should be noted that these practices are not unique to the Islamic movement. In Jordanian society in general there is gender segregation at various levels, and many men believe that women should remain in the household. Proponents of this view have become increasingly vocal as more women run for the Lower House of Parliament. It is thus as much a cultural phenomenon as an Islamist practice.

Islamic NGOs share similar male and Palestinian dimensions, but visits to these organizations indicated that the degree of religiosity varies widely. In some instances, volunteers dressed in jeans and without the traditional beard, while others wore traditional Islamic clothing with well-manicured beards. Typically, the group at each society was relatively homogenous with regard to religious fervor, although differences among participants existed. Some were motivated by a desire to help the community, while others were driven by the desire to create a more Muslim society. All of the respondents, aside from the members of one cultural organization, were clearly moderates and articulated support for the regime, the state, and democracy. When asked whether Jordan was an Islamic state, most replied that it was, but that improvements could be made by more accurately applying the *shari'a*. This contrasts sharply with more radical groups, which argue that the entire system is un-Islamic and that any change must entail new political and social institutions. In general, there is support for regime policies, except in one area—the peace process. Almost every volunteer interviewed opposes the peace process, though the level of opposition varies. Some believe in peace at a conceptual level, but argue that the current peace process is insufficient and does not support the Islamic cause. Others adamantly oppose peace in any guise. Most respondents articulated a position somewhere in the middle. After the deterioration of the peace process in 1996, opposition increased.[13]

The majority of Islamic NGO volunteers are between forty and sixty years old; a generation which more critical groups argue has become increasingly moderate over the years. This generational composition is an important issue for NGO members given that the majority of the Jordanian population is less than eighteen years old. Organizers recognize that they need to appeal to a younger audience if they want to ensure long-term organizational survival. As a result, some organizations are trying to expand activities to include sports programs in an effort to attract young people to participate in the NGO.

The nonconfrontational nature of these organizations is to a large extent due to selective registration practices that tend to favor groups connected to the regime. Organizations with a membership connection to the state are less likely to devote resources to oppositional activities; and direct links exist between NGO participants and the regime through personal relations, political connections, and employment. The single largest employment source for respondents at these NGOs is the public education system. A substantial proportion of volunteers work either as teachers in government schools or in the Ministry of Education. Others work with the Ministry of Awqaf, particularly in Sanduq al-Zakat and the department charged with building new mosques. In many instances, former ministers and government officials are often either in leadership positions or part of the general membership, and organizations utilize these connections to advance the interests of the NGO. This relationship is viewed as an organizational advantage since it can open opportunities.

For some members, the relationship with the regime is more personal. In Zarqa, for example, the president of one Islamic charitable organization is friends with the director of the local branch of the Ministry of Social Development. While this is most likely a result of their mutual interest in the field of charity work, it still represents a connection to the state, one that is frequently called upon when engaging in activities or attempting to expand the scope of work. At another Islamic charitable organization in Amman, the Syrian family running the society has personal ties to the Hashemite family. This particular NGO was founded by Tysir Thubian, who enjoyed close relations with King Abdullah I. Upon Abdullah's request, Thubian moved his newspaper operation from Syria to Jordan and began publishing the first Jordanian newspaper. He later founded a local school and was active in social development projects. Thubian's sons took over the society when he passed away and are extremely proud of the family's historical link to the Hashemite regime. At one point, the older brother gave me a copy of the personal pass King Abdullah I issued to his father, which granted him unlimited access to any of the king's palaces. In another example, the president of an Islamic medical clinic received financial support from King

Hussein to send his son to a Western hospital for medical treatment. Still other organizations cooperate with the government in joint activities. For example, Islamic NGOs often use the space provided by the Ministry of Awqaf at King Abdullah Mosque to hold events and activities. At other times, volunteers coordinate with government officials to determine more effective ways for promoting socioeconomic development and religious change. Islamic NGOs and the state are partners, connected through personal relations, employment, and mutual interest in charity work.

In addition, there is no broad, unified organizational network. In many social movements, there is an organizational network that allows activists to cooperate and coordinate resources to achieve movement goals. Though there may be disagreements among the members of an organizational network as to the precise strategy, tactics, or message, there are linkages, whether through cooperation in action or membership. Leadership overlap and coordinated activities are generally viewed as constituting the linkages of a social movement organizational network, and both are generally lacking in the Islamic NGO community. First, Islamic NGOs rarely coordinate activities. As the president of one Islamic organization stated, each "works in its own way." Respondents unanimously indicated that they do not cooperate with other organizations in activities, though they share a common "spiritual orientation." Each group believes in a certain perspective and manner of achieving its goals and is hesitant to coordinate with others for fear of diluting effectiveness. In one case, volunteers from an Islamic cultural society contacted other Islamic organizations to pool resources and coordinate efforts, but were rebuffed and thwarted by interorganizational differences over the aims and methods of cooperation.

The limited coordination that does occur is at a very informal level and is minimal. One cultural society sent volunteers from the organization to teach members of an Islamic charitable organization how to memorize the Qur'an. Another society sent some of its members to help an organization set up lectures and a budget. In other instances, if particular services are not offered at one Islamic organization, members may recommend another Islamic NGO, as opposed to secular organizations.

Second, there is very little leadership overlap. Network analysis of philanthropic work in the United States typically focuses on the composition of the executive board to determine whether there is significant overlap. Again relying on the sample of thirty-one Islamic organizations and the leadership previously discussed, there is very little overlap among administrative board members. This was confirmed in numerous interviews with organizational leaders who indicated that their main work is at a single society where they hold a leadership position. This is not to say that a network does not exist among grassroots volunteers, only that there is no *organizational* network. The exception to this is the Muslim Brotherhood organizations (discussed later in the chapter).

There may be a network at the general membership level, but this has not led to any coordination between or among organizations. Most respondents belong to an average of three to six Islamic NGOs, and in many cases are members of non-Islamic organizations as well. The pattern of joining reflects personal interests, not the imperative of some larger organizational movement. For example, many volunteers are interested in Palestinian issues and as a result joined Palestinian organizations, regardless of whether these societies were Islamic. These decisions are personal choices, not part of a broader social movement design. Participation in multiple organizations is also the result of administrative practices that prevent any single organization from fulfilling a wide range of activities. Because individual volunteers are interested in affecting change in multiple areas of voluntary work, they are forced to join other organizations to do so.

The volunteers at these organizations are predominantly moderate Muslims driven by socioeconomic concerns for their communities. They do not represent an ideological opposition movement and do not articulate a counterdiscourse of Islam that could serve as the basis of a fundamental critique of the state or regime. On the contrary, they generally support the regime, democracy, and the current system, even while criticizing specific government policies such as the peace process. They are not a threat to state power nor do they represent the rudimentary foundations for an Islamist challenge to the passive Islamic discourse of the state. This composition results from the selective administrative practices of the state, which shapes and molds opportunities for voluntary work. The Muslim Brotherhood's experience demonstrates how Islamic groups that do not threaten the regime can utilize formal organizations in the pursuit of social movement goals.

THE MUSLIM BROTHERHOOD AND COOPERATION

The Muslim Brotherhood in Jordan has a rich historical record that details its relationship with the Hashemite regime and the movement's organizational experience. Its long history in Jordan and success in organizing present a good case study for understanding how the relationship between a social movement and the regime can impact concomitant organizational opportunities. The Brotherhood's consistent, though dynamic, support for Hashemite legitimacy and political stability has opened organizational opportunities that are unavailable to other social movement groups. Although there have been moments of tension, the historical relationship is predicated upon a balance between the ideological objectives of the Brotherhood and the need to assuage the survival imperatives of the Hashemites. The result is a symbiosis in which the regime allows the Brotherhood to organize and promote its objectives, while the movement upholds the regime's right to rule and refrains from challenging Hashemite Islamic legitimacy.

Reform, Not Revolution

The Muslim Brotherhood in Jordan is not seeking to destroy the current political system; rather, it proposes reform from within. Statements by leaders and working members of the movement reflect this outlook. Abdul Majid Thunaybat, the current leader of the Muslim Brotherhood, describes the movement's approach to change:

> [O]ur approach to education is to begin with the individual and then move on to the family and then ultimately the Islamic government that rules as provided for in God's *shari'a*. Our mission does not envisage an overthrow of the regime in the sense of holding the reins of power regardless of people's temperament or whether they approve of this regime or not. We seek the creation of faithful grassroots that receive these instructions and this order, and government by Islam comes later. . . . We renounce violence and say that the alternative is political reform and respect for Islamic *shari'a*, which constitutes the base of powers as approved by all Arab and Islamic constitutions.[14]

Other members of the Muslim Brotherhood echo Thunaybat's views. In his outline of the Islamic position on political involvement,

Ishaq Farhan, a leader in the Brotherhood, reemphasizes the movement's support for the stability of Jordan and argues that "no matter how much the political stands differ between the Islamic movement and the official stand, things must never end up with using violence and the opposite violence [counterviolence]."[15] Of paramount importance is that the movement supports the "state of law and institutions while adopting the gradual reform means in order to shift towards the application of the Islamic sharia in society."[16] Elsewhere, Farhan states that the Brotherhood "will not spill one drop of blood or vandalize any public or private property." This derives from a belief that "Sometimes words speak louder than swords."[17] The Muslim Brothers articulate a gradualist agenda for change that begins with "the Muslim individual, up to the Muslim family, the Muslim community, and then the Muslim state."[18]

The Brotherhood's method of change is not the erection of a new system of politics; it is a reformist strategy of working through the current system to imbue it with more Islamic tones.[19] Leaders in the movement characterize themselves as "reformists, not revolutionaries," and argue that the strategy of change is "evolution, not revolution."[20] It is an attempt to renew the system, not to radically change or alter it. Members of the Brotherhood view themselves as partners with the government in providing social and moral guidance. Bassam Umush echoes these sentiments when he argues that any change should be pursued by "making an effort toward reforming government rather than through an attempt to overthrow the regime."[21] Various members of the movement have labeled their relationship with the regime as one of "peaceful coexistence."[22]

Movement outsiders recognize the peaceful nature of this relationship as well. In a series of articles in the Jordanian Arabic daily *al-Ra'y*, numerous observers outside the Muslim Brotherhood describe the relationship between the regime and the movement as one of mutual cooperation. Many argue that there has never been any real contradiction or confrontation because peaceful coexistence brought "mutual benefit" for both parties.[23]

The Brotherhood's stance vis-à-vis the regime can be viewed in terms of "opposition as support of the state."[24] This is where the opposition operates within the constraints of the system in a manner that reifies the structure of the state. Though the movement may disagree with policies or articulate opposition, it continues to act through the institutions of the political system without challenging the raison d'être of state or Hashemite power. The regime and the Muslim Brotherhood share an interest in maintaining the system since both benefit from its continuance. The regime benefits from the Muslim Brotherhood because the movement checks other more confrontational social movements and channels Islamic activism into a nonviolent agenda. The Muslim Brotherhood, on its part, has benefited from organizational opportunities produced by the incumbent regime. State support has allowed the movement to extend its reach in society and has enabled the Brotherhood to more effectively deliver its religious message. This creates what I. William Zartman terms "role complementarity," whereby the "government and opposition have interests to pursue within the political system."[25] It is a "coordination game" in which each actor coordinates with the other to achieve different ends.[26] The goals are not necessarily the same, but in pursuing different goals through the same means (i.e., the current political system), each hopes to achieve its own objectives. The regime seeks to perpetuate its power and control, while the Muslim Brotherhood hopes to promote a more Muslim society. By working through the system, the Muslim Brotherhood acts as a "loyal opposition,"[27] not as the revolutionary vanguard of Islamic change.

The Relationship with the Regime

The historical record supports the Muslim Brotherhood's rhetoric of moderation. It has never seriously challenged the legitimacy or power of the ruling regime. While the Egyptian Brotherhood experienced violent clashes with President Abd al-Nasser and has been repressed by Presidents Sadat and Mubarak, the Jordanian movement has enjoyed a relatively cordial and cooperative relationship with the Hashemite monarchy. Although moments of tension have surfaced over the years, the relationship has remained one of mutual understanding and cooperation, reinforced by common interests and institutionalized through repeated episodes of interaction. Though earlier years in the relationship witnessed serious disagreements and mutual suspicion,[28] conflict diminished as the result of extended interactional experiences. Each actor has, in essence, learned the limits and objectives of the other. Despite its advocacy of a more Islamic society, the Jordanian Muslim Brotherhood has never sought a radical or revolutionary change in political arrangements that would threaten the survival of the regime, nor has it sought the dissolution of monarchical rule. On the contrary, it has actively supported the regime and its claims to legitimacy, and has served as a source of stability throughout Jordan's tumultuous history.

Its relationship with the regime began when the movement was founded in Jordan on 19 November 1945. King Abdullah I provided patronage for the inauguration of the general offices and granted the movement legal status in January 1946 as a charitable society. The king was a personal associate of the Jordanian Brotherhood's founder, Abdul Latif Abu Qura, and included the movement's secretary, Abdul Hakim Adin, in the government's cabinet, proclaiming that "Jordan is in need of the Brotherhood's efforts."[29] Abdullah allowed the Brotherhood to establish branches throughout the kingdom, enabling the movement to extend its influence during the initial period of state formation.

In 1953, the Brotherhood was granted legal status as an "organized group," which allowed it to broaden its activities beyond charity work and operate as a "general and comprehensive Islamic committee."[30] The comprehensiveness of its agenda and organizational reach grew, and the movement developed interests in all areas of social life. Abdul Rahman Khalifa, leader of the Brotherhood in 1953, described the movement as follows:

> We are not a political party, though we believe that Islamic action is part of Islam. Neither are we a charitable society, though charitable action is an indivisible part of our call. And, we are not a sports club, though physical training goes hand-in-hand with our spiritual education and ideological culture.[31]

King Abdullah I supported the religiously conservative agenda of the Brotherhood and viewed the movement as a strategic ally in combating leftist and communist forces in the kingdom. The Muslim Brotherhood, on its part, supported the king's annexation of the West Bank and respected the religious credentials of the Hashemites. The mutual amicability and cooperation was colored by periods of tension but established the foundations for a long-lasting relationship. The Brotherhood became an active partner in the construction of the new Jordanian entity and has maintained an important role in shaping the affairs of the country.

Ishaq Farhan divides the historical development of the Brother-

hood into four tactical periods. In the 1950s, the movement focused on *al-da'wa*. As a broad religious committee, the Muslim
Brotherhood enjoyed access to the mosques and other religious institutions and used these opportunities to support missionary work.
In the 1960s, the movement promoted Islam through education.
In the third stage during the 1970s, the movement formed grassroots
charitable organizations and became active in professional associations. In the 1980s and 1990s, particularly after political liberalization, the Brotherhood became more directly involved in politics by
participating in parliamentary elections, briefly joining the
government's cabinet, and forming the IAF. Farhan believes that
despite these shifts in focus, the movement has maintained its "strategic objective" of promoting Islam.[32]

Throughout these stages, the Muslim Brotherhood has consistently supported the regime during periods of crisis. During the
height of the regime's confrontation with Arab nationalists and the
coup attempt in the 1950s, the Brotherhood openly declared its
loyalty to King Hussein, supporting martial law to combat destabilizing movements. At that point, both the regime and the Brotherhood felt threatened by Nasserist forces. The king feared that
Nasserists would undermine his power and control, a fear that was
affirmed by the attempted coup led by Nasserist officers. The Muslim Brotherhood's antipathy toward Nasserism stemmed from the
experience of the Egyptian branch. After a 1954 assassination attempt against Nasser, which was blamed on the Brotherhood, he
brutally cracked down on the movement.[33] The Brotherhood in Jordan feared a similar fate if Nasserists gained political control of the
kingdom. Both the regime and the movement thus shared a common enemy and worked in tandem to combat the Nasserist movement. Both also opposed communists, leftists, and Ba'thist forces.
The Brotherhood objected to the atheistic nature of these movements, while King Hussein feared an erosion of his power and control. The Brotherhood's support for the king was reaffirmed during
the 1970–71 civil war when the movement refrained from entering
the conflict, reinforcing its allegiance and commitment to stability.

The regime has also directly requested Muslim Brotherhood assistance to promote political stability. For example, after unrest ex-
ploded in the Palestinian refugee camps following a 1990 incident
in which Israelis killed twelve Palestinians near a Tel Aviv train sta-
tion, the regime asked Brotherhood leaders to use their influence to

regain order since they had strong ties to the camps. The Muslim Brotherhood complied with the request and order was subsequently restored.[34]

In another recent example of Brotherhood moderation, during the 1989 and 1996 riots that erupted over subsidy reductions, the Muslim Brotherhood was careful not to criticize King Hussein, focusing its attacks on the cabinet and not the system of power or legitimacy. The Brotherhood actively worked to ease tensions and looked to the king as an unbiased arbiter during the crisis, publicly praising his wisdom and political acumen. In 1996 during a public speech, the king publicly recognized the Brotherhood's restraint during the riots.

As a result of this alliance, borne from opposition to common enemies, the regime has actively supported the Muslim Brotherhood and fostered its growth. While all other political parties were banned after the implementation of marital law in 1957, the Muslim Brotherhood was allowed to continue its activities through its charitable organizations and the mosques. Through its umbrella organization, the Islamic Center Charity Society, the movement expanded its power through a host of civil society institutions, including schools, medical centers, Qur'anic centers, and the mosque. Its ability to organize and operate during the martial law period provided the Brotherhood with organizational opportunities that other social movements were denied.[35] The regime also supported the Brotherhood in elections to professional association boards, student councils, and faculty boards in its effort to counter other social movements.

In the 1980s, the regime allowed the Jordanian Brotherhood to organize against Syria. The Brotherhood's opposition to the Asad regime in Syria, which attempted to crush the Syrian Muslim Brotherhood movement, coincided with King Hussein's own antipathy and foreign policy. During the 1970s and 1980s, the king allowed the Brotherhood to form training grounds in Jordan for military operations against Syria. This provided the movement with a safe haven for armed campaigns and served as a launching point for attacks against Asad.[36]

The regime has also invited members of the Brotherhood to participate in governance. High profile moderates, such as Ishaq Farhan, have served as ministers in the government and have been appointed to the Senate. In 1991, members of the Brotherhood were given the most important domestic portfolios, including the Ministries of Education, Health, Justice, Social Development, and Awqaf. Although this Gulf War cabinet only lasted six months, it demonstrated cooperation between the regime and the Brotherhood movement.

Despite this collaboration, the relationship has experienced downturns as well. In 1956, the Muslim Brotherhood organized protests against policies that permitted a substantial British presence in the country. Later, divisions between the movement and the crown emerged over the regime's policy toward Iran. Before the 1979 Iranian revolution, King Hussein attempted to bolster the faltering Shah by visiting Iran three times in 1978. Since the majority of Jordanians supported the Iranian revolution, the king's actions in support of the Shah were used by the Brotherhood as an opportunity to attack the government's policies as un-Islamic. King Hussein's later support of Iraq during the Iran-Iraq war further emphasized these differences.

Another clash occurred during Egypt's rapprochement with Israel. Despite King Hussein's public condemnation of the peace efforts, he refused to break ties with Egypt, continuing economic relations after the Camp David Accords in 1978. The Muslim Brotherhood expressed dismay at what it viewed as inadequate action against Egypt's independent break with the united Arab front against Israel.

Still another breakdown in relations occurred in the 1980s when political circumstances between Syria and Jordan improved. The king's rapprochement with Syria led to a crackdown on the Brotherhood to prevent further military attacks against the Asad regime. This included an assortment of measures designed to repress the movement's foreign operations as well as domestic activities.[37] Other areas of confrontation have emerged over issues such as economic liberalization, relations with the West, the peace process, and the election law.

Regardless of these differences, however, the Muslim Brotherhood has remained loyal to the political system and the Hashemite regime. It has never operated underground, attempted to destabilize the kingdom, or used violence. Though there have been disagreements, it is like any relationship and has experienced ups and downs. The historical record has demonstrated the movement's loyalty to the system, and a long history of interaction has created a predictable relationship in which the actors are well known to one another. As Hilmi Asmar, member of the Muslim Brotherhood and former editor of the Islamist weekly *al-Sabil*, argues,

> There is an accumulation of trust building because we have been dealing with decision-makers for a long time. There is a gentleman's agreement between the royal court and the Muslim Brotherhood. King Abdullah opened the first headquarters of the Muslim Brotherhood in Jordan so trust started from the beginning. There was no real conflict between the Muslim Brotherhood and the regime. . . . We are partners; we are not revolutionaries. We have disagreements, different points of view, but we do not go boxing.[38]

This cooperation and participation has been criticized by more radical groups within the broader Islamic movement who argue that the Muslim Brotherhood has compromised its ideological and religious message for political and social power. From this perspective, the pragmatism of the Muslim Brotherhood has superseded its original intent. Layth Shubaylat's objections to the movement reflect the view of many Islamists outside the Muslim Brotherhood:

> I do not think they are serious. I think they are part of the regime. I think they are not serious and they are tame. And their duty is to tame the new followers. They give them a lot of rhetoric and tell then to obey and they say this is why and that it is the wisdom.[39]

An Islamist from the Mu'tazila movement lamented that the Muslim Brotherhood is concerned with "small, trivial things, like preventing alcohol from being served on planes or stopping pornographic movies; but these are very trivial matters and are not effective in social change."[40] Another Islamist complained that "their nature, their very thought, is pragmatic," and argued that the Muslim Brotherhood will never affect real Islamic change in Jordan because it has been "captured by the system." Even radical members of the Muslim Brotherhood itself articulate this perspective, charging that the leadership is more concerned with political power than with producing an Islamic society. Despite such internal disagreements, however, radical members of the Brotherhood do not propose a violent or confrontational approach that would threaten the power of the king or the political system. Their approach is more one of nonparticipation, which includes boycotts and statements opposed to government policies. They believe that the Brotherhood should remain outside parliament and the cabinet, and that the movement should pursue change through other venues such as grassroots projects. This wing of the Brotherhood, which is not a majority, fears that cooperation could lead to co-optation and the "domestification of the opposition" (if this has not occurred already).[41]

While there are a few individuals outside the Brotherhood who believe the movement may eventually resort to violence, they are in the minority.[42] Scholars, intellectuals, independent Islamists, and the Muslim Brotherhood itself recognize the long and cooperative relationship between the Brotherhood and the regime. A historical record of participation and cooperation supports the public rhetoric of the Muslim Brotherhood. They have consistently defended the regime and peaceful mechanisms of change, even during periods of crisis when the Brotherhood could have mobilized against the king. They have participated in state and government institutions, and have remained within the rules of the political game, as defined by the regime.

As a consequence, the Muslim Brotherhood has been awarded maneuvering room for social movement activism. Beginning in the late 1950s, the movement expanded through a variety of formal organizations, at a time when all other social movements were repressed. This created mutual trust that, while not perfect, did provide the foundations for "peaceful coexistence." Because the regime is experienced in dealing with the Brotherhood and recognizes its participation in the system, the movement has been allowed to effectively operate through formal organizations in civil society.

MUSLIM BROTHERHOOD ORGANIZATIONS

The Muslim Brotherhood took advantage of its special relationship with the regime during the period of martial law to institutionalize its presence through formal NGOs. The movement built schools, health care facilities, cultural centers, youth centers, and a plethora of charitable societies. Most of these activities operate through the Islamic Center Charity Society, which was licensed in 1963 and serves as the charitable arm of the Muslim Brotherhood. The center's activities grew during the 1970s with the influx of oil-related revenues and financial support. With expenditures in 1993 of JD1,148,573

($1,640,820), the financial resources of the center dwarf the resources of all other NGOs except those sponsored by the royal family.[43]

The center runs a variety of organizations. Some of its most successful enterprises are educational institutes. The society operates a network of kindergartens and schools, including the reputable Dar al-Arqum and Dar al-Aqsa schools (the latter had seventeen branches throughout Jordan as of 1993).[44] These schools combine the mandatory national curriculum with special religious classes and hold special Islamic events, such as Islamic book festivals. Nonreligious classes, such as biology, are imbued with an Islamic dimension by explaining scientific information in terms of the Qur'an and *hadiths*. The society also built the Islamic Community College in Zarqa and Zarqa University, a coed school that institutes norms of gender segregation in classes and promotes Islamic behavior. Other organizational activities through the center include health clinics, sewing centers, Qur'anic reading courses, orphanages, scholarships for students, and financial and in-kind distribution for the poor.

The Center's most successful charitable project is the Islamic Hospital in Amman. During the initial phase of state building in Jordan, missionaries and foreign nationals operated most health and educational institutions. Following the 1967 war with Israel, members of the Muslim Brotherhood decided to establish their own health care facilities. Construction of the hospital began shortly thereafter in 1970 and it was opened in 1982. Initially, the hospital had 60 beds, but it has since expanded to 360. All kinds of specialties are available, as at most modern hospitals. Administrators are particularly proud of the one to three daily heart surgeries performed at the hospital. Occupancy during the summer months is around a hundred patients per day, but this drops to between sixty-five and seventy patients per day during the winter. There are eleven hundred employees at the hospital, a third of which are nurses. There are eighty-seven resident doctors, including seventy specialists.[45]

There is a special fund for the poor at the hospital that disburses approximately JD10,000 ($14,000) per month to patients who cannot afford payment. A committee, independent of the hospital management, determines whether patients are eligible for the special fund and the amount of financial support disbursed.[46] Between 1982 and 1990, free treatment was provided to 10,831 patients at a cost of JD1,311,655 ($1,873,793).[47]

The hospital attempts to promote Islamic values, standards, and norms. For employees, certain rules are applied to ensure Islamic behavior. Nurses are issued standard Islamic attire, which includes a *hijab* to cover the hair and a long, modest dress. Women working at the hospital are not permitted to wear the more constrictive veil because, as Zaid Abu Ghamineh, an administrator at the hospital, states, "The face of the nurse always affects the patient."[48] While some employees do wear the veil outside the hospital, less conservative dress is required while at work. The hospital also tries to implement norms of gender segregation, though in practice this is often difficult to achieve. Intermingling of male and female employees is minimized where possible, and the hospital tries to match female medical personnel with female patients and male staff with male patients. In general, this has been successful at the nursing level, but because of the low number of female doctors, it is more difficult where patients must see a doctor. Employees are required to pray five times a day; but this is not always enforced or practiced, particularly among medical specialists. There are also Islamic educational activities held at the hospital for employees, including lectures and weekly lessons on subjects such as the Qur'an, *hadith*, Islamic *fiqh* (jurisprudence), and Qur'anic recitation. These activities are not obligatory, but the hospital encourages employees to attend.[49]

Patients are exposed to Islamic values through employee practices at the hospital and special Islamic activities. The staff is encouraged to discuss Islam with patients, and Islamic programming and videos are shown on hospital televisions. Books and pamphlets on Islam are also readily available to patients. While some patients come to the hospital because of its specifically Islamic character, more often they are attracted by the availability of medical technology.[50]

The activities at the hospital and other centers affiliated with the Islamic Center Charity Society are not political in nature. They synthesize Islamic values and grassroots socioeconomic needs. As with other Islamic and non-Islamic NGOs in Jordan, the state prevents the use of the Islamic Center Charity Society for political activities. The movement has succeeded through formal organizations precisely because it has not challenged the legitimacy of the regime or the terms of conditional participation. While the Muslim Brotherhood has opposed specific policies, it has never utilized the center to mobilize against the regime. This is not unique to the Brotherhood; it is part of a broader pattern of NGO activity in Jordan, a pattern structured by the state's control of organizational space.

Because of the Muslim Brotherhood's relationship with the regime and its consistent support for working through the system, it has enjoyed special treatment in organizing through the Islamic Center Charity Society. Not only was it permitted to organize when all other political organizations in the country were banned during the martial law period, but it has also been allowed to expand the scope of its activities, broadening the reach of its appeal. For example, the law requires that NGOs first obtain permission to open branches. Though the center has opened only four official branches, it has sidestepped regulations by opening thirty-two "committees."[51] These committees are not a secret; they are well known to the state apparatus, and their existence is due to state tolerance and tacit approval, an acceptance that is not forthcoming for many other social movements. In addition, while the Ministry of Social Development strictly monitors the financial records of NGOs through annual audits, the Islamic Center Charity Society has frequently been exempt.

The Muslim Brotherhood operates through other NGOs as well. The Yarmuk Sports, Social, and Cultural Club was founded in 1967 as an athletic club with an Islamic orientation. It primarily focuses on children and young adults. The society sponsors a number of athletic teams, including soccer, table tennis, basketball, and handball teams. There is also a swimming pool where gender segregation is practiced. Additional activities at the Club include a scouts team, pilgrimages to Islamic sites, Islamic lectures, Islamic book exhibits, *iftar* banquets during Ramadan, Qur'anic recitation, *fiqh*, and the Yarmuk Club Troupe for Islamic singing, which performs songs with an Islamic message that often address the Palestinian struggle.[52] The club's focus on athletics reflects the Muslim Brotherhood's view of the movement as an "athletic movement aiming to prepare the soldiers of tomorrow."[53]

The Brotherhood's Islamic Studies and Research Association (ISRA), located in the Jebel Webdeh neighborhood of Amman, was licensed in 1980 at the Ministry of Culture. Its purpose is to conduct scientific research in various areas of knowledge that impact Muslim societies. The research agenda and strategy is constructed within a broad Islamic framework to facilitate an Islamic philosophy that incorporates contemporary political, social, economic, and intellectual issues. To this end, the society hosts seminars, lectures, and conferences; publishes Islamic research papers and books; and has established ties with research institutes in other countries. The board members include non-Muslim Brotherhood Islamists, but members of the Brotherhood are an important component. Ishaq Farhan is the president of the society and is actively involved in its projects. The society shares space with the Jordanian branch of the International Institute for Islamic Thought (IIIT), registered in Jordan in 1990 to pursue similar research, cultural, and educational interests.[54] The president of IIIT also sits on the administrative board of ISRA and is a member of the Muslim Brotherhood. The two organizations often jointly sponsor lectures and events. At one lecture, they invited a member of the Higher Council for Islamic Studies in Algeria to discuss intercultural issues. While the discussion and lectures do address some limited political issues, the orientation is apolitical and focuses more on culture. Transgressions into political subjects are subsidiary to the main thrust of the activities. Any political dimensions are limited to discussions and do not involve organizing or activism.

Following political liberalization, members of the Muslim Brotherhood continued to branch into the cultural arena through the Society for the Preservation of the Qur'an, founded in 1990. The society engages in a variety of activities intended to promote the application of the Qur'an because of a belief that "there is no way man can be happy unless they take their knowledge from the Qur'an, read it, and understand."[55] The society teaches Muslims, especially younger Muslims, to read and memorize the Qur'an. It also educates participants in fields related to the Qur'an, such as the *shariʿa*, *fiqh*, and the Sunna. In July, it holds the National Project for the Conservation and Learning of the Qur'an, which encourages children to participate in Qur'anic education and activities. During Ramadan, the society holds a national contest for students who have memorized more than five parts of the Qur'an. During this month, members of the society also bring people in from the street for general lessons on understanding and memorizing the Qur'an.

This society enjoys an amicable relationship with the state. While a similar cultural society comprised of critical Salafis, discussed in the next chapter, was routinely denied permission to open branches, despite its legal prerogative to do so, the Society for the Preservation of the Qur'an has successfully opened one hundred centers throughout the kingdom, far exceeding the Ministry of Awqaf's own twenty-six cultural societies. This provides access to a variety of neighborhoods in different cities. It is the strongest and best organized of

the nine Islamic cultural societies. While other Islamic cultural societies are routinely denied permission to form branches without an
explanation, the only barriers for this society are "financial, strictly
financial."[56] It enjoys a good relationship with the regime and the
state apparatus. As the director of the society states, "The Ministry
of Culture understands perfectly the goals of the society. We have all
the moral support we need from the Ministry of Culture. The only
obstacle is financial, and we keep the ministry informed of our activities."[57] In fact, the society's bylaws, approved by the minister of
culture, state that it can open branches whenever it wants and inform the ministry after the fact. In most cases, NGOs require prior
permission to open branches. In addition, the society works directly
with the Ministries of Culture, Education, and Awqaf, often utilizing state-owned facilities such as the Islamic Center at King Abdullah
Mosque in Amman. Given this supportive relationship, it is not sur-
prising that the director of the society is also an employee at Sanduq
al-Zakat at the Ministry of Awqaf.[58]

Volunteers at these NGOs typically downplay their relationship
with the Brotherhood because of legal requirements. Administrative distinctions require a formal separation between the Brotherhood and various Brotherhood-operated NGOs. However, although
these organizations are not formally attached to the Brotherhood,
they are recognized as part of the movement because they are run
and operated by members of the Muslim Brotherhood. While the
administrative, financial, and decision-making structures of these
organizations are independent, the participants and the message are
the same. Volunteers are tied to the mission and goals of the Muslim
Brotherhood movement. This emphasis on organizational independence reflects the members' understanding of administrative distinctions. At these Muslim Brotherhood-affiliated societies members
consistently emphasized that they operate under different organizational structures, follow Law 33, and are part of the ministerial apparatus where they are registered. For example, when asked about
a relationship with the Muslim Brotherhood, the director of The
Society for the Preservation of the Qur'an responded as follows: "We
have no ties to any parties in this country. We were established by the
law of charitable and cultural societies in the country." After further
questioning about the society's relationship with the Brotherhood,
he agreed that many members of the Muslim Brotherhood volunteer at the society, and claimed that "this is known to the Ministry

of Culture," indicating his concern for administrative and organizational separation in accordance with legal restrictions.[59] The distinction is a formality, and the membership is composed of members of the Muslim Brotherhood, including the society's president, Abdul Latif Arabiyyat.

This perspective mirrors responses by organizational leaders at other Muslim Brotherhood societies. At the Islamic Hospital, Zaid Abu Ghamineh was asked a similar question, and he too emphasized the legal and administrative distinction, though recognizing the Muslim Brotherhood membership composition:

> The organizers and owners of the hospital are the Islamic Center [Charitable] Society. Most of the founders of this society were and still are members of the Muslim Brotherhood Society. So from this there is the belief that this hospital belongs to the Muslim Brotherhood Society. This is wrong. It belongs to the Islamic Center [Charitable] Society, and this Islamic Center [Charitable] Society has a relationship with the Ministry of Social Development, not with the Muslim Brotherhood. But we are Muslim Brotherhood members working here.[60]

These NGOs have allowed the Brotherhood to organize in multiple spheres of activity at once and form an organizational network that can be used to mobilize support for the movement. While these organizations are not used for political purposes or to organize against the regime, they do provide an extended organizational reach. The Muslim Brotherhood is able to use organizations to promote a religious message in different areas of Islamic work, thus transcending administrative barriers through multiple organizations.

In addition, many Muslim Brotherhood institutions, such as the Islamic Hospital and Zarqa University, serve as sources of movement patronage. According to Ra'if Nijim, the engineer responsible for the construction of both institutions and the former director of the fund for the poor at the Islamic Hospital, the vast majority of employees at these organizations are members of the Brotherhood, a fact that Nijim believes brings down the quality of services:

> Now the hospital here, the Islamic Hospital, all the employees there, all the doctors, are members of the Muslim Brotherhood, regardless of their knowledge or the ability for work. I go and visit the hospital always and I can see with my own eyes. There are

many workers and many employees [who] do not deserve to be employed in that hospital because this is a big, standard hospital in the country and should employ better staff. They do not employ anyone who is not a member of the Muslim Brotherhood.[61]

In reality, there are non-Muslim Brotherhood employees as well, but Nijim estimates that 90 percent of the staff is from the movement.

The substantial number of Brotherhood employees reflects the patronage function of these organizations. It creates a social network for the movement, which attracts new followers and rewards participants. Hamam Sayyid, a hard-liner in the Brotherhood, stated:

When we were children, the movement (the Muslim Brotherhood organizations) took care of us. We would sit together with the old shaykhs, and I do not think this exists in other religious movements. The social network which they built for us children attracted us to the movement.[62]

By providing these services for communities and members, the Brotherhood can utilize its organizations to garner support, a fact well known to the government and to movement outsiders. It provides a point of contact with communities and an opportunity to publicly display movement achievements through concrete projects. As Ra'if Nijim observed,

All of these projects—cultural, political, and social projects—they prove this movement is helping the people, that these projects are for the people. So when you do such projects, it is better than being only an association talking to people, calling them to Islam, calling them to pray, calling them to go for pilgrimage. This is how they succeed and because of this they have succeeded. Not because they are the only Muslim movement, but because they have done a lot of projects for the country.[63]

Although these organizations do not engage in political activities, there is a political effect. Beneficiaries provide political support to the Brotherhood because of its social service provision. Zaid Abu Ghamineh argues:

Our success is in building a practical model for how Islam can serve. It has raised the confidence of the community that Islam can solve people's problems. That is why people now support the

Islamic movement and this is reflected. Poor people, especially those served by the hospital, they pay us back in elections and meetings. They interact with us. The hospital has influenced them. . . . This influence is not direct. We do not require that people either support the movement or we will not help. . . . It is not a requirement that they become members of the Muslim Brotherhood. They voluntarily find themselves morally indebted to the movement and that is why they do not pay us [immediately for charitable work]. When the movement is in elections or needs support, they repay the debt.[64]

The Muslim Brotherhood's activities in organizations are not part of an insidious political scheme to uproot the regime. The history of the Brotherhood demonstrates otherwise. It is a grassroots attempt to promote a religious message through formal organizations in civil society. The Brotherhood has adhered to administrative distinctions, emphasizing organizational differentiation rather than the unity of organization activities. It respects the limits of organizational space, as determined by the logic of administrative practices and regime survival. The movement has supported the state, and the state, in turn, has reciprocated by allowing the Brotherhood to organize effectively.

CONCLUSION

The regime's control of organizational space means that critical Islamist groups cannot use NGOs to attack the state's Islamic discourse. Its ability to remove individuals from the voluntary sector and prevent their participation is coupled with absolute discretion in issuing permits. This discretion and the administrative/repressive capacity of the state have produced the Islamic NGO community outlined in this chapter. There are indeed more Islamic NGOs since political liberalization, but the expansion of freedom has not seeped to the level of organizational content. Islamic NGOs remain, like other NGOs, apolitical and nonconfrontational.

The Muslim Brotherhood's organizational success has benefited both the Brotherhood and the regime. Not only has the Brotherhood's expansion in civil society allowed it greater opportunities for reaching new constituencies and garnering support, but its high profile and moderate stance serve to counter radical Islamic groups.

From the perspective of regime survival, the Muslim Brotherhood's most important function is that it marginalizes more militant Islamic groups that propose revolutionary changes in the political and social system. As a moderate, supportive, and legal Islamic movement, the Brotherhood is viewed as a means of absorbing the increased religiosity that began in the 1970s to divert it away from more radical groups. At times, the Brotherhood uses its high profile and legitimacy to delegitimize the claims and ideologies of groups that espouse violence in the kingdom. Any new, more radical Islamic group, which might construct a material or ideological challenge to the regime, would first need to successfully diminish the Muslim Brotherhood's status in the community. This creates a legitimating buffer that protects the regime from revolutionary discursive challenges. The Brotherhood, in effect, serves as a mechanism of internal social movement discipline that the regime hopes will prevent the growing power of more threatening Islamic groups.

CHAPTER 4

The Salafi Movement and Informal Networks

This is My straight path, so follow it. Follow not the other ways,
lest ye be parted from His way. This hath He ordained for you
that ye may ward off (evil).

—Qur'an 6:154

For Muslims, the correct way to practice Islam is outlined in the
Qur'an and Sunna. These sources represent the foundations of the
Islamic faith and detail the "straight path" to salvation. Throughout
centuries of Islamic history, religious reform movements have
emerged to combat what they view as deviations from the straight
path. These movements promoted *islah* (reform) and *tajdid* (renewal) to encourage Muslims to return to the path of God as delineated by the Qur'an and Sunna. Contemporary *mujaddinun*, or those
who facilitate this religious renewal, are typically literalists who rely
upon a narrow scriptural approach to religious understanding. These
reformists believe that the Qur'an and Sunna outline the perfect
model of the Muslim community. By returning to the fundamentals
of the faith and following the example of the Prophet Mohammed,
they hope to recreate the Muslim society that existed during the
period surrounding the divine revelations. The past represents the
ideal of community and an unchanging standard.[1] Because the Qur'an
is the word of God and the Prophet Mohammed represents the
Muslim exemplar whose path (behavior, sayings, deeds, decisions,
etc.) in religious affairs was perfect, these sources of religion are immutable. While circumstances and contexts may change, religious
practice must not be altered to accommodate contemporary challenges. Muslims must instead address new challenges with unchanging religious principles.

The contemporary Salafi movement is the most recent resurgence of this puritanical reformism. The term *salafi* derives from the
Arabic *salaf*, which means "to precede." In the Islamic lexicon, *salaf*

111

refers to *al-salaf al-salih*, the virtuous forefathers of the faith who were companions of the Prophet Mohammed. Application of the term *salaf* generally includes not only *al-salaf al-salih*, but also their followers *(al-tabi'un)* and their followers' followers *(tabi'u al-tabi'in)*, in other words, the first three generations of Muslims. The last *salaf* is the jurist and founder of the Hanbali school of jurisprudence, Ahmad Ibn Hanbal, though the term is frequently extended to include renown reformists who adhered to the model of the companions, such as Hamid al-Ghazali (d. 1111), Taqi al-Din Ahmad Ibn Taymiyya (d. 1328), Ibn Qaiyyim al-Jawziya (d. 1350), and Mohammed Bin 'Abd al-Wahhab (d. 1792).[2] Those who adhere to the example of the *salaf* and strictly follow the Qur'an and the Sunna of the Prophet as the only sources of religious understanding are considered Salafis.

Salafis argue that since the first three generations of Muslims learned about Islam directly from the Prophet or those who knew him, they commanded a pure understanding of the religion. Subsequent understandings, they argue, were sullied and distorted by the introduction of innovations and the development of schisms within the Muslim *umma*. Salafis therefore seek to eradicate impurities introduced during centuries of religious practice. They are attempting to institute religious rituals and understandings that capture the purity of Islam, as interpreted and understood by practitioners during the initial phases of its development. Interpretations that do not rely upon the original sources of the religion are viewed as distortions that lead Muslims away from the straight path of God and into the fires of hell. Decisions in every aspect of life must be based upon evidence from the Qur'an, Sunna, and the *salaf*, which indicates whether particular actions or behaviors are permitted. In instances where action or behavior was not sanctioned or practiced by the Prophet, it is rejected as a new invention in religion.

In pursuing its goals of purifying Islamic practice according to the *salaf* model, the Salafi movement predominantly relies upon informal social networks rather than formal organizations. Unlike the Muslim Brotherhood, the Salafis in Jordan never enjoyed a strong relationship with the regime. Its literalist interpretation leaves little room for the kinds of pragmatic compromises espoused by the Brotherhood. Anything less than absolute implementation of Salafi doctrine is tantamount to abandoning the straight path. As a result, Salafis have always been highly critical of regime actions and have been unwilling to sacrifice ideological purity for practical political gains, an intransigent position that has been exacerbated by the emergence of more violent factions within the Salafi movement. Because of the Salafi challenge to the religious credentials and legitimacy of the Hashemites, the regime has selectively utilized administrative and repressive mechanisms in the management of collective action to prevent the emergence of a Salafi opposition organized through SMOs. This has led Salafis to instead mobilize through informal social networks, which operate outside the disciplinary gaze of the state apparatus and serve as alternative institutional resources for the production and dissemination of the Salafi interpretation of Islam. Networks represent an indigenous model of mobilization that allows Salafis and other critical Islamist groups to act outside the system of control instituted through techniques of management.

SALAFI IDEOLOGY

Based upon *salaf* understandings of Islam, the Salafis have constructed a *manhaj*, or approach to religion. The Salafi *manhaj* is a methodology for determining proper religious interpretations based upon the Qur'an, the Sunna, and the *salaf* model. It is predicated upon certain accepted "truths" about Islam, which were espoused by the Prophet and recorded in authentic *(sahih) hadiths*. Important issues include *tawhid* (belief in the oneness of God), the evils of *shirk* (ascribing partners to God in worship), and the problem of *bid'a* (innovation in religion). Salafis also emphasize the role of *hadith* science and the weakness of blindly following one *mathhab* (school of Islamic jurisprudence) rather than religious "truth." The objective of the Salafi movement is to promote this understanding of Islam.

Tawhid and Shirk

The central concept in Salafi thought is *tawhid*—belief in the oneness of God.[3] *Tawhid* begins with the *shahada* (the testimony of faith that is required to become a Muslim): "I testify that there is no god except Allah, and that Mohammed is His messenger." Because of its emphasis on the oneness of God, the *shahada* is sometimes referred to as "the phrase of *tawhid*."[4] Following Wahhabi doctrine, Salafis break the concept of *tawhid* into three constituent elements.[5]

The first is *tawhid al-rububiyya*—the state of being the only true *rabb*, or lord. This dimension of *tawhid* describes God as the sole Lord and sovereign of the universe, and is based upon the *suras* (chapters of the Qur'an), "Allah is Creator of all things, and He is Guardian over all things,"[6] and, "No calamity befalleth save by Allah's leave. And whoever believeth in Allah, He guideth his heart. And Allah is Knower of all things."[7] This dimension of *tawhid* is accepted by all Muslims and is not a point of contention.

The second element of *tawhid* is *tawhid al-asma' wa al-sifat*—belief in the unity of the names and attributes of God. Salafis interpret this dimension of *tawhid* to mean that references to the names and attributes of God in the Qur'an must be understood in their literalist meaning, without likening them to human characteristics.[8] Throughout the Qur'an, there are references to the uniqueness of God and His attributes, such as, "He is Allah the One! Allah, the eternally Besought of all! He beggeteth not nor was begotten. And there is none comparable to Him."[9] Another *sura* states that, "Naught is His likeness, and He is the Hearer, the Seer."[10] In essence, *tawhid al-asma' wa al-sifat* is a rejection of anthropomorphism.

This dimension of *tawhid* is an important source of vociferous disagreement among Muslim groups over *'aqida* (creed or doctrine). Throughout Islamic history, there has been a strain between rationalist and literalist tendencies in Islamic thought over the consequences of the uniqueness of God's attributes.[11] The rationalists are represented by Islamic groups such as al-Mu'tazila who interpret God's attributes as metaphors. They argue, for example, that God cannot have sight per se because this implies that He has eyes. Because God created eyes and He does not share attributes with His creatures, this is impossible. Rationalists therefore interpret references to God's sight as His knowledge.

The literalist tendency is represented by groups such as the Salafis who argue that the Qur'an, as the word of God, is not open to interpretation. They argue that while God's attributes are not comparable to those of His creations, they are not metaphors either. Instead, such descriptions are considered incomprehensible to humans and part of the knowledge of *ghayb* (domains beyond human senses and perceptions). The Qur'an mentions God's hands, so Salafis believe that He has hands, though they are not like human hands.

As humans, we cannot comprehend such things as God's hands because they are beyond our range of understanding. These attributes are nonetheless real since they are mentioned in the Qur'an. Salafis reject *tahrif* (distortion), *ta'til* (stripping God of His attributes), and *tamthil* (comparison of God with His creations). Muslims should believe in God's attributes without question because the Qur'an is the literal word of God. Salafis charge that the rationalist tendency to interpret Qur'anic references as metaphors is equal to "suspending or neutralizing Allah's attributes."[12] Salafis and the rationalists have engaged in heated debates over this aspect of *tawhid,* and the volume of Salafi publications devoted to this issue attests to its importance. These debates, however, are often more polemical attacks than real theological divisions. Salafis often critique theological positions held by major schools of thought in Islamic history that are not necessarily prevalent today.[13]

The third component is *tawhid al-ilahiya*—worshipping only God. The basis of this element of *tawhid* is *suras* such as, "And the places of worship are only for Allah, so pray not unto anyone along with Allah,"[14] and *hadiths* such as, "Allah's right upon the creatures is that they worship Him without taking any partners with Him."[15] While this may seem to be a noncontroversial element of monotheism, there are in fact interpretative complexities that have fostered divisions among Muslims. The primary disagreement within the Muslim community over *tawhid al-ilahiya* is related to the role of saints. Over centuries of religious practice, certain cultural and religious innovations emerged. Sufi groups in particular introduced many popular practices, such as praying to saints as intermediaries between Muslims and God. Salafis interpret *tawhid al-ilahiya* as a prohibition against such practices, and Sufis and Salafis are diametrically opposed over this issue. In some instances, conflicts between Sufis and Salafis have led to violence. In Jordan, especially during the late 1970s and early 1980s when Sufism was more prevalent, there were several violent clashes.[16]

The opposite of *tawhid* is *shirk*—ascribing partners in worshipping God. For Salafis, *shirk* includes religious practices such as visiting tombs and using saints as intermediaries to God. The Qur'an is filled with direct prohibitions against *shirk:*

[A]nd be not one of those who ascribes partners (unto Him).[17]

Lo! Whoso ascribeth partners unto Allah, for him Allah has forbidden Paradise. His abode is in the Fire. For evil-doers there will
be no helpers.[18]

Lo! Allah forgiveth not that a partner be ascribed unto Him. He
forgiveth (all) save that to who He will. Whoso ascribeth partners
to Allah, he hath indeed invented a tremendous sin.[19]

There are primarily two kinds of *shirk*: minor and major. The former
is sometimes referred to as "secret *shirk*" because the person guilty
of minor *shirk* often does not realize that it is an infraction. Examples include such things as swearing by other than God and show-
ing off. Major *shirk* is more serious and includes innovations in worship and religious rituals.[20] Salafis fight against both forms, but con-
centrate their efforts against major *shirk*.[21]

Bid'a

Those of you who live long after me will see a lot of differences, so
hold fast to my Sunnah and to the Sunnah of the Rightly-Guided
Khaleefahs after me. Cling to it tightly and beware of newly-invented matters, for every newly-invented matter is an innovation,
and every innovation is misguidance, and all misguidance is in the
Fire.[22]

Salafis argue that because the Qur'an and Sunna reveal the per-
fection of Islam, any innovations are a distortion of the straight path.
Whatever is not outlined in the Qur'an or was not practiced by the
Prophet is a deviation from the original and pure framework of Islam. If there is no evidence of a particular practice in the Qur'an or
Sunna, it is *bid'a* (an innovation in faith). Even acts intended to
bring Muslims closer to God are innovations and evil if they are not
outlined in the original sources of Islam. For example, Salafis chas-
tise Muslims who pray more than five times a day in an attempt to
venerate God because such practices were never prescribed or sanctioned by the Prophet and are therefore invented. Salafis attack Sufis
for practices such as those involving belief in *baraka* (grace or "good
blessing"), claiming that such beliefs and actions were never endorsed or practiced by the Prophet. There is even a linguistic *bid'a*
when referring to religion or religious issues. At a seminar, Mohammed Abu Shaqra, a prominent Jordanian Salafi sheikh, was asked his

opinion on Islamic extremism and violence in Algeria. He responded by rejecting the term Islamic extremism as *bid'a* (and thus avoided answering the intent of the question):

> I say that the word "extremism" that we now know was not known by our *salaf* and is not a part of our religion. In our religion, there was another word that should be commonly used. . . . The terms should all come from the *shari'a*. The word "extremism" is not a religious term; it is a modern term. And there is a similar term that is used—Islamic fundamentalism. This term is also not a *shari'a* term. Extremism and fundamentalism are two terms that mean, linguistically speaking, that you rectify the path of a nation that has lost its way. The right term that should be used for people who have lost their way is *gulu* [a nation that overdoes things]. And the Prophet says to the people of the Book, "Do not overdo your worship to God." This term *gulu* is what should be used to describe such a condition. And people who use these other terms [extremism and fundamentalism] are just imitators of the people whose clothes we wear and behavior we copy [e.g., the West]. So the word *gulu* should be used.[23]

For Salafis, it is a priority to fight *mubtadi'un* (those who innovate) since innovators do not teach "true" Islam and lead people astray and into damnation. The path of *bid'a* is not the straight path and leads people away from the word of God and the Sunna of the Prophet.

The concept of *bid'a* is often extended to entail a rejection of outside traditions and cultures. Many Salafis reject blue jeans, skirts, pants for women, consumerism, and other Western cultural practices as foreign to Islam. These practices are part of an outside culture and are therefore considered alien to Muslim traditions. Instead, many Salafis propose practices allegedly performed during the time of the Prophet, such as wearing white, flowing robes, which come down to the mid-calf.[24] In extreme cases, this can even include the rejection of technology as a Western invention, though this view is not prevalent among Salafis.

The Importance of Hadith

Because Salafis rely on the model of the Prophet and the *salaf*, Salafi scholars devote their attention to the science of *hadith* and refer to Salafis as *Ahl al-Hadith* (the people of *hadith*). The *hadiths* are reported sayings and traditions of the Prophet Mohammed and comprise a written record of his Sunna. Many of the Companions collected the Prophet's sayings in written books called *sahifas*, which were later used for religious lectures and lessons. Literally, the Companions collected thousands of *hadiths*. Next to the Qur'an, *hadiths* form the most important source of religious knowledge and guidance, since they provide a picture of how Islam was practiced when it was first introduced.

Like any endeavor of this magnitude, there were inevitable forgeries produced by heretics *(zanadiqa)*, sectarian preachers and sycophants who sought caliphal largess, storytellers *(qasasiyun)*, and devout traditionalists who attempted to attract people to Islam by forging *hadiths*. Mohammed Ibn 'Ukkasha and Mohammed Ibn Tamin are said to have forged over ten thousand *hadiths*. Ahmad al-Marwazi reportedly fabricated ten thousand himself. A large number of forgeries by men such as Ziyad Ibn Mayun, Shurayk Ibn 'Abd Allah, and Talha Ibn 'Amr are still used in sermons today.[25] Though the core of authentic *hadiths* was preserved, the existence of even a small number of inaccurate *hadiths* threatens the Salafi *manhaj* and strikes at the center of Salafi understandings of Islam. False *hadiths* represent the devils of the "other paths" and threaten to pull Muslims away from the straight path of Islam.

Many Salafi scholars, therefore, devote themselves to the science of *hadith*, a science intended to cleanse Islam of false or weak *hadiths* in order to present an accurate record of the Sunna.[26] Until the third century of Islam, each tradition recorded in a *hadith* collection included the chain of narrators who transmitted it. This chain is referred to as an *isnad*, or authority. In tracing *isnads*, scholars assemble biographies of the transmitters (to ascertain their reliability) and use established rules for verification.[27] The *hadiths* fall into one of three categories: *sahih* (sound), *hasan* (fair), and *da'if* (weak). The first two categories are comprised of *hadiths* whose transmissions are considered reliable. The last category is divided into several subcategories, which include questionable *isnads*, broken chains of transmission, and forged *hadiths*.[28] Determining the authenticity of *isnads* and *hadiths* is one of the cornerstones of the Salafi mission since Salafis are devoted to eliminating false Islamic practices. Some of the most famous Salafi scholars, such as the late Mohammed Nasir al-Din al-Bani in Jordan, are foremost in the field of *hadith*. In principle, Salafis only accept sound *hadiths*, though in practice one can find them using fair *hadiths* as well.

Mathhabs

Islamic jurisprudence is traditionally divided into four *mathhabs*, or schools: Maliki, Hanbali, Hanafi, and Shafi'i.[29] Though referred to as "schools," *mathhabs* are more accurately described as methods. Each presents a set of criteria for determining religious rulings based upon sources such as the Qur'an, *hadiths*, the opinion of jurists, consensus, scholarly interpretations, notions of public interest, and reason. Muslim communities typically follow one of the four *mathhabs* to the exclusion of others (though in some instances there is overlap or other *mathhabs* are used in particular types of rulings). The *mathhabs* agree on the most fundamental and basic aspects of Islam, but there are divergences over particulars and the application of religion to modern issues and problems.

For Salafis, the division of Muslims into separate *mathhabs* is an unacceptable practice because there can be only one right answer and ruling—that which is according to God. They argue that one of the pitfalls of Muslim practices is blind adherence *(taqlid)* to particular *mathhabs*. Those who blindly follow one *mathhab* are inevitably blind to the truth because it prevents them from questioning their own school of thought. This does not mean that *mathhabs* are useless or irrelevant, only that Muslims cannot blindly follow them or disregard evidence from the Qur'an and Sunna that may reveal the truth and correct religious rulings. Salafis argue that the truth lies in the sources of the religion, not in the texts of jurists from particular *mathhabs*. They therefore turn directly to the Qur'an and authentic *hadith*, rather than imitate the findings and understandings of scholars, even epic scholars. Scholars known to employ the Salafi *manhaj* are used as sources of religious rulings, but only in conjunction with direct evidence from the Qur'an and Sunna. Even central figures in Salafi thought are not immune to criticism and challenges from the Salafi community.

The Salafi movement is thus in part a search for religious truth; a desire to practice Islam as it was revealed to the Prophet. Avoidance of *bid'a* and *shirk*, strict adherence to *tawhid*, and a willingness to transcend *mathhab* divisions reflect the Salafi mission to locate evidence and rules in the original sources of Islam. For Salafis, there are no intermediaries between religion and ordinary Muslims. Individuals should refer directly back to the Qur'an and Sunna. As a result, Salafis like to refer to themselves as "knowledge-seekers."

They believe that in following this path they will find salvation. They refer to themselves as the Aided Group *(ta'ifat al-mansura)* and the Saved Sect *(al-firqa al-najiyya)*, groups mentioned in the Qur'an.[30] The Prophet predicted that the *umma* would fracture into sects after his death and warned his followers to remain focused on his Sunna and the Qur'an for guidance: "I am leaving you two things and you will never go astray as long as you cling to them. They are the Book of Allah and my Sunnah."[31] Salafis believe that by relying only on these sources of religion, they are preserving the straight path and will be protected by God on judgment day. They cite several *hadiths* to support this contention:

> And this *Ummah* will divide into seventy-three sects all of which except one will go to Hell and they [the saved sect] are those who are upon what I and my Companions are upon.[32]

> This Ummah will split into seventy-three sects: seventy two will be in the Fire and one in Paradise and that is the Jamaa'ah.[33]

For Salafis, this sect is comprised of those who agree upon the truth. From the Salafi perspective, those who agree upon the truth are those who strictly follow the Qur'an and Sunna and strive to establish the standards of the *umma* from the period of the *salaf.* They consider themselves saved because they believe they are practicing Islam as God intended it to be practiced. By spreading this interpretation and restructuring society to adhere to this model, Salafis believe they offer Muslims salvation.

THE SALAFI CHALLENGE

The Salafi movement in Jordan began during the 1970s as the result of individuals exposed to Salafi thought while studying abroad in Lebanon, Syria, and Egypt. At that point in time, it was common for students of religion to study outside the kingdom because there were few religious scholars or centers of religious learning in Jordan. In particular, groups of Salafis traveled to Syria to study with Mohammed Nasir al-Din al-Bani (d. 1999), a renowned Salafi sheikh, and over time the number of students traveling from Jordan increased. As interest in Salafi thought spread, a group of Salafis began to bring al-Bani to Jordan to give lessons, and the relationship strengthened. In 1979, during a brutal campaign by the Asad regime in Syria to crush the Islamic movement, al-Bani moved to Jordan.

Al-Bani's arrival on the Muslim scene in Jordan precipitated an explosion in Salafi activism. Because al-Bani was one of only a handful of well-known Muslim scholars in Jordan at the time, he became a natural focal point for young students seeking guidance in Islam, and the number of Salafis rapidly increased. The period after 1979 is considered the "second wave" in the movement because most of the young Salafis who joined at that time have now become leaders and scholars in the contemporary movement. Salafi lessons, sermons, and speeches increased; and the movement gathered large numbers of people, mostly because of al-Bani's reputation. In his first lesson in Jordan, al-Bani gave an unadvertised lecture on the roof of a house that drew between five hundred and six hundred people, who filled the surrounding streets. Disconcerted by the large masses gathered around a single sheikh, the regime subsequently banned al-Bani from delivering public speeches.

As waves of fighters from the Afghan war returned after 1979, some Salafi groups adopted a more critical and militant posture vis-à-vis the political system and the regime. Many individuals who fought in the war not only gained military experience, but were exposed to Salafi thought by Salafis involved in the fighting. They returned to Jordan with a more critical framework and understanding of Islamic legitimacy, which was coupled with military training. These Salafi "jihadi groups" formed militant, underground organizations designed to directly challenge the state through violence.

Jihadi thought among Salafis increased dramatically after the Gulf War in 1991, as a result of the Saudi regime's decision to allow non-Muslim foreign troops in the holy land. Disillusionment with Muslim regimes and frustration with the pace of political change resulted in the emergence of several militant groups in the early 1990s.[34] In 1994, a Salafi group known as "the Afghans" (because of their previous experience in the war in Afghanistan) was convicted of cinema and liquor store bombings. In addition to the bombings, the group had also plotted to assassinate leading Jordanian officials involved in the Jordanian-Israeli peace negotiations and to bomb symbols of

Western culture, such as nightclubs and video rental stores.[35] In October 1996, members of another jihadi Salafi group, called Bay'at al-Imam (Pledge of Allegiance to the Leader), were arrested and convicted of attempted sabotage and lèse-majesté. The group was led by Abu Mohammed al-Maqdisi (also known as Mohammed Tahir Mohammed), a leading proponent of the jihadi perspective. One tract by al-Maqdisi, which circulated underground in 1996, argues that Muslims are exempt from the laws of current regimes because contemporary rulers do not govern according to Islam and are therefore illegitimate. It calls for revolutionary struggle against the regime in an effort to create a true Muslim state. Maqdisi's publications have influenced other Salafi groups in the Arab world, including those responsible for the November 1995 bombing in Riyadh, Saudi Arabia, that killed five Americans and two Indian nationals.[36] Later, the Salafi "Reformation and Challenge Group" was convicted of a series of bombings and arsons in May 1998, including attacks against the American School in Amman, a traffic police compound, and a car parked in front of the luxury Jerusalem International Hotel.[37] Prior to millennium celebrations in 1999, another Salafi group affiliated with Osama Ben Laden was arrested for plotting to carry out acts of terrorism in the kingdom.

The issue of whether violent measures and jihad are permissible against incumbent regimes is the primary point of contention among Salafis and has fractured the movement, not only in Jordan but throughout the Muslim world. One Salafi informant described the division as follows:

> In dealing with the system, the government, you have to describe it. There are two descriptions: it is either a Muslim leadership or non-Muslim. There is a sect of Salafis that believe that [even if] a Muslim leader is doing injustice, we have to tolerate this and try to resurrect the people, including the leader, by praying for change. There is another way of thinking among Salafis that describes the leader of the government differently. They say that the leader is a *kafir* (a person who becomes a Muslim and then is non-Muslim) to begin with because he adopted an ideology that is not in accordance with Islam, such as communism or liberalism. The first way is by peaceful means. The second is more violent and is called jihad. Because the leader is a *kafir*, he deserves to die; he deserves elimination. That is why there are two theories among Salafis and

this is the center of the argument between the two ways of thinking among Salafis.

The primary point of disagreement between these two groups is over *takfir*—declaring someone a *kafir*—for which there are specific rules.[38] There are those Muslims who violate Islamic rules out of ignorance or because they are foolish. In such cases, the individual is guilty of un-Islamic behavior, but is given the opportunity to repent and change once the error is understood. A Muslim is not considered a *kafir* unless they know the truth and choose otherwise. This is based upon the sura, "Forgiveness is only incumbent upon Allah toward those who do evil in ignorance (and) turn quickly (in repentance) to Allah."[39] In any application of *takfir*, there must be a clear violation and this violation must be proven. The most important debate within the Salafi community at this point is whether governments and regimes are *kafir*. If a regime is Muslim, then according to the *shari'a* Muslims cannot organize or rise against it. But if it is indeed *kafir*, then jihad applies.

At one end of this debate are those within the movement who argue that leaders are Muslims and not *kafirs* because there is no clear evidence that can directly prove apostasy. This group does not reject jihad as a legitimate tool of change, but believes that the rules condoning its use against incumbent regimes in Muslim countries require narrow and absolute proof, something that is rarely available. From this perspective, it is impossible to know with certainty what is in a person's heart; and as a result jihad against the regime is not permitted.[40] Instead, this reformist faction believes religious change must come through stages and that the current context necessitates *tarbiya* (education and cultivation to encourage proper Muslim practices).[41] Only when society properly applies Islam will jihad become a possible alternative for change.

In addition, premature action could engender harsh regime reprisals, which would make even rudimentary *da'wa* difficult. Salim al-Hilali, a prominent Jordanian Salafi scholar, argues that Muslims "should not say that the state is *kufr* [in a state of being *kafir*] and change it with force. Otherwise the mosques would be closed and scholars would be put in prison. Change in Islam must be for the better."[42] Another Salafi sheikh phrased the same perspective differently: "The hand cannot fight a fist of iron." In essence, he argues, "if you cannot achieve your objective through jihad, then it is *haram* [forbidden according to Islam]." Reformists believe that engaging in violent struggle will create a greater evil.

This group instead endorses a tactic of grassroots change that begins at the level of the individual and personal transformation without directly challenging the system of power. The hope is that religious change will filter upward through individuals who will eventually create a more Muslim system. *Tarbiya* is viewed as a mechanism for creating change through the individual that will affect the heart and then broaden to eventually change society. 'Ali Hasan al-Halabi, a former al-Bani student and one of the most respected Salafi scholars in the world, supports this view of change:

> [I]f the Muslims desire good, unity and establishment upon the earth, then they should make their manners and behavior like that of the Salaf of this *Ummah* and begin by changing themselves. However, he who is unable to change even himself, will not be able to change his family, not to mention changing the *Ummah*.[43]

Change should come from education and research in *hadith* science, which produces an accurate account of the Sunna of the Prophet.

This faction views itself not as revolutionaries, but as guardians of the true faith. A Salafi imam explained that,

> A group of pioneers with the right vision should try to resurrect society, and it should not be done through the army, a coup, or violence. This is not the time for such things. Change should happen at the personal level. . . . To rectify our society, we have to bring the individual back to Islam. We need to start by returning to the Qur'an and Sunna and then expand the circle. This is the rational way. If the circle expands to others, then laws and regulations would be rectified and there would be a societal resurrection in all areas—politics, economics, administration.

Violent tactics, in contrast, are viewed as counterproductive because the prospects of success are low and regime reprisals would prevent Salafis from promoting their religious message. Sheikh Mohammed al-'Uthaymin of Saudi Arabia decries the use of unrest: "Let those who riot know that they only serve the enemies of Islam; the matter cannot be handled by uprising and excitement, but rather by wisdom."[44] Mohammed Nasir al-Din al-Bani warns, "The way to salvation is not, as some people imagine, to rise with arms against the rulers, and to conduct military coups. In addition to being among contemporary *bid'as* (innovations), such actions disregard texts of Islam, among which is the command to change ourselves. Furthermore, it is imperative to establish the basis upon which the building will stand."[45] 'Ali Hasan al-Halabi adds, "Anyone who examines the past and present of *Islam* would clearly see that excessiveness has brought for the *Ummah* disasters, bloodshed, eviction, and harm that cannot be known to the full extent except by Allah. It suffices in this regard to remember the turmoils of the [Khawarij] and the advocates of Takfir from past to present."[46]

The reformist Salafi group benefits from a sponsorship of discourse. The Saudi regime and other governments promote this variant of Salafi thought, as opposed to radical interpretations, in an effort to prevent the emergence of a more dangerous and challenging Salafi discourse, which could undermine state control. Through financial assistance and publication support, the Saudis provide reform-oriented Salafis with resources to propagate their interpretation. This support allows its proponents to act as full-time scholars without economic burdens. Financial assistance allows this group of Salafis to publish widely in a variety of languages, including English, while more critical groups suffer from a resource deficit and cannot spread their interpretation as effectively. There is thus an economic dimension to internal movement divisions, at least among the scholars of the movement, whereby individuals are rewarded with financial support for purporting a nonviolent Salafi doctrine. Salafi sheikhs, such as al-Halabi, receive generous donations for *da'wa* work and reap financial gains from their publications. Al-Bani reportedly received between $50,000 and $60,000 for some of his books, a large sum of money for publications in the Arab world. Because such sheikhs have a vested interest in protecting their view of Salafi thought, they act as mechanisms of internal movement discipline by using their high visibility, publishing instruments, and status to delegitimize violent Salafis. In most instances, the Salafi scholars I met from this group were financially secure and enjoyed substantial resources for pursuing their objectives. Because of this perceived linkage between regimes (especially the Saudis) and these scholars, more critical Salafis refer to them as "sheikhs of authority," implying that they represent the interests of regime power.

This economic dimension may not result from conscious choices to pursue a perspective that enjoys financial resources, but the sponsorship of discourse encourages a certain direction. It is much easier to live a comfortable life as a scholar than to pursue revolutionary ideology in poverty. More radical Salafis argue that al-Halabi and others who are "tied to Saudi" are "opportunists." This may be a strong charge, but it demonstrates the linkage between financial gains and tactics within the Salafi movement, produced by patterns in the sponsorship of discourse. The direction of material rewards is clear.[47]

The second faction within the Salafi movement is the jihadi group, which focuses upon Ibn Taymiyya's interpretation of jihad.[48] Ibn Taymiyya lived during the Crusades and the Mongol invasions, and it was the latter experience that shaped his understanding of jihad. As the Mongols conquered Muslim societies, they were exposed to Islam and eventually converted. The dilemma faced by Islamic scholars was whether the war against the Mongols could still be considered a jihad or had become a war between two Muslim entities, in which case it was no longer a jihad. In his *fatwa* on the Mongols, Ibn Taymiyya recognized that the Mongols practiced the pillars of the faith, but questioned whether this made them true Muslims. The dominant interpretation was that the *shariʿa* considered such groups Muslim, regardless of their actions, because they fulfilled the basic Muslim obligations. Ibn Taymiyya introduced a new criterion for this evaluation. He argued that regardless of whether a person follows the basics of the faith, if an individual fails to uphold any aspect of the *shariʿa*, that person is no longer considered a Muslim. Such people become *kafirs* (unbelievers) because they embraced Islam but through actions left the faith. They are therefore subject to jihad.

Like Ibn Taymiyya, the jihadi Salafis argue that actions by rulers can be used as evidence in *takfir*. Rulers who promote un-Islamic policies can be considered *kafir* regimes and are therefore subject to jihad. The ambiguity of this argument is that it is unclear where the threshold for jihad lies. Some radical groups argue that any single transgression can constitute apostasy and have used *takfir* to condemn anyone who disagrees with radical religious interpretations. But Salafis themselves have difficulty living up to the pristine model of the Prophet, even while trying to emulate his example, and any number of reasons could be used to declare a regime *kafir*. *Takfir* thus becomes a blanket weapon that can be used to oppose any regime through violent means. The jihadis do not disavow other reform measures, such as individual change, but they believe that all tactics should be pursued at once.

Many jihadis in Jordan imply that the Hashemites are *kafirs* because they pursue policies derived from liberalism and support peace with Israel. In underground publications found in Jordan, the jihadis rarely directly name members of the Hashemite family in their arguments, but the message is clear, even when delivered in the abstract— any regime that does not pursue Islamic policies, as defined by jihadi Salafis themselves, is *kafir* and subject to violence. The assessment is not based upon the ruler's beliefs, but upon his actions.

At least in Jordan, the jihadis are financially strained and do not have the publication reach of the reformist faction. Most of the scholars from this group, who like to call themselves "independent" to emphasize their autonomy from governments such as Saudi Arabia, are from poorer neighborhoods. Most are employed in nonreligious occupations and pursue religious scholarship in their free time. There are few publication and resource routes for those who espouse violent means, especially since the regime actively cracks down on this group. The result is that the jihadi faction must secretly disseminate photocopied manuscripts through informal networks.

Although nonviolent reformists still dominate the Salafi movement, jihadi thought is becoming increasingly popular. This is reflected in the growing number of jihadi publications, which began to appear in Jordan during the 1990s. Pamphlets and religious tracts calling for the destruction of incumbent Arab regimes have become more common. During the period of research for this project, there were two sets of arrests of Salafis for distributing such literature.[49] Many of the younger Salafis I interviewed had either been members of an underground group at one point in time or had been arrested or detained by the regime under suspicion of terrorism. The actual rate of participation in militant Salafi activities is extremely low and limited, but more individuals hold jihadi ideas, even if they do not act upon them.[50] This has raised concerns among reformists who denounce the jihadis as non-Salafis. Muhammad Abu Shaqra, for example, a leader in the reformist faction, claims that members of the Reformation and Challenge Group are not Salafis. Such denunciations are becoming increasingly common.

The difficulty for the regime is that both the nonviolent and jihadi Salafi factions utilize the same principles and textual references. As one jihadi Salafi argued, "The split is not in thought, it is in strategy." The importance of this foundational ambiguity from the point of view of the regime is that there is a fine line separating these two groups, and it is unclear at what point reformist Salafis might shift their perspective to a more radical stance. Even Salafis who on the surface appear quiescent and supportive of the regime privately discuss its lack of legitimacy and the need for eventual change. The difference is that while jihadi groups seek immediate change, the reformist faction believes that circumstances are not right for a direct challenge and that they must bide their time before acting.

Another dilemma for the regime is that regardless of tactical differences, both factions in Jordan do not work through the current political system. There are exceptions, such as Muhammad Abu Shaqra who works with the regime, but these are rare. Most Salafis believe that, as one Salafi put it, "If you enter into this game, into this structure, you become a part of it. You cannot change it. The change comes from outside." This view of political participation informs Salafi critiques of the politically active Muslim Brotherhood. As al-Halabi argues,

> The senators and members of parliament of the Muslim Brotherhood, when they entered parliament or the ministries, they became part of the system. And they think they are going to be able to force change and affect [the system], but in reality it is they who are affected, changed, and weakened.[51]

Another Salafi argued that this compromise with the regime means the Brotherhood has been "captured by the system" and will never affect real Islamic change. The Salafis believe that in the race for power the Muslim Brotherhood has abrogated some its ideological constants. From this perspective, pragmatism superceded ideology and belief. In contrast, Salafis, especially those sympathetic to the jihadi perspective, view themselves in "total contradiction with the system."

ORGANIZATIONAL EXPERIENCE

Unlike the Brotherhood, the Salafis have never enjoyed a close relationship with the regime. Not only do Salafis articulate a more radical Islamic discourse, but the growth of jihadi groups directly threatens the regime, the state, and the stability of the political system. As a result, the organizational opportunities for Salafis are quite limited, especially in comparison to the Brotherhood's organizational network.

In the mid-1980s, a group of Salafis tried to establish an organization called the Sunna Society but failed to garner enough support. More recently in 1993, however, this same group succeeded in forming the Qur'an and Sunna Society, a cultural NGO devoted to promoting Salafi thought through lectures, small publications, and seminars. There are general lessons in Salafi doctrine as well as more specialized training in *hadith*, *fiqh*, and other areas of the Islamic sciences. The members believe that the current deprived condition of Muslim societies is a result of deviations from the fundamentals of Islam. By teaching people about the Salafi understanding of Islam, they hope to provide the foundations for a better society. Because of the specialized nature of these activities, members must have an expertise in the Qur'an and Sunna and be considered strong Salafi followers. Material resources are limited and the society is located in a stark building in a less affluent section of East Amman. There are only about fifty members and the NGO is limited, but it provides a glimpse into Salafi organizational experiences and points to some of the factors underlying the strategic decision to utilize informal networks.

In contrast to the Muslim Brotherhood, which has experienced little state opposition in forming organizations, the Qur'an and Sunna Society applied for a permit several times prior to the 1989 political liberalization measures, but was rejected. Even after 1989 and despite new political openings, it still took four years before the Ministry of Culture would issue a license. During this four year period, the *mukhabarat* harassed this group of Salafis and threatened to affect their employment opportunities, passport status, and well-being. Eventually the organization was formed, but it has continued to encounter difficulties and repression.

There are several limitations to this organized work. First, although the internal law states that the society can form branches, it has thus far been prevented from branching beyond its current location, despite numerous offers for assistance from individuals in other neighborhoods in Amman. The members submitted multiple proposals to open ten additional centers but have been systematically rejected by the Ministry of Culture. This is in sharp contrast to the

Muslim Brotherhood's Society for the Preservation of the Qur'an, which engages in similar activities and has been permitted extensive expansion. Because the Qur'an and Sunna Society cannot open branches, its organizational reach is limited.

Second, activities at the society clash with the administrative logic of the state bureaucracy, which limits civil society activities to a particular set of nonpolitical functions. Like other Islamic groups, Salafis argue that Islam is at once political, economic, cultural, social, and religious. It serves as a framework that should regulate and guide behavior and action in all aspects of social existence. Because the Salafis believe in a unified Islamic discourse, many of the seminars and lessons blur the line between politics and culture. For example, a Salafi sheikh who is an expert on the Egyptian ideologue Sayyid Qutb presented a lecture that mixed religious, cultural, and political issues.[52] In the lecture, he used Sayyid Qutb's arguments and interpretations as a framework for understanding contemporary political issues, such as the crisis in Bosnia, the role of the United Nations, the hegemony of the United States, the Taliban movement in Afghanistan, and the Palestinian struggle. The lecture was obviously not simply cultural. It was imbued with political meaning. The following day, the *mukhabarat* came to the society and accused members of attempting to organize a political movement. One of the members was arrested and the society was searched. Not only did the state view the lesson as provocative and political, but the sheikh who gave it led an underground jihadi group in 1979 as well, thus furthering regime suspicion.

Finally, the regime targets this Salafi organization for ongoing repression and harassment. After the permit for the organization was issued in 1993, the *mukhabarat* attempted to intimidate members and potential recruits, and the harassment continued. As a result, many of the members quit the organization and potential recruits were prevented from joining. The state also utilized its prerogative to interfere with the membership and leadership composition. In particular, the state prevented several volunteers from participating in the society because of their radical ideology and forced one member of the executive committee to remove himself from a position of leadership. Of the ten members I met, every one had been arrested or detained by the *mukhabarat*, both prior to and following registration; and during my period of research, all three of my primary informants from the society were brought in by the *mukhabarat*.

This kind of harassment is a constant burden for members. It also has a residual effect—the organization is unable to encourage new members because of fear. People are suspicious when the *mukhabarat* interfere and would rather not place themselves in a position where they could become targets. The result is that individuals who might have joined stay away because of repression. For a fledgling organization such as the Qur'an and Sunna Society, this is devastating for organizational survival.

Members of the society believe that the regime represses the organization because it fears Salafis will educate people about "proper" Islam and provide them with a framework for critiquing the current political system. The president of the society summarized the members' opposition to the current system:

> The separation between religion and government or social practice is really not credible. It is not right. There are things like liberalism, which the government applies and would like to continue applying, but we have a different ideology. Islam as an ideology is different.

Another member of the society added, "If people understand Islam and apply it, then they would ask the governors about what they did and why they did it." In other words, the regime would have to demonstrate its Islamic legitimacy in the face of a Salafi critique. Regime concerns about such critiques are further complicated by the fact that it is difficult to determine whether the jihadi faction might use these organizations at some point.

In addition to these considerations, Salafis also base their view of formal organizations on the Syrian experience. Al-Bani's negative experience with formal organizations in Syria before he emigrated to Jordan has colored perceptions among Salafis about organizational efficacy. The Asad regime's crackdown on visible manifestations of the Islamic movement in 1979 led al-Bani to issue a *fatwa* when he first arrived in Jordan, which stated that Muslim activism through organizations is *haram*. He believed that organizations prompted harsh reprisals from state authorities and therefore stunted the spread of the Islamic message. He instead preferred Islamic work through the traditional structure of lessons, the mosque, and meetings in homes. Though there are certain Islamic textual readings that support this ruling, most Salafis argue that al-Bani's decision was heavily influenced by his own personal experience. Further evidence of the experiential basis of this ruling is provided by the fact that when political circumstances changed in Jordan after political liberalization in 1989, al-Bani issued a second *fatwa* stating that organizational work is allowed. Despite this reversal, however, the first *fatwa* has had a lasting effect, and the vast majority of Salafis oppose work through formal organizations.[53]

The inability of the movement to effectively sponsor its religious discourse through formal organizations is recognized by the Salafis themselves. Members of the Qur'an and Sunna Society claim that the organization is really only a superficial dimension of their work and that the real action is "behind the scenes." Many expressed disillusionment about the prospects for affecting change through the organization. They feel betrayed by the lure of organizational opportunities, which seem to have stunted, rather than supported, their objectives. The members echo al-Halabi's argument:

> We have to go back to the teachings of the Qur'an and Sunna and not be affected by the materialistic world we live in. And we should not be restricted to a center or a society. If we want something specific and it does not agree with what leaders want, they would close it and finish off the organization. This is what we are trying to avoid. . . . They [other Islamic groups] are organized. They have societies and centers. But if they print a book or hold a lecture, they have only a few people who attend. But us Salafis, we do not have an organization or a center, but we have people who ask for the knowledge, people who agree on one thought. Much more than them. Many times these societies and organizations ask us to participate; and if they were more effective, they would not ask us to do so.[54]

The conditions for participation in formal organizations and state management strategies require that social movements make concessions and limit their objectives; but the ideological imperative that drives the Salafi movement makes it difficult for Salafis to give up the dogmatism of their beliefs for pragmatic reasons. They believe that operating through a formal organization means surrendering to regime control and forfeiting religious integrity. One Salafi scholar made this observation: "What we have seen through formal organizations is that these institutions give up some Islamic constancies. Organized work is frightening because it often means you give up some principles."[55]

INFORMAL NETWORKS AND SALAFI ACTIVISM

Salafi evaluations of the tactical efficacy of formal organization have led them to rely upon the informal networks that have characterized the transmission of Islamic knowledge through centuries of practice. Jonathan Berkey's study of Islamic education in medieval Cairo captures many of the dynamics of the Salafi network:

> Islamic education took place in a vibrant world of fluid categories in which social, cultural, and institutional barriers became indistinct. What will emerge is less a formal system than a dynamic network, loose but comprehensive in its inclusion of disparate social groups, and extraordinarily effective, not just in transmitting knowledge, but also in forging a common Muslim cultural identity.[56]

In transmitting the Salafi understanding of Islam, members of the Salafi movement mobilize through personal, face-to-face interactions where they communicate, recruit, educate, and facilitate the movement's goal of transforming society through religious education. This network structure provides the Salafis with institutional resources that are more difficult to repress because of their fluidity and informal nature. This provides the movement with an alternative to formal organizations and facilitates activism.

Recruitment and Network Growth

Social networks play a critical role in social movement recruitment. While ideological congruence creates structural availability, personal contacts and relationships typically pull individuals into a social movement or religious group.[57] The Salafi movement recruits through social networks that are created by personal relationships and/or shared religious beliefs and practices. While some individuals become Salafis by reading books written by Salafi scholars, networks of personal relationships represent the more typical recruitment pattern.

The initiatory Salafi network in Jordan began with a small group of friends who traveled to Syria to sit with Mohammed Nasir al-Din al-Bani during the late 1960s. Muhammad Salik is considered the first Salafi in Jordan by many in the movement and began following al-Bani after learning about Salafi thought while in Lebanon. Others involved in the early period of the movement include Muhammad Abu Shaqra, Hamdi Murad, and Yusuf Barqawi. Most of the early Salafis were from Hasmimi in the Zarqa area near Amman, which is why the movement is so strong in Zarqa today. These individuals promoted Salafi thought and gave lessons to members of the "second Salafi wave," which includes Salafi figures such as 'Ali Hasan al-Halabi, Salim al-Hilali, 'Umar Abu Qattadeh, Hasan Abu Haniya, and Wafiq Nadif. This latter group spent more time with al-Bani once he emigrated to Jordan in the late 1970s. At the time, the second wave Salafis were around sixteen years old. Later in 1985, Mashhur Hasan Salman was brought to al-Bani by this younger group and quit the Muslim Brotherhood to devote his time to Salafi thought. He is currently considered one of the most knowledgeable Salafi scholars in Jordan. Each of these scholars has his own following and has adopted a slightly different path, though they are joined by the fundamentals of Salafi thought. The network thus grew around al-Bani through his students who eventually developed their own independent followings. In some cases, the relationship with al-Bani was maintained, such as with al-Halabi, while for others there was a more distinct break over disagreements.

Virtually every Salafi interviewed described the involvement of friends and colleagues in their "conversion" to the Salafi perspective. The process of recruitment is quite straightforward and occurs through discussions about Islam. Pious Muslims typically socialize in friendship circles where Islam plays an important role in participants' lives. In such circles, religion is a common topic of everyday conversations, whether sitting and sipping tea or visiting for dinner. Through these everyday interactions, Salafis expose friends to Salafi thought. In many cases, religious issues or interpretations of Islam are discussed, and Salafis use these opportunities to explain their beliefs to others. One of the most important ways in which Salafis promote the "conversion" of friends is by encouraging them to attend lessons by Salafi scholars. The conversion is not an unconditional acceptance of new ideas; there is discussion, debate, and dialogue. The process of recruitment takes place over a protracted period and through multiple interactions until the individual is convinced that the Salafi perspective represents the straight path of Islam and seeks more knowledge about Salafi thought. Within informal networks, Salafis thus engage in what Bert Klandermans calls "consensus mobilization"—a "deliberate attempt by a social actor to create consensus among a subset of the population."[58]

In most instances, entire groups of friends eventually become Salafis, most likely because they are exposed to the same lessons, discussions, and thoughts. In various Salafi groups or clusters, participants indicated that they were friends with one another before they became Salafis. Groups grow over time as individuals help convert more friends to the Salafi cause. This overlays friendship and religious networks, creating a high sense of group solidarity within the Salafi movement. The movement includes many of these friendship-religious clusters, which are incorporated into the broader Salafi movement through lessons and other activities. These groups constitute cells of participants with high degrees of intragroup trust.[59]

At the periphery of the Salafi network are "weak ties" that form the basis of recruitment.[60] These linkages are not predicated upon shared Salafi beliefs (though there is usually a common religious commitment), but connect the Salafi network to other social networks and communities. They serve as bridges to diverse publics and enhance the network's "linkage breadth."[61] While strong ties foster solidarity, as in Salafi clusters or groups, weak ties provide linkages to incorporate new members and expand the network.

The majority of new recruits and converts come from other Islamic movement groups. Muslims from a variety of Islamic groups interact in mosques, lessons, and religious gatherings. Most share general religious goals and objectives, such as obtaining religious knowledge and promoting a more Muslim society, and are linked through friendship circles. As a result of religiosity and connections, there is a level of predisposition toward Salafi thought that does not exist for individuals outside the broad Islamic movement. For non-Islamists, the leap to dogmatism and the puritanical approach of the Salafis is simply too great. Members of the Islamic movement, in contrast, already possess a certain degree of receptivity to the Salafi message because of their religiosity. This makes the "framing process"— the conscious attempt to create shared understanding and foster collective action— less problematic in recruitment.[62] In addition, some members of these other groups hold Salafi ideas, but have not made the full transition to the Salafi *manhaj*. As this direction becomes clear, members of the Salafi movement target these individuals for direct recruitment. Salafis are thus linked to recruitment pools through other Islamic groups.

There are two Islamic groups that serve as the primary pools of recruitment. The first is Jama'at Tabligh (The Islamic Missionary Society).[63] Tabligh is a religious movement predicated upon *da'wa*. Members of the movement travel throughout the country and enjoin friends and strangers alike to practice Islam. It is purely a missionary movement and eschews involvement in politics or social change issues. In Jordan, members of Tabligh who begin to articulate a more socially conscious message are ostracized by other members and driven from the group. These more socially conscious members are the potential recruits of the Salafi movement. Some Salafis remain in Tabligh and attempt to use its organizational structure, but they are usually found out and expelled before they can affect the direction of the movement.[64]

The second major recruitment pool is the Muslim Brotherhood. Several prominent scholars, such as Mohammed Rafat and Mashhur Hasan Salman, left the Brotherhood to pursue Salafi thought. Each time a scholar leaves the Brotherhood, he typically brings many of his followers with him. Rafat studied with al-Bani, and Salafi thought influenced many members of the Muslim Brotherhood who studied under Sheikh Rafat. Some of these individuals have Salafi tendencies but chose to remain in the Muslim Brotherhood to pursue Brotherhood goals rather than Salafi objectives. These Salafi-leaning Muslim Brothers include well-known hard-liners such as Hamam Sayyid, Mohammed Abu Faris, Ahmed Nawfal, and 'Abd Allah Azzam.

Network Structure

Like other social movements predicated upon informality, the structure of the Salafi network is decentralized and segmented.[65] Decentralization reflects the fact that there is no hierarchical leadership that guides or regulates the movement. There are numerous Salafi scholars with various followings, and this creates overlapping clusters and a high degree of fluidity. The movement is also segmented by differences over tactics and religious interpretations. Groups of scholars can be identified that disagree on particular points of doctrine and the best tactical means for achieving Salafi goals. The single most important disagreement is between the reformists and the jihadi groups, and this division has become heated as proponents of each side denounce the other faction as unknowledgeable.[66] Despite these divisions and the decentralized nature of the movement, however, there is a certain locality to the movement that results from the importance of spatial proximity for face-to-face interactions.

In contrast to formal SMOs, which typically have hierarchical structures for bureaucratic effectiveness, the Salafi movement is not predicated upon a strict hierarchy. There is, however, a loose and informal ranking based upon the reputation of various scholars, as recognized by the Salafi community and determined by levels of knowledge. Recognition is developed over years of interaction within the Salafi community through lessons, religious rulings, and informal meetings. Strong scholars develop large followings based upon students who recommend them to friends because of a high level of knowledge. Recognition by established scholars also helps develop a newly emerging scholar's reputation. Weak scholars, on the other hand, will not enjoy high praise or extensive references, and their influence remains limited. The title "scholar" or "sheikh" is not a formal or official appointment. It is a title bestowed by the community through an informal process of recognition. The term "knowledgeable" is thus essential in determining a particular Salafi's reputation (or lack thereof).

Until his death in October 1999, Mohammed Nasir al-Din al-Bani was at the top of this informal ranking. He was considered the greatest Salafi scholar in Jordan, and his work in the science of *hadith* is renowned throughout the Muslim world. The next level consists of al-Bani's best students. This includes al-Halabi, al-Hilali, Abu Shaqra, and Salman. Because al-Bani was prevented from giving public lessons, this tier of scholars became more active in promoting Salafi thought in Jordan (though al-Bani continued to publish prolifically). These sheikhs are considered "tied to Saudi" because they receive Saudi financial support through *da'wa* contributions and publication opportunities and are unwilling to articulate a challenging discourse that would threaten the Saudi regime.[67] Beneath this second tier of scholars are less well-known Salafi sheikhs who either work without giving lessons (such as in *hadith*) or enjoy small followings.[68] All of these scholars are tied to less erudite Salafis, who are seeking knowledge about Salafi thought, through the student-teacher relationship (i.e., through lessons).

In the Salafi movement, the proliferation of scholars means that there is no single leadership elite. There is no centralized figure that determines the overall direction of the movement or makes binding decisions. Even al-Bani could not dictate direction or tactics. The Salafi movement is instead led by multiple leaders with different, but overlapping, followings of students and knowledge seekers. These scholars may be able to influence a cluster of individuals who are tied to particular sheikhs, but there is no regulatory power over the rest of the network. This makes state repression difficult since there is no central figure or institution that can be targeted to weaken the movement. If one group or leader is repressed, the network itself continues to function.

While students may spend more time with one sheikh as opposed to others, they attend lessons with more than one scholar. This is partially the result of specialization among Salafi scholars. Each aspect of the Islamic sciences constitutes a discipline of study, and expertise requires concentrated effort and focus. Most Salafi scholars are educated in various aspects of the Islamic sciences, but usually specialize in a particular area of application, such as *hadith*. If Salafi students want exposure to a comprehensive Salafi ideology, they must sit with multiple sheikhs. Patterns of attendance also depend upon a student's personal field of interest. Students seek out specialists in their preferred field of study, including non-Salafi sheikhs if they are considered experts in the relevant specialization.

This student-teacher relationship is the most important social tie in the Salafi community since it connects Salafi groups to one another and perpetuates the movement. Because the Salafi movement is based upon the sponsorship of Salafi thought through education, the student-teacher relationship represents the primary conduit for the movement's message. This relationship is a nexus that links network clusters together. Salafi groups that might otherwise remain isolated from one another are connected through interactions at lessons and shared student-teacher experiences. The student-teacher relationship is also an engine for network expansion. As more students are incorporated into lessons, meetings, and informal interactions, they learn about the Salafi belief system through informed and knowledgeable Salafi scholars, and the network grows. The scholars thus represent important nodes that connect individual Salafis through a common ideological orientation.

The ideological system that fosters these connections and a certain level of unity in the Salafi network, however, is also the principle cause of segmentation and division. While there is a certain level of "cognitive closure," whereby core beliefs are no longer subject to questioning,[69] there are different views, which creates internal movement divisions. Personal rivalries, differences in interpretation, and tactical disagreements have engendered divisions within the movement. These disagreements often obtain personal dimensions because of the importance of reputation in the Salafi community. Attacks against a particular perspective are frequently interpreted as threats to a scholar's sense of self. In addition, scholars are building their own base of students through the Salafi network, and there is a certain modicum of competition. Each scholar claims he espouses the true understanding of the *salaf* (and thus the straight path) and argues that those who disagree are misguided, even though they share many of the same Salafi understandings. Because there can only be one correct understanding of Islam, this in effect delegitimizes other Salafi interpretations.

In addition to the decentralized and segmented dimensions of the Salafi network, there is also a certain degree of spatial locality to the movement. The reliance on face-to-face interactions through informal networks requires that participants are able to physically gather and meet. To attend lessons, scholars must be physically accessible. Long distances can serve as a discouraging impediment to students who want to sit with knowledgeable Salafi sheikhs. While individuals can learn about Salafi thought through books, the sheer volume of published materials on Salafi doctrine requires some measure of guidance from scholars and teachers. Learning about Salafi thought through books is certainly one of the catalysts that encourage individuals to seek out like-minded Muslims, but it is a difficult and rare trajectory of joining. Recruitment more often occurs through social interactions, which require a person's physical presence. Geographic proximity matters.

As a result, the movement is located in the cities and centers where Salafi scholars live. The movement began in the Zarqa area, and the city of Zarqa represents the strongest center of Salafi activism. There are numerous scholars, students, bookshops, and lessons in Zarqa, and it constitutes the geographic center of the movement. There are also many scholars in Amman, and Salafis are active there as well. There are some Salafis in the Salt area because of extended student-teacher linkages, but they are not scholars in the movement as yet. The absence of scholars in Salt means that there is little opportunity for building a strong Salafi presence in the area. This does not, however, preclude the possibility; and the existence of even one strong Salafi scholar could facilitate the emergence of a Salafi group tied to Salt.

This locality is not inevitable, and the student-teacher relationship can serve as a vehicle for network expansion by transcending geographic barriers. Students often bring their teachers to new neighborhoods, quarters, and cities in order to promote Salafi thought. Because some students do travel to sit with a sheikh, they serve as connections to other locations. In at least a few observed instances, students invited teachers to give lessons in their home town or neighborhood. While giving lessons, a scholar may encourage new followers, thus extending the informal network. The student-teacher relationship serves as a mechanism for transcending the limitations of physical distance by creating "geographical peel-off."[70]

Micromobilization Contexts

In disseminating Salafi beliefs, the movement utilizes several mechanisms that are rooted in informal networks. These include informal interactions, mosque-related activities, seminars, and conferences. These activities constitute what Doug McAdam refers to as "micromobilization contexts"— "small group setting[s] in which the processes of collective attribution combine with rudimentary forms of organization to produce mobilization for collective action."[71] Comparative examples include churches, informal groups of people, and friendship networks. The micromobilization context is where social psychological processes occur, and it provides rudimentary forms of organization and solidary incentives necessary to override the free rider dilemma.[72] In the process of such interactions, participants negotiate and renegotiate their collective identity and construct new meaning.[73] Participants define what it means to be a Salafi while promoting particular Salafi perspectives.

Initially, the primary micromobilization context for the Salafi movement was the religious lesson, or *dars*, in mosques. The mosque represents a context of religiosity, and individuals gathered in mosques or who attend lessons are predisposed to religious learning. Without announcing themselves as Salafis, Salafi sheikhs give lessons in mosques about various religious rituals and issues. While some members of the audience may already recognize the teacher as a Salafi, this is not always the case; and in many instances scholars may purposely obfuscate their identity to avoid discouraging members of other Islamic groups from attending the lesson. Sometimes these lessons are impromptu while others are institutionalized and held at regular times. Lessons serve not only as an opportunity to propagate the Salafi message to an interested audience, but can also inspire individuals to seek more information about Salafi thought, thus pulling them farther into the network.

The preeminence of lessons in mosques has dissipated since the peace process with Israel, at which point the regime tightened its control of the mosque to limit Muslim opposition to the peace treaty. Legally, a sheikh must receive government permission to give lessons in the mosques. So long as the sheikh does not challenge state policy or the regime's Islamic legitimacy, permission is obtainable. More radical interpretations are not permitted. Because the mosques are controlled by the regime, it does not permit the articulation of Islamic discourse that is not in accordance with understandings sanctioned by the Ministry of Awqaf.[74]

Salafi lessons have instead moved into private homes where they are less vulnerable to the surveillance and control of state officials. These lessons are more difficult for the regime to control because they are advertised within the Salafi community and avoid formal government monitoring mechanisms. Advertising occurs by word of mouth, and the content of the lessons is Islamic education, ostensibly not a direct threat to state power. The state can still utilize informants, but private homes are outside state-controlled religious space; and as a result Salafis enjoy more latitude in propagating their message in such fora. These lessons are popular and as many as 150 people may attend, depending upon the teacher. The lessons address a number of religious issues from a Salafi perspective, including rituals, *hadith*, and *da'wa*.

The lessons in private homes are institutionalized and usually held at particular times and places each week. Outside the northern city of Salt, for example, a group of Salafis holds weekly gatherings where outside speakers are invited to give lessons. Since Salafi thought is not strong in this geographic area, these lessons are used to promote Salafi thought in the community, especially among teenage boys and young men. Most of the lessons are held every Wednesday for boys ages sixteen years and younger who are interested in learning more about their religion. They attend without their parents and there is a consistent following. By focusing on the young, the Salafis hope to indoctrinate the next generation of Muslims.

Although these lessons are ostensibly nonpolitical, such gatherings provide an opportunity to discuss politics and issues related to regime legitimacy and state power. Prior to one lesson on the psychological obstacles to *da'wa* work, a Salafi from Amman began by explaining the concept of jihad to the young audience and criticized the late King Hussein for "fighting against the Islamic movements." He also critiqued the current political system as un-Islamic and argued that jihad is more than simply fighting—it means liberating human beings from constrained circumstances. A lecture on *da'wa* thus began with political tones and represented an opportunity to further construct and disseminate a critique of the system, within an educational context. For impressionable youth, this kind of presentation can have a lasting impact since someone who is considered a respected scholar in the religious community articulates it. After the lesson ended, the adults who organized the lesson remained and discussed other political issues in more depth. While these informal lessons are not utilized explicitly to organize opposition to the regime, they do act as fora where an oppositional discourse can be constructed and presented without direct government surveillance.

Other informal contexts are more akin to study circles where groups of friends meet to discuss particular books or religious issues. Such gatherings are difficult for the regime to monitor because they overlap with friendship networks. It is simply impossible for the regime to monitor all personal relationships, even when it watches particular groups of friends for subversive activities. Again, although these meetings are not intended as opportunities to organize underground militant operations, they do provide a social space for the construction and dissemination of a Salafi discourse outside formal organizations.

In addition, though there are few Salafi-based conferences in Jordan, Salafis frequently attend general seminars and meetings sponsored by Islamic NGOs.[75] During these seminars, Salafis have an opportunity to present their views and arguments to the broader Islamic movement community through lectures, debates, and dialogue. These seminars are arenas where Salafis can present their message to Islamists who may already be predisposed to literalist ideas and interpretations. NGO-sponsored seminars, however, fall under the purview of the state apparatus and are constrained. As a result, Salafis utilize these fora not as an organizing mechanism, but as an opportunity to expand the Salafi network and advertise Salafi thought. The informal network thus penetrates formal organizations without actually tying the movement to an NGO.

These informal interactions endow the network with a collective mentality. Rather than simply linking one individual to the next, the micromobilization contexts gather groups together to reinvigorate their sense of commonality and collective ties. While the network of overlapping individual linkages provides a structure for communication and information dissemination, these micromobilization contexts are responsible for creating a collective identity and collective action. The shared purpose, social movement goals, and micromobilization contexts distinguish the structure of the Salafi movement from other traditional social networks, such as patron-client ties, kinship, or *wasta*.

Publications

Publication is also an important mechanism for the Salafi movement. Salafi scholars are prolific and their writings are widely distributed throughout the Muslim community. Written publications are usually inexpensive paperbacks that address a variety of issues from a Salafi perspective. Cassettes have also become increasingly popular; and because they are inexpensive and readily accessible, sales are quite robust. Cassettes reproduce lessons and sermons by Salafi scholars and are popular not only because of the low cost, but because they allow Muslims to listen to some of the greatest Salafi sheikhs in the world.[76] Many leading Salafi scholars have strong oratory skills that inspire Muslims to believe. The tone, the fluctuating pitch and tenor of speech patterns, and the learned classical Arabic all combine to create a religious experience that ties the religious message to an emotive dimension. This experience also directly links individuals to prominent sheikhs and connects Salafis across time and space, drawing the community closer (even at the international level). The fact that a Salafi in Jordan can directly experience a sermon by Sheikh Ibn Bin of Saudi Arabia through a cassette fosters a stronger sense of "imagined community" that transcends national boundaries and links Salafis through a shared religious discourse.[77] The use of publications and cassettes helps transcend the limits of spatiality.

In Amman, there are a number of Salafi bookshops, predominantly located next to the King Hussein mosque downtown.[78] There are also some bookshops located in other cities, especially in Zarqa, many of which are owned by prominent Salafis sheikhs. Al-Halabi, for example, owns one of the largest Islamic bookshops in Zarqa. While passing along one of the main streets of the city, one is assaulted by Salafi cassettes blasted over a speaker outside the store. Smaller shops also exist throughout Amman, Salt, Zarqa, and other cities. Because these stores do not want to provoke regime ire, which could lead to closure, jihadi publications are extremely rare in Islamic bookstores.

CONCLUSION

The Salafi network is not a rigid matrix of intersecting and overlapping linkages; it is characterized by dynamic change as linkages grow, disappear, and reorient themselves toward other nodes. Not only do new individuals become participants and add to the expanding network, but individuals leave as well. Islamic interpretations are not indelible or immutable, and in various instances Salafis adopt different leanings or approaches, even while remaining within the movement. This creates opportunities for forging new relationships with similar-minded Salafis and new linkages across groups or clusters. There is constant dynamic change introduced by shifts in attitudes, beliefs, and values, as participants learn new information about Salafi thought or are drawn to alternative arguments and ideas. Exogenous factors in the social and political environment also ineluctably impinge upon how beliefs are formulated and the salience of perspectives at a particular moment. Ideas are not static; they change as a result of interactions, experience, and new information.

This fluidity and the network structure of the movement have led many observers, including non-Salafi Islamists and Jordanian academics, to argue that the Salafis are not a movement. For example, Hilmi Asmar argued that the Salafis are not organized and therefore do not constitute a social movement.[79] From this perspective, there must be some concrete and articulated goal through a well-organized and structured formal organization. As Luther Gerlach and Virginia Hine note,

There is a marked tendency . . . to identify an organization as something which has a clear-cut leadership and which is centrally directed and administered in a pyramidal, hierarchical pattern. It is assumed that a well-defined chain of command ties the whole organization together from top to bottom. People may sense that a popular mass movement does not have all the bureaucratic administrative machinery that such formal organizations have, but they still feel that it must possess central direction. If there is not observable bureaucratic organization, a single charismatic leader or a very small elite is assumed to be controlling the movement . . . In the minds of many, the only possible alternative to a bureaucracy or a leader-centered organization is no organization at all.[80]

In several instances, even Salafis themselves rejected references to a Salafi "movement," instead preferring terms such as *manhaj*, thought, approach, or idea.

But such understandings reflect a refusal to conceptualize social movements in less directed terms. Movements are often informal and based upon transformative fluidity in which meaning is changed, rather than rigid organization. There may not be a directed or linear logic, but social activism can flow through informal structures.[81] The Salafi movement uses informal social networks rather than formal organizations to transform individual understandings and create new meaning. Rejection of the term "social movement" for the Salafis reflects the conflation of movements with formal organizational structures, something that is lacking among Salafis.[82]

This conflation leads other Islamists and Jordanian academics to underestimate the influence and impact of the Salafi movement. While the nature of informal networks makes it impossible to provide a precise measurement of size, Salafis estimate that the movement is at least as large as the Muslim Brotherhood, a view shared by other Islamists as well.[83] Salafis are located in almost every neighborhood in the major cities, such as Amman and Zarqa, and the network is continuing to expand. The fact that the major sources of recruitment are other Islamic groups means that the Salafis are becoming a larger component of the overall Islamic movement. Its size and breadth are obscured by its informal patterns of interaction, but the movement is an important and growing social force in Jordan.

While these informal networks allow the movement to operate outside state-controlled organizational space, there are important limitations. Despite weak ties that connect the Salafi movement to other groups, informal networks are limited in their ability to connect non-Islamist groups to the Salafi cause. The reach of the network is thus constrained, and the Salafis are unable to mobilize the cross-section of society that would be necessary for a broader revolutionary movement. In addition, the reliance on the student-teacher relationship means that the network will remain spatially constrained until more Salafi scholars relocate to other areas of the country. Given that Salafi "intellectual" life revolves around central locations in Zarqa and Amman, it is unlikely that scholars will move to new locations with few students or Islamist intellectual exchanges. As a result of these limitations, it is more likely that the Salafis will change the face of the Islamic movement and push it in a more literalist direction than that they will successfully mobilize society against the regime.

Conclusion

Understanding patterns of Islamic activism necessitates elucidating the political context of mobilization. While formal organizations are often viewed as effective mechanisms of collective empowerment, the political context may render them vulnerable to repression. Formality creates visibility, and Islamists who choose to operate through civic organizations are frequently subject to legal restrictions and administrative practices that diminish their effectiveness. Under such circumstances, informal social networks, such as those utilized by the Salafi movement in Jordan, offer an institutional alternative for social movements to escape state regulation.

The process of democratization and its limitations structure the political context of Islamic activism in Jordan. Political change unleashed expectations about political life, freedom, and the human condition; and Jordanians experienced new optimism about the prospects for political participation as greater political freedom replaced patterns of exclusion. Many hoped that freedom in the political arena would eliminate state violence, intimidation, and authoritarian practices to uphold the dignity of civil liberties and freedoms. But despite the implementation and consolidation of democracy as political discourse and praxis, the regime continues to repress dissent and opposition. Various forms of repression have accompanied the expansion of political parties and the implementation of elections—the symbol and underlying institutional face of democracy. There is ample opportunity to form political parties, yet civic organizing remains limited. Members of parliament are bolder in their opposition to government policies, while the press remains circumscribed. Relatively free

and fair elections at the local and national level reflect the institutionalization of democratic practices, but peaceful demonstrations and
public political meetings are prohibited. Greater political freedom is
marred by lingering authoritarian tendencies that have persisted long
after the first democratic vote was counted.

To a large extent, the fitful transition to democracy is due to the
underlying imperative of political change. In Jordan, political liberalization was part of a controlled process of "managed liberalization," dictated by the interests of the regime.[1] Unlike in Eastern
Europe or Latin America where democratization resulted in part
from sustained grassroots pressure, the transition in Jordan was initiated by King Hussein to prevent widespread instability during an
economic crisis. As a result, the process has been carefully crafted
and coordinated, dictated by the logic of stability rather than a benevolent desire for greater political participation.

This stability imperative informs the regulation of civil society
and points to the limits of social movement organization in the kingdom. Since 1989, numerous social actors have taken advantage of
new opportunities to act collectively through formal grassroots organizations. Human rights activists, women's movement members,
Palestinian leaders, Islamists, and a host of other groups have created NGOs in civil society to pursue goals through formal institutions. These organizations, however, are embedded in a web of laws
and administrative procedures, and the state uses these to circumscribe organizational activities through a process I term "the management of collective action." Law 33 of 1966, for example, prohibits political activities at NGOs; and the regime has utilized this
ambiguous regulation to crack down on any whisper of politicization
in civil society. Other regulations provide the state with the necessary instruments for monitoring collective action through formal
organization to ensure that there are no "surprises" that might challenge regime power and control. Mandatory financial statements
and general reports, strict regime control over permits, and the de
facto power of the security apparatus to control NGO membership
and leadership all arm the regime with instruments for controlling
who has access to formal organizations and the range of permissible
activities. Rather than using overt repression to crush collective action, the state subtly manages activism to limit its effects.

At the same time, alternative forms of collective action, such as public demonstrations or informal gatherings, are repressed. Such acts constitute challenges to the system of administrative oversight since they operate outside the scope of the bureaucracy. These transgressions are usually met by the techniques of social control that characterized the martial law period, and it is here that more overt forms of authoritarian repression become readily apparent. Collective action outside the reach of the administrative apparatus is less visible, and therefore potentially threatening. The regime attempts to limit this possibility by requiring that collective action operate through grassroots organizations, which are vulnerable to state control.

Overt, brutal forms of physical coercion thus no longer characterize continued repression in Jordan; rather, it is embedded in bureaucratic processes, masked beneath the surface of visible state practices. Wrapped in the sanctity and rhetoric of democracy, the regime cannot afford the visible brutality and repression that characterize China, Iraq, and other authoritarian systems. Instead, social control is projected through an array of legal mechanisms and manipulated administrative regulations, which are systematically applied to limit dissent, opposition, and associational life. Legal and bureaucratic instruments have become the new weapons of repression, hiding brutality in a complex web of laws and regulations.

This allows the regime to claim the mantle of democracy while expanding social control and repression through the bureaucracy and regulative practices. Because elections are held, political parties are legalized, and political participation is expanded, the regime can point to concrete indicators of procedural democracy. At the same time, alternative political views and collective action are limited by the politics of regulation, which prevents real opposition from forming in civil society. It is a "façade democracy," concerned more with regime maintenance and control than the values of freedom and human dignity.[2] The veneer of democracy masks regime power.

This system of social control cautions against an optimistic assessment of the potentially democratizing role of civic organizations in the Middle East. Many scholars emphasize the possible, though still limited, role of civil society in the mobilization of opposition, dissent, and alternative voices.[3] Where political participation is constrained, civic organizations are viewed as mechanisms of social empowerment for groups excluded from the formal political arena. But while civic organizations have proliferated throughout the region,[4] they are frequently constrained by administrative and regulative practices. Such controls exist in Egypt, Morocco, and other Arab countries and have led to objective organizational growth without substance.

Because the Jordanian regime is particularly concerned with the management of Islamic activism, it uses the regulation of civic organizing to limit which Islamic groups can mobilize effectively through NGOs in civil society. The Jordanian regime, like others in the region, relies upon Islamic credentials for legitimacy. The precise level of religiosity is certainly an issue of contention within Jordan, but the regime nonetheless claims the mantle of Islam in its legitimation strategies. As a result, it is concerned with controlling Islamic discourse. Religious interpretations that challenge the Hashemites' historical role in Islam or the state's religious functions undermine regime power. The recent growth of Islamic opposition movements has prompted the Jordanian state to tighten control over the religious institutions responsible for propagating meaning, such as the mosque, the *khutba*, imams, and those issuing *fatwas*. Such concerns have also led the regime to selectively use administrative practices to empower moderate Islamic groups that do not challenge its control, while limiting the formal institutionalization of more radical groups.

The Muslim Brotherhood, in particular, has benefited from these selective administrative practices. It is a moderate reform movement with a history of supporting the regime, and it has benefited accordingly. Even during periods of political instability, when there were opportunities to move against King Hussein, the Brotherhood acted as an ally, rather than an enemy. Disagreements have emerged over specific policies, but the Brotherhood has never attempted to overthrow the regime. Instead, it acts as a loyal opposition by working through the political system. The regime has rewarded this moderation and support with abundant organizational opportunities in civil society, both during and after martial law. Prior to political liberalization, when all other political organizations were banned, the Brotherhood was allowed to mobilize through its Islamic Center Charity Society. After 1989, it received preferential treatment in organizing opportunities and successfully built an organizational network through NGOs, including schools, hospitals, cultural societies, and charitable centers. These organizations are not vanguards of revolutionary change and do not articulate a radical, politicized Islamic discourse. They are designed to provide basic goods and services to communities while promoting a moderate Islamic vision.

The expanding Salafi movement, however, has not enjoyed the same historical relationship with the regime or concomitant organizational opportunities. There has been little opportunity for the kind of trust building that led to preferential treatment for the Brotherhood. This is especially the case since the 1990s, when a number of violent jihadi groups emerged. These groups argue that the regime is *kafir* and therefore subject to violent overthrow. Though such groups remain limited, jihadi thought, which legitimates the use of violence for political change, is growing in Jordan and elsewhere in the Muslim world. Even reform-oriented Salafis work outside the political system and question regime legitimacy, though they do not believe violence is an effective means of change.

As a result, the regime has mobilized the administrative apparatus to limit the organizational efficacy of Salafis. Harassment, permit denials, and regulations limit the ability of Salafis to effectively articulate and disseminate their interpretation of Islam through formal organizations. The state's control is simply too debilitating. The experience of the Salafis' Qur'an and Sunna Society is a case in point. Its activities are limited by legal constraints; it is unable to form multiple branches because of state opposition; and it suffers from *mukhabarat* intervention. Salafis understand this political context and believe that formal organizations are ineffective for achieving social movement goals.

This rejection of organization is not driven by ideological concerns with *formality* itself. Formal Salafi organizations exist throughout the world in diverse country contexts. In the United States, for example, there are several Salafi organizations, including the Qur'an and Sunna Society (unrelated to the Jordanian organization by the same name), the Islamic Association of North America (IANA), the Salafiyya Society, the Preservation of the Qur'an, and the Society for Adherence to the Sunna.[5] In Britain, there is an assortment of Salafi organizations; many of them organized under the umbrella Jami'iat Ihyaa' Minhaaj al-Sunnah. The Mohammed Sourour Center in Britain is active as well. Salafis have also formed organizations in the Middle East, though to a more limited extent. In Kuwait, for example, not only do Salafis run the Revitalization of Heritage Society, but they also control several seats in parliament. In Egypt, the Ansar al-Sunna Society led by Sheikh Safwat has produced several

Salafi scholars, including many who emigrated to Jordan. Where formal organizations are evaluated as effective instruments of Salafi collective action, they have been utilized. Where they are affected by state control, however, Salafis such as those in Jordan often instead turn to informal social networks, which constitute the underlying matrix of many societies.

As with other social movements, the Salafis in Jordan rely upon informal networks for recruitment. Typically, friends are approached and brought to lessons given by Salafi sheikhs. Repeated interactions through friendship linkages pull others into the movement, though certainly not everyone is "converted" to Salafi ideology. Because recruitment patterns often reflect friendship cliques, there is a high degree of solidarity in the movement.

Salafi networks also provide a foundation for informal fora of activism. Lessons, study circles, informal meetings, and a myriad of other activities are rooted in informal networks. Participants use their personal connections to other Salafis to advertise their activities and ideology; and social networks and informal institutions are used as vehicles for the production, articulation, and dissemination of the Salafis' interpretation of Islam. Because they are rooted in personal relationships and informality, networks are less vulnerable than formal organizations to state social control mechanisms.

These divergent patterns of Islamic activism indicate that a less formal understanding of social movements is necessary to understand the range of contention. While it is certainly true that formal social movement organizations (SMOs) are often effective vehicles of mobilization, this is not always the case; and the assumption of organizational efficacy that underlies much of social movement theory has obfuscated the role of informally structured movements. As Piven and Cloward argue,

> Whatever the intellectual sources of error, the effect of equating movements with movement organizations—and thus requiring that protests have a leader, a constitution, a legislative program, or at least a banner before they are recognized as such—is to divert attention away from many forms of political unrest and to consign them by definition to the more shadowy realms of social problems and deviant behavior. . . . Having decided by definitional fiat that nothing political has occurred, nothing has to be explained, at least not in terms of political protest. And having contrived in this

way not to recognize protest or study it, we cannot ask certain rather obvious and important questions about it. [6]

Collective action research frequently reserves the term "social movement" for movements with formal organizations. As a result, informally structured collective action becomes more diffuse and ambiguous, like shifts in public opinion or personal transformation. Movements such as the Salafis in Jordan are thus excluded from analysis by a narrow definition. This prevents us from asking important questions about informally structured activism, which while less visible may still have an impact on politics or society.

The decision to act informally does not mean collective action is outside the boundaries of a social movement; instead, it often reflects the impact of political context on strategic mobilization choices. The Jordanian case demonstrates that movement decisions are informed by the realities of exogenous factors; and understanding the full range of Islamic activism, or collective action in general, requires examining both formal and informal modes of organization, and why movements choose one over the other.

Notes

INTRODUCTION

1. This is not to say that all social movements in liberal democracies enjoy unlimited freedoms or that they have not experienced varying levels of repression. One need only look at the Kent State incident, FBI surveillance of civil rights organizers and environmental activists, or crackdowns on recent right-wing movements in the United States to recognize that there are limits to proclaimed freedoms. However, comparisons with the majority of other countries in the world community indicate that there is *relative* openness and freedom.

2. For the conceptualization of "exit" from a system, see Albert O. Hirschman, *Exit, Voice and Loyalty* (Cambridge: Harvard University Press, 1970).

3. For more information on the initial period of the Muslim Brotherhood, see Richard P. Mitchell, *The Society of the Muslim Brothers* (London: Oxford University Press, 1969).

4. Linda Schull Adams, "Political Liberalization in Jordan: An Analysis of the State's Relationship with the Muslim Brotherhood," *Journal of Church and State* 38, 3 (Summer 1996): 507–28; Hanna Y. Freij and Leonard C. Robinson, "Liberalization, the Islamists, and the Stability of the Arab State: Jordan as a Case Study," *Muslim World* 86, 1 (January 1996): 1–32; Glenn E. Robinson, "Can Islamists Be Democrats? The Case of Jordan," *Middle East Journal* 51, 3 (Summer 1997): 373–88; and Najib Ghadbian, *Democratization and the Islamist Challenge in the Arab World* (Boulder: Westview Press, 1997), 117–37.

5. Amnon Cohen, *Political Parties in the West Bank under the Jordanian Regime, 1949–1967* (Ithaca: Cornell University Press, 1980); Beverley Milton-Edwards, "A Temporary Alliance with the Crown: The Islamic Response in Jordan," in *Islamic Fundamentalisms and the Gulf Crisis*, ed. James Piscatori (Chicago: Fundamentalism Project of the American Academy of Arts and Sciences, 1991); Anne Sofie Roald, *Tarbiya: Education and Politics in Islamic Movements in Jordan and Malaysia* (Stockholm: Almqvist & Wiksell, 1994); Sabah El-Said, *Between Pragmatism and Ideology: The Muslim Brotherhood in Jordan*, policy paper no. 39 (Washington, D.C.: The Washington Institute for Near East Policy, 1995); Lawrence

155

Tal, "Dealing with Radical Islam: The Case of Jordan," *Survival* 37, 3 (Autumn 1995): 1398–56; Lisa Taraki, "Islam Is the Solution: Jordanian Islamists and the Dilemma of the Modern Woman," *British Journal of Sociology* 46, 4 (December 1995): 643–61; idem, "Jordanian Islamists and the Agenda for Women: Between Discourse and Practice," *Middle Eastern Studies* 32, 1 (January 1996): 140–58; and Marion Boulby, *The Muslim Brotherhood and the Kings of Jordan, 1945–1993* (Atlanta: Scholars Press, 1999).

6. Although various labels are used to describe the movement (such as the "new Islamism," the Salafiyyun, the Salafists, and neo-Wahhabis), the term "Salafi" is used here because this is how Jordanians in the movement describe themselves. In addition, rather than using the Arabic *al-salafiya*, I use "Salafi" since this is what appears in most English publications produced by the movement itself.

7. For example, see Misagh Parsa, *Social Origins of the Iranian Revolution* (New Brunswick, N.J.: Rutgers University Press, 1989); John Foran, ed., *A Century of Revolution: Social Movements in Iran* (Minneapolis: University of Minnesota Press, 1994); and Charles Kurzman, "Structural Opportunity and Perceived Opportunity in Social Movement Theory: The Iranian Revolution of 1979," *American Sociological Review* 61 (February 1996): 153–70.

8. It is important to note that the study of religious movements in general has been divorced from social movement theory. For an attempt to synthesize these two streams of research, see John A. Hannigan, "Social Movement Theory and the Sociology of Religion: Toward a New Synthesis," *Sociological Analysis* 52, 4 (1991): 311–31.

9. For an overview of the resource mobilization approach in social movement theory, see Mayer N. Zald and John D. McCarthy, eds., *Social Movements in an Organizational Society* (New Brunswick, N.J.: Transaction Books, 1987).

10. Aldon D. Morris, *The Origins of the Civil Rights Movement: Black Communities Organizing for Change* (New York: Free Press, 1984).

11. Anthony Oberschall, *Social Conflict and Social Movements* (Englewood Cliffs, N.J.: Prentice Hall, 1973).

12. Jo Freeman, "The Origins of the Women's Liberation Movement," *American Journal of Sociology* 78 (1970): 792–811.

13. William A. Gamson, *The Strategy of Social Protest* (Homewood, Ill.: Dorsey Press, 1975).

14. Ibid., 108.

15. Russell L. Curtis, Jr. and Louis A Zurcher, "Stable Resources of Protest Movements: The Multiorganizational Field," *Social Forces* 52 (September 1973): 53–61; Dieter Rucht, "Environmental Movement Organizations in West Germany and France: Structure and Interorganizational Relations," in *Organizing for Change: Social Movement Organizations in Europe and the United States*, ed. Bert Klandermans, Hanspeter Kriesi, and Sidney Tarrow, vol. 2 of *International Social Movement Research* (Greenwich, Conn.: JAI Press, 1989; Bert Klandermans, "Introduction: Interorganizational Networks," in Klandermans, Kriesi, and Tarrow, *Organizing for Change;* Bert Klandermans, "Linking the 'Old' and the 'New': Movement Networks in the Netherlands," in *Challenging the Political Order: New Social and Political Movements in Western Democracies*, ed. Russell J. Dalton (New York: Oxford University Press, 1990); Susan D. Phillips, "Meaning and Structure in Social Move-

ments: Mapping the Network of National Canadian Women's Organizations," *Canadian Journal of Political Science* 24, 4 (December 1991): 755–82; Robert D. Benford, "Frame Disputes within the Nuclear Disarmament Movement," *Social Forces* 71, 3 (March 1993): 677–701; and Paul Burstein, Rachael L. Einwohner, and Jocelyn A. Hollander, "The Success of Political Movements: A Bargaining Perspective," in *The Politics of Social Movement Protest: Comparative Perspectives on States and Social Movements*, ed. Craig Jenkins and Bert Klandermans (Minneapolis: University of Minnesota Press, 1995).

16. For example, most studies of informal networks in social movement research focus on their use during movement recruitment rather than conceptualizing them as enduring structures of mobilization. See David A. Snow and Robert D. Benford, "Ideology, Frame Resonance, and Participant Mobilization," in Klandermans, Kriesi, and Tarrow, *From Structure to Action;* Rodney Stark and William Sims Bainbridge, "Networks of Faith: Interpersonal Bonds and Recruitment to Cults and Sects," *American Journal of Sociology* 85, 6 (May 1980): 1376–95; Doug McAdam, "Recruitment to High-Risk Activism: The Case of Freedom Summer," *American Journal of Sociology* 92 (1986): 64–90; Roger V. Gould, "Multiple Networks and Mobilization in the Paris Commune, 1871," *American Sociological Review* 56, 6 (December 1991): 716–29; and Doug McAdam and Ronnelle Paulsen, "Specifying the Relationship between Social Ties and Activism," *American Journal of Sociology* 98 (1993): 640–67.

17. Frances Fox Piven and Richard A. Cloward, *Poor People's Movements: Why They Succeed, How They Fail* (New York: Vintage Books, 1979); and idem, "Normalizing Collective Protest," in *Frontiers in Social Movement Theory*, ed. Aldon D. Morris and Carol McClurg Mueller (New Haven: Yale University Press, 1992).

18. Piven and Cloward, *Poor People's Movements*, xv.

19. For the concept of an organizational repertoire, which focuses on various types of formal organizations, see Elisabeth S. Clemens, "Organizational Repertoires and Institutional Change: Women's Groups and the Transformation of U.S. Politics, 1890–1920," *American Journal of Sociology* 98, 4 (January 1993): 755–98.

20. Luther P. Gerlach and Virginia H. Hine, *People, Power, Change: Movements of Social Transformation* (Indianapolis: Bobbs-Merrill, 1970); Pamela E. Oliver, "Bringing the Crowd Back in: The Nonorganizational Elements of Social Movements," in *Research in Social Movements, Conflict and Change*, vol. 11, ed. Louis Kriesberg (Greenwich, Conn.: JAI Press, 1989); Alberto Melucci, *Nomads of the Present: Social Movements and Individual Needs in Contemporary Society*, ed. John Keane and Paul Mier (Philadelphia: Temple University Press, 1989); idem, *Challenging Codes: Collective Action in the Information Age* (Cambridge: Cambridge University Press, 1996); Roger V. Gould, *Insurgent Identities: Class, Community, and Protest in Paris from 1848 to the Commune* (Chicago: University of Chicago Press, 1995); and Matthew Schneirov and Jonathan David Geczik, "Alternative Health's Submerged Networks and the Transformation of Identity," *Sociological Quarterly* 37, 4 (1996): 627–44.

21. Steven M. Buechler, *Women's Movements in the United States* (New Brunswick, NJ: Rutgers University Press, 1990), 61. For a further application of the "social movement community" concept, see Verta Taylor and Nancy E. Whittier, "Collective Identities in Social Movement Communities: Lesbian Feminist Mobilization," in

158   *Notes to the Introduction*

Morris and Mueller, *Frontiers in Social Movement Theory;* and Randy Stoecher, "Community, Movement, Organization: The Problem of Identity Convergence in Collective Action," *Sociological Quarterly* 36, 1 (1995): 111–30.

22. Ibid., 42.

23. See Melucci, *Nomads of the Present.*

24. James Scott, *Weapons of the Weak: Everyday Forms of Peasant Resistance* (New Haven: Yale University Press, 1986); and idem, *Domination and the Arts of Resistance: Hidden Transcripts* (New Haven: Yale University Press, 1990).

25. See, for example, Karl Dieter Opp and Christiane Gern, "Dissident Groups, Personal Networks, and Spontaneous Cooperation: The East German Revolution of 1989," *American Sociological Review* 58 (1993): 659–80; Cathy Lisa Schneider, *Shantytown Protest in Pinochet's Chile* (Philadelphia: Temple University Press, 1995); Mara Loveman, "High-Risk Collective Action: Defending Human Rights in Chile, Uruguay, and Argentina," *American Journal of Sociology* 104, 2 (September 1998): 477–525; and Dingxin Zhao, "Ecologies of Social Movements: Student Mobilization during the 1989 Prodemocracy Movement in Beijing," *American Journal of Sociology* 103, 6 (May 1998): 1493–1529.

26. Steven Pfaff, "Collective Identity and Informal Groups in Revolutionary Mobilization: East Germany in 1989," *Social Forces* 75, 1 (September 1996): 99.

27. Jiping Zuo and Robert D. Benford, "Mobilization Processes and the 1989 Chinese Democracy Movement," *Sociological Quarterly* 36, 1 (1995): 131–56.

28. Ira M. Lapidus, *Muslim Cities in the Late Middle Ages* (Cambridge: Cambridge University Press, 1967); idem, "Hierarchies and Social Networks: A Comparison of Chinese and Islamic Societies," in *Conflicts and Control in Late Imperial China*, ed. F. J. Wakemann (Berkeley: University of California Press, 1975); Samih K. Farsoun, "Family Structure and Society in Modern Lebanon," in *Peoples and Cultures of the Middle East*, ed. Louise Sweet (Garden City, N.Y.: National History, 1970); Ernest Gellner and John Waterbury, eds., *Patrons and Clients in Mediterranean Societies* (London: Duckworth, 1977); Guilain Denoeux, *Urban Unrest in the Middle East: A Comparative Study of Informal Networks in Egypt, Iran, and Lebanon* (Albany: State University of New York Press, 1993); Diane Singerman, *Avenues of Participation: Family, Politics, and Networks in Urban Quarters of Cairo* (Princeton: Princeton University Press, 1995); Asef Bayat, *Street Politics: Poor People's Movements in Iran, 1977–1990* (New York: Columbia University Press, 1997); idem, "Un-Civil Society: The Politics of the 'Informal People'," *Third World Quarterly* 18,1 (1997): 53–72; and Sato Tsugitaka, ed., *Islamic Urbanism in Human History: Political Power and Social Networks* (London: Keagan Paul International, 1997).

29. Singerman, *Avenues of Participation.*

30. Bayat, *Street Politics.*

31. Denoeux, *Urban Unrest.*

32. See, for example, the political process argument presented in Charles Tilly, *From Mobilization to Revolution* (Reading, Mass.: Addison-Wesley, 1978); Doug McAdam, *Political Process and the Development of Black Insurgency, 1930–1970* (Chicago: University of Chicago Press, 1982); and Sydney Tarrow, *Power in Movement: Social Movements, Collective Action, and Politics* (Cambridge: Cambridge University Press, 1994).

33. Herbert P. Kitschelt, "Political Opportunity Structures and Political Protest: Anti-Nuclear Movements in Four Democracies," *British Journal of Political*

Science 16 (1986): 57–85; Charles D. Brockett, "The Structure of Political Opportunities and Peasant Mobilization in Central America," *Comparative Politics* 23 (1991): 253–74; Hanspeter Kriesi, Ruud Koopmans, Jan Willem Duyvendak, and Marco G. Giugni, *New Social Movements in Western Europe: A Comparative Analysis* (Minneapolis: University of Minnesota Press, 1995); and Dieter Rucht, "The Impact of National Contexts on Social Movement Structures: A Cross-Movement and Cross-National Comparison," in *Comparative Perspectives on Social Movements: Political Opportunities, Mobilizing Structures, and Cultural Framings,* ed. Doug McAdam, John D. McCarthy, and Mayer N. Zald (Cambridge: Cambridge University Press, 1996).

34. For Jordan's political history, see Naseer H. Aruri, *Jordan: A Study in Political Development (1921–1965)* (The Hague: Martinus Nijhoff, 1972); Shaul Mishal, *West Bank/East Bank: The Palestinians in Jordan, 1948–1967* (New Haven: Yale University Press, 1978); Clinton Baily, *Jordan's Palestinian Challenge, 1948– 1983: A Political History* (Boulder: Westview Press, 1984); Mary Wilson, *King Abdullah, Britain and the Making of Jordan* (Cambridge: Cambridge University Press, 1987); Uriel Dann, *King Hussein and the Challenge of Arab Radicalism: Jordan, 1955–1967* (Oxford: Oxford University Press, 1989); Kamal Salibi, *The Modern History of Jordan* (London: I. B. Tauris, 1993); and Robert Satloff, *From Abdullah to Hussein: Jordan in Transition* (Oxford: Oxford University Press, 1994).

35. Baily, *Jordan's Palestinian Challenge.*

36. Bahgat Korany, Rex Brynen, and Paul Noble, eds., *Comparative Experiences,* vol. 2 of *Political Liberalization and Democratization in the Arab World* (Boulder: Lynne Rienner Publishers, 1998). For this argument applied to Jordan in particular, see Laurie Brand, "Economic and Political Liberalization in a Rentier Economy: The Case of the Hashemite Kingdom of Jordan," in *Privatization and Liberalization in the Middle East,* ed. Iliya Harik and Denis J. Sullivan (Bloomington: Indiana University Press, 1992); Rex Brynen, "Economic Crisis and Post-Rentier Democratization in the Arab World: The Case of Jordan," *Canadian Journal of Political Science* 25, 1 (March 1992): 69–97; and Katherine Rath, "The Process of Democratization in Jordan," *Middle Eastern Studies* 30, 3 (July 1994): 530–57.

37. Hazem Bablawi and Giacomo Luciani, eds., *The Rentier State* (London: Croom Helm, 1987).

38. Giacomo Luciani, "Economic Foundations of Democracy and Authoritarianism: The Arab World in Comparative Perspective," *Arab Studies Quarterly* 10, 4 (Fall 1988): 463.

39. Singerman, *Avenues of Participation,* 245.

40. Malik Mufti, "Elite Bargains and the Onset of Political Liberalization in Jordan," *Comparative Political Studies* 32, 1 (February 1999): 104. See also Robert Satloff, "Jordan's Great Gamble: Economic Crisis and Political Reform," in *The Politics of Economic Reform in the Middle East,* ed. Henri Barkey (New York: St. Martin's Press, 1992).

41. Satloff, "Jordan's Great Gamble."

42. Daniel Brumberg, "Survival Strategies vs. Democratic Bargains: The Politics of Economic Reform in Contemporary Egypt," in *The Politics of Economic Reform in the Middle East,* ed. Henri Barkey (New York: St. Martin's Press, 1992).

43. Daniel Brumberg, "Authoritarian Legacies and Reform Strategies in the Arab World," in *Theoretical Perspectives,* ed. Rex Brynen, Bahgat Korany, and Paul

Noble, vol. 1 of *Political Liberalization and Democratization in the Arab World* (Boulder: Lynne Rienner, 1995), 230.

44. Glenn Robinson, "Defensive Democratization in Jordan," *International Journal of Middle East Studies* 30 (1998): 387–410.

45. John D. McCarthy, David W. Britt, and Mark Wolfson, "The Institutional Channeling of Social Movements by the State in the United States," in *Research in Social Movements, Conflict and Change*, vol. 13, ed. Louis Kriesberg (Greenwich, Conn.: JAI Press, 1991).

Chapter 1. The Management of Collective Action

1. Michel Foucault, *Discipline and Punish* (New York: Vintage Books, 1979)

2. Various studies explore disciplinary power in such diverse settings as the classroom, the barracks, prisons, the workplace, the criminal justice system, nursing, and colonialism. See R. V. Ericson and P. M. Baranek, *The Ordering of Justice: A Study of Accused Persons as Dependents in the Criminal Process* (Vancouver: University of British Columbia Press, 1982); Stanley Cohen, *Visions of Social Control: Crime, Punishment, and Classification* (Cambridge: Polity Press, 1985); Timothy Mitchell, *Colonising Egypt* (Berkeley: University of California Press, 1988); Graham Sewell and Barry Wilkinson, "'Someone to Watch over Me': Surveillance, Discipline, and the Just-in-Time Labour Process," *Sociology* 26, 2 (May 1992): 271–90; and Sam Porter, "Contra-Foucault: Soldiers, Nurses, and Power," *Sociology* 30, 1 (February 1996): 59–79.

3. Foucault, *Discipline and Punish*, 187.

4. Ibid.

5. Peter Wagner, *A Sociology of Modernity: Liberty and Discipline* (London: Routledge, 1994), 99.

6. The *mukhabarat* are the General Intelligence Directorate, tied to the office of the prime minister.

7. Information on the *mukhabarat* and their pattern of repression was provided by various Islamic activists and members of other social movements who were arrested, questioned, and even tortured during the period of martial law. These sources, of course, will remain anonymous.

8. The national security blanket allowed the *mukhabarat* to indiscriminately detain activists since any social movement activity was viewed as potentially destabilizing and thus a threat to national security. When this group activity was combined with an Islamist discourse and ideas that challenged the current system and its legitimacy, it was considered intolerable since it linked collective action to an agenda for political change.

9. This does not include popular association through the tribal system, which persisted. The tribes constitute the backbone of Hashemite power and staff the army and important social control institutions. They have supported the royal family and are not viewed as a collective threat to the regime. On the contrary, the tribes reify and perpetuate monarchical rule. In any event, social movement activism never overcame, nor did it try to overcome, the dominant logic of tribal affiliation to usurp its structures for movement goals.

10. Abdullah El Khatib, "The Impact of the Third Sector in Economic Development of Jordan," paper presented at the ISTR Second International Conference, Mexico City, 18–21 July 1996.

11. General Union of Voluntary Societies, *Profiles, Programs, Projects* (Amman: GUVS, 1996), 4.

12. Law 33 is similar to laws governing voluntary work in other Arab countries as well. For a discussion of the parallel Egyptian law, see Ibn Khaldoun Center for Development Studies, *An Assessment of Grass-Roots Participation in Egypt's Development*, unpublished study, 1993; Denis J. Sullivan, *Private Voluntary Organizations in Egypt: Islamic Development, Private Initiative, and State Control* (Gainesville: University Press of Florida, 1994), 17–18; Amani Kandil, *Civil Society in the Arab World: Private Voluntary Organizations* (Washington, D.C.: Civicus, 1995); and Moheb Zaki, *Civil Society & Democratization in Egypt, 1981–1994* (Cairo: Konrad Adenauer Foundation, 1995), 56–65.

13. *Law of Societies and Social Organizations* (in Arabic), Law 33 of 1966, Article 2, published in the *Official Gazette* no. 1927, 11 June 1966.

14. The state requires that all members of the administrative board are elected democratically. This is an important point for scholars who argue that democratic indicators may be found in grassroots organizations. It is an imposed democracy, not a selection process that is freely chosen. This is not to say that organizational activists would not otherwise invoke democratic principles in the selection process, but that it is impossible to argue that it is an indication of the potential for democratic consolidation in Jordan.

15. President of this charitable organization, interview by author, Zarqa, 18 March 1997. Members of this society still *informally* provide marriage services.

16. *Law of Societies and Social Organizations*, Article 15.

17. Ibid., Article 14.

18. Ibid., Article 17. A GUVS official confirmed that this is enforced in practice.

19. GUVS official, interview by author, Amman 28 October 1996; Administrative Committee for the Union of Voluntary Societies, Amman Governate, minutes for meeting no. 21 (in Arabic), 14 December 1996.

20. General Union of Voluntary Societies, *Executive Council Report* (in Arabic) (Amman: GUVS, 1996), 39.

21. Mahmoud Kafawee, director of charitable organizations at the Ministry of Social Development, interview by author, Amman, 28 March 1997.

22. The state also routinely issues warnings to organizations.

23. *Law of Societies and Social Organizations*, Article 18.

24. Hashem Azzan, interview by author, Amman, 17 February 1997. Azzan was a member of the appointed temporary committee.

25. *Political Party Law*, Law 32 of 1992, Article 14, published in the *Official Gazette* no. 3851, 1 September 1992, p. 1670.

26. *Law of Societies and Social Organizations*, Article 2.

27. Director of cultural exchange, Ministry of Culture, interview by author, Amman, 8 October 1996; Mahmoud Kafawee, director of charitable organizations, Ministry of Social Development, interview by author, Amman, 28 March 1997.

28. *Jordan Times*, 4 November 1997.

29. *Star*, 6 November 1997.

30. This is not to argue that political parties will remain weak indefinitely. They have only been legal since 1992 and there is room for maturation. But to date, they remain financially strapped and do not dominate the political arena.

31. Leader in this organization, interview by author, Amman, 5 November 1996.

32. Shubaylat is considered one of the most radical opposition figures in the country. He considers himself an opposition figure first and an Islamist second. He was also the president of the Engineers' Association. He has directly criticized the royal family in various speeches, for which he has served time in jail at numerous points. Members of the Islamic movement have mixed views of Shubaylat. Some view him as an inspiration, while others describe him as an egomaniac. One Islamist went so far as to imply that Shubaylat suffers from mental illness (though in my interview with Shubaylat I never saw any signs of such an illness) (Layth Shubaylat, interview by author, Amman, 13 March 1997).

33. Women's movement activist who presented a lecture at the society just prior to its cancellation, interview by author, Amman, 20 March 1997.

34. *Star*, 23 January 1997.

35. Human Rights Watch, *Jordan: Clamping Down on Critics: Human Rights Violations in Advance of the Parliamentary Elections*, vol. 9, no. 12 (October 1997) (New York: Human Rights Watch).

36. Ibid., 31–33.

37. *Jordan Times*, 20 September 1997.

38. Abdullah El Khatib, "The Experience of NGOs in Jordan (A Brief Description)," paper presented at the Experts Meeting on Strategies for Strengthening NGO Networking and Research in the Middle East, Arab Thought Forum, Amman, 26 March 1994, pp. 20–21.

39. In all registration decisions, the governor of the district where the organization would operate is consulted. Islamists and other social movement actors claim that the governor acts on behalf of the *mukhabarat*.

40. For a general discussion of corporatism in the Middle East, see Robert Bianchi, *Interest Groups and Political Development in Turkey* (Princeton: Princeton University Press, 1984); idem, *Unruly Corporatism: Associational Life in Twentieth-Century Egypt* (Oxford: Oxford University Press, 1989); and Shahrough Akhavi, "Shi'ism, Corporatism, and Rentierism in the Iranian Revolution," in *Comparing Muslim Societies: Knowledge and the State in World Civilization*, ed. Juan Cole (Ann Arbor: University of Michigan Press, 1992).

41. General Union of Voluntary Societies, *GUVS, An Overview* (Amman: GUVS, 1995), 3.

42. General Union of Voluntary Societies, *GUVS, An Overview*, 4; El Khatib, "The Experience of NGOs in Jordan," 11.

43. General Union of Voluntary Societies, *Profiles*, 19.

44. El Khatib, "The Experience of NGOs in Jordan," 15.

45. General Union of Voluntary Societies, *Profiles*, 16.

46. El Khatib, "The Impact of the Third Sector," 17.

47. *Jordan Times*, 29 July 1996.

48. Abdul Latif Arabiyyat, interview by author, Amman, 27 November 1996.

49. United States Department of State, *Jordan Human Rights Report* (Amman: United States Embassy, 1996), 9.

50. Toujan Faisal was the first women elected to parliament and served from 1993 to 1997, where she was a staunch critic of the government. She was defeated in the 1997 elections and filed fraud charges to contest the loss. Khalil Haddadin, a member of the Jordanian Ba'th Arab Socialist Party, won a seat in the parliament in the 1997 elections. He was also a member of parliament from 1993 to 1997.

51. *Jordan Times*, 20 November 1997.

52. *Jordan Times*, 22 November 1997.

53. E. E. Schattschneider, *The Semi-Sovereign People* (New York: Holt, Rinehart, & Winston, 1960).

54. *Jordan Times*, 11 February 1998.

55. *Jordan Times*, 12 February 1998.

56. *Jordan Times*, 14 February 1998.

57. *Star*, 19 February 1998.

58. He was arrested for inciting the riot and lèse-majesté (attacks against the royal family).

59. The coroner's report indicated that the bullet did not come from a police-issued gun (*The Star*, 26 February 1998).

60. *Star*, 26 February 1998.

61. *Star*, 5 March 1998.

62. Even when a demonstration receives permission, there is no guarantee that it will be allowed to proceed. In 1994, Hamza Mansour, then an IAF parliamentarian, was granted permission to hold a demonstration in Irbid to protest the Jordanian-Israeli peace accords. Despite receiving permission, before the demonstration could proceed paratroopers intervened at the Grand Mosque in the center of Irbid (*Jordan Times*, 29 October 1994). The IAF sent a letter of protest to the government, but never received a response (Ishaq Farhan, interview by author, Amman, 10 October 1996).

63. *Law of Public Meetings* (in Arabic), Law 60 of 1953, Article 2, published in the *Official Gazette* no. 1139, 1 April 1953, p. 651.

64. This legal prohibition in effect prevents traditional meeting formats such as the *diwaniyya*, common in the Gulf and Iran. *Diwaniyya* are meetings, often held in private homes, to discuss various issues, including politics, and can serve as venues for political mobilization. See James A Bill, "The Plasticity of Informal Politics: The Case of Iran," *Middle East Journal* 28, 2 (1973): 131–51; and Shafeeq Gharba, "Voluntary Associations in Kuwait: The Foundation of a New System," *Middle East Journal* 45, 2 (Spring 1991): 199–215.

65. *Law of Public Meetings*, Article 3.

66. Ibid., Article 4.

67. Ibid., Article 5.

68. Ibid., Article 6.

69. Ibid., Article 7.

70. Ibid., Article 8.

71. Organization leader, interview by author, Amman, 14 December 1996.

72. A founder of the Coalition for Jordanian Women, interview by author, Amman, 5 November 1996.

73. Doug McAdam, "Tactical Innovation and the Pace of Insurgency," *American Sociological Review* 48, 6 (December 1983): 735–54.

74. Ibid.

75. Samih K. Farsoun and Lucia P. Fort, "The Problematics of Civil Society: Intellectual Discourse and Arab Intellectuals," unpublished paper, 1992, p. 42.

76. S. E. Finer, *Comparative Government* (London: Pelican, 1970); Mahfound Bennoune, "Algeria's Façade Democracy," *Middle East Report* (March–April 1990); and Beverley Milton-Edwards, "Façade Democracy and Jordan," *British Journal of Middle East Studies* 20, 2 (1993): 191–203.

77. One reform proposal that has recently circulated is to make professional association membership voluntary. Currently, individuals employed in particular fields must be members of the appropriate association and must abide by its rules and regulations. This gives association leaders substantial power and possible political influence. The new proposal would eliminate this power.

CHAPTER 2. STATE POWER AND THE REGULATION OF ISLAM

1. Dale F. Eickelman and James Piscatori, *Muslim Politics* (Princeton: Princeton University Press, 1996), 5.

2. Ibid., chapter 4.

3. Michael C. Hudson, *Arab Politics: The Search for Legitimacy* (New Haven: Yale University Press, 1977).

4. Charles Tripp, "Islam and the Secular Logic of the State in the Middle East," in *Islamic Fundamentalism*, ed. Abdel Salam Sidahmed and Anoushiravan Ehteshami (Boulder: Westview Press, 1996), 66.

5. Jamil Abun-Nasr, "The Salafiyya Movement in Morocco: The Religious Bases of the Moroccan Nationalist Movement," *Middle Eastern Affairs (St. Anthony's Papers)* 16 (1963): 90–105; Leon Carl Brown, "The Islamic Reformist Movement in North Africa," *Journal of Modern African Studies* 2, 1 (1964): 55–63; Jean-Claude Vatin, "Popular Puritanism versus State Reformism: Islam in Algeria," in *Islam in the Political Process*, ed. James P. Piscatori (Cambridge: Cambridge University Press, 1983); Abdelbaki Hermassi, "The Political and Religious in the Modern History of the Maghrib," in *Islamism and Secularism in North Africa*, ed. John Reudy (New York: St. Martin's Press, 1994); and Mohamed El Mansour, "Salafis and Modernists in the Moroccan Nationalist Movement," in Reudy, *Islamism and Secularism in North Africa*.

6. See, for example, the argument made by Mahmud Shaltut, a rector of the Islamic university al-Azhar in Cairo, presented in John J. Donahue and John L. Esposito, eds., *Islam in Transition: Muslim Perspectives* (New York: Oxford University Press, 1982).

7. Vatin, "Popular Puritanism versus State Reformism," 99.

8. James P. Piscatori, "Ideological Politics in Sa'udi Arabia," in Piscatori, *Islam in the Political Process*, 56–72.

9. Hermassi, "The Political and Religious," 91.

10. Bianchi, *Unruly Corporatism*, 180.

11. Piscatori, "Ideological Politics in Sa'udi Arabia," 60–61. For a general treatment of the state and religion in Saudi Arabia, see Ayman al-Yassini, *Religion and State in the Kingdom of Saudi Arabia* (Boulder: Westview Press, 1985).

12. Fouad Ajami, "In the Pharaoh's Shadow: Religion and Authority in Egypt," in Piscatori, *Islam in the Political Process*, 14.

13. Vatin, "Popular Puritanism versus State Reformism," 98.

14. Mohammed Tozy, "Islam and the State," in *Polity and Society in Contemporary North Africa*, ed. I.W. Zartman and W. M. Habeeb (Boulder: Westview Press, 1993), 117.

15. For a discussion of the Prophet's night journey, see Annemarie Schimmel, *And Muhammad Is His Messenger: The Veneration of the Prophet in Islamic Piety* (Chapel Hill: University of North Carolina Press, 1985), 159–75. Richard Antoun provides an interesting discussion of five different interpretations of the night journey by Muslim preachers in Jordan. See Richard Antoun, *Muslim Preacher in the Modern World: A Jordanian Case Study in Comparative Perspective* (Princeton: Princeton University Press, 1989), 219–34.

16. In 1993, the king changed the electoral system from bloc voting to a one-person one-vote system (see *Provisional Law 5 of 1993, Amendment to the Law of Election to the House of Deputies, Law 22 of 1986* [Amman: Press and Publications Department, 1993]). In the previous system, voters were given a bloc of votes that could be used for various candidates. They could use all these votes for a single candidate if they wished, thus amplifying the influence of political groups capable of mobilizing disciplined voters. This system provided advantages for the Muslim Brotherhood, whose army of loyal cadres was able to effectively utilize the bloc-voting system to benefit its own candidates in the 1989 elections. Prior to the 1993 elections, however, the king implemented the electoral changes. Under the new law, individuals are only given one vote, thus excluding the possibility of saving votes for single candidates. This change is generally recognized as an attempt to curb the growing influence of the Islamists in electoral politics and raised criticism from the Muslim Brotherhood and other groups which argued that the law was undemocratic since it had never been voted on by parliament.

17. International Press Office, Royal Hashemite Court, *Selected Speeches by His Majesty King Hussein, The Hashemite Kingdom of Jordan, 1988–1994*, 2d ed. (Amman: International Press Office, Royal Hashemite Court, 1994), 91.

18. Ibid., 105.

19. Wilson, *King Abdullah, Britain, and the Making of Jordan*.

20. For the social and political role of mosques in communities, see Akbar S. Ahmed, "Mosque: The Mosque in Politics," in *The Oxford Encyclopedia of the Modern Islamic World*, ed. John Esposito (Oxford: Oxford University Press, 1995), 3:140–43; Juan Eduardo Campo, "Mosque: Historical Development," in Esposito, *Oxford Encyclopedia of the Modern Islamic World*, 3:133–35; and Patrick D. Gaffney, "Mosque: The Mosque in Society," in Esposito, *Oxford Encyclopedia of the Modern Islamic World*, 3:143–47.

21. In instances where demonstrations are announced, regimes typically prohibit them and take security measures. Even when demonstrations are unannounced but there is potential because of current events or conditions, regimes take precautionary measures such as police armed with tear gas. This is also a common tactic of the Israeli army in Jerusalem where their presence is increased in the old city on Fridays and during religious holidays to preempt any possible collective action.

22. A *waqf* is a religious endowment, often in the form of land. The revenues

of the *waqf* are generally supposed to be used for charitable or religious purposes, though historically there has been some abuse of the system. *Awqaf* is the Arabic plural of *waqf.* For more on the *waqf,* see Monzer Kahf, "Waqf," in Esposito, *Oxford Encyclopedia of the Modern Islamic World,* 4:312–16.

23. For a discussion of private and public mosques and government versus popular Islam, see Vatin, "Popular Puritanism versus State Reformism"; Antoun, *Muslim Preacher in the Modern World,* 212–18; and Patrick D. Gaffney, "The Changing Voice of Islam: The Emergence of Professional Preachers in Contemporary Egypt," *Muslim World* 81, 1 (January 1991): 27–47.

24. Morroe Berger, *Islam in Egypt Today: Social and Political Aspects of Popular Religion* (Cambridge: Cambridge University Press, 1970); and Gaffney, "The Changing Voice of Islam," 38–40.

25. *Jordan Times,* 3 August 1997. The number of mosques in Egypt has been the source of debate and numbers vary. For a good discussion of different estimates, see Gaffney, "The Changing Voice of Islam," 47.

26. While the Department of Preaching and Guidance currently supervises mosques, there are plans to establish a new Department of Mosque Administration.

27. Ministry of Awqaf, *Annual Report* (in Arabic) (Amman: Hashemite Kingdom of Jordan, 1996), 191, 208.

28. It should be noted that, as Gaffney argues, this does not always mean that there are no oppositional figures in government controlled mosques. There is often a lack of qualified preachers and imams and regimes therefore encounter difficulty excluding oppositional figures (see Gaffney, "The Changing Voice of Islam"). In Jordan, the director of preaching and guidance indicated that many of the imams are not qualified to give Friday sermons. This makes it difficult to completely exclude oppositional figures, particularly when they are highly qualified. In addition, many of the private mosques in the Middle East showcase popular preachers whose removal could very well incite unrest. Regardless, states do try to control the content of the message by oppositional imams or preachers in official mosques, often removing them from their position or suspending their duties.

29. For more on the role of imams, see Hamid Algar, "Imam," in Esposito, *Oxford Encyclopedia of the Modern Islamic World,* 2:182–83.

30. *Al-da'wa* is the call to Islam. It entails both spreading Islam to nonbelievers as well as calling Muslims who have strayed from religious practice back to the Islamic faith.

31. This practice of hiring only moderate imams has increased in recent years. In an interview, one imam noted that he would never have been hired today because his views are not moderate enough. He also pointed to a systematic effort by the regime to remove any imams whose views do not support the state.

32. Antoun, *Muslim Preacher in the Modern World,* 85.

33. Saudi Arabia reportedly funnels donations through individuals, a practice allegedly tolerated by the Jordanian regime because it defrays costs.

34. Mifli Adabas, director of preaching and guidance, interview by author, Amman, 5 October 1996.

35. This community transcends ethnic and national identities and ties all Muslims together through their religion.

36. Antoun, *Muslim Preacher in the Modern World;* and idem, "Themes and

Symbols in the Religious Lesson: A Jordanian Case Study," *International Journal of Middle East Studies* 25 (1993): 607–24.

37. Bruce Borthwick, "The Islamic Sermon as a Channel of Political Communication," *Middle East Journal* 21, 3 (1967): 299–313; Asghar Fathi, "Preachers as Substitutes for Mass Media: The Case of Iran, 1905–1909," in *Towards a Modern Iran*, ed. Elie Kedourie and Sylvia G. Haim (London: Cass, 1980), 169–84; and idem, "The Islamic Pulpit as a Medium of Political Communication," *Journal for the Scientific Study of Religion* 20 (1981): 163–72.

38. For an overview of the *khutba* and its role in Muslim communities, see Asghar Fathi, "Khutba," in Esposito, *Oxford Encyclopedia of the Modern Islamic World*, 2:432–35.

39. The most comprehensive studies of the Muslim preacher to date are Antoun, *Muslim Preacher in the Modern World*; and Patrick D. Gaffney, *The Prophet's Pulpit: Islamic Preaching in Contemporary Egypt* (Berkeley: University of California Press, 1994).

40. Gaffney, "The Changing Voice of Islam."

41. In Egypt, in addition to attempts to control all mosques and imams, the government issued a new law in early 1997 that requires all mosques, regardless of whether they are private or government controlled, to register their preachers with the Ministry of Awqaf (*Jordan Times*, 8 March 1997). Also, the sermons of preachers in Egyptian government mosques are no longer written by the local preacher, but by officials at the ministry (Ahmed, "Mosque," 141). The goal is to control who speaks on behalf of Islam and channel the effects of the *khutba* into support for the state, or to at least prevent opposition. The state thus sponsors its own legion of cultural brokers programmed to interpret Islam in a light that is favorable to those in power. Of course, this extension of state control has historical precedent in Egypt. The trend began much earlier with Mohammed Ali, considered by many to be the great modernizer of Egypt, who took over many of the religious institutions and reduced the role of Islamic scholars to ritual and display.

42. Antoun, *Muslim Preacher in the Modern World*, 93–94.

43. Ibid., 97, 139–40.

44. Ibid., 93–94.

45. Calculated using information from Ministry of Awqaf, *Annual Report*, 191, 208.

46. This is not uncommon in Muslim countries where mosque building frequently outpaces the ability of the state to provide qualified personnel, straining the state's capacity to effectively control mosques. This often times necessitates the use of non-state personnel, including outside preachers. In Algeria in 1981, the minister of religious affairs openly admitted this fact when he commented that three-fifths of the imams at official mosques were not qualified to comment on the Qur'an and Sunna (see Vatin, "Islamic Puritanism versus State Reformism," 112). Various governments have attempted to rectify this by creating training and educational courses for preachers and imams. For Algeria, see Vatin, "Islamic Puritanism versus State Reformism," 112–13; and Hugh Roberts "From Radical Mission to Equivocal Ambition: The Expansion and Manipulation of Algerian Islamism, 1979–1992," in *Accounting for Fundamentalisms: The Dynamic Character of Movements*, ed. Martin E. Marty and R. Scott Appleby (Chicago: University of Chicago Press, 1994), 428–89.

47. Mifli Adabas, director of preaching and guidance, interview by author, Amman, 5 October 1996.

48. A good example is the *khutbas* that discussed traffic. Traffic accidents in Jordan have risen dramatically over recent years, predominantly as a result of young drivers who are frequently the cause. In conjunction with a program to highlight traffic accidents in the press, *khutbas* were given to raise awareness of the issue.

49. Mifli Adabas, director of preaching and guidance, interview by author, Amman, 5 October 1996.

50. *Law of Preaching, Guidance, and Teaching in Mosques* (in Arabic), Law 7 of 1986, Article 3, booklet provided by the Department of Preaching and Guidance, Ministry of Awqaf and Religious Affairs.

51. Ministry of Awqaf, *Annual Report*, 38.

52. *Law of Preaching, Guidance, and Teaching in Mosques*, Article 7.

53. 'Ali Hasan al-Halabi, interview by author, Zarqa, 26 October 1996.

54. *Jordan Times*, 29 October 1994.

55. *Jordan Times*, 26 January 1995.

56. *Jordan Times*, 30 September 1999; *Jordan Times*, 2 October 1999.

57. Mohammed Raoud, interview by author, Amman, 1 April 1997.

58. These sources will remain anonymous for their safety.

59. Abdullah al-Sheikh, "Zakat," in Esposito, *Oxford Encyclopedia of the Modern Islamic World*, 4:366–70.

60. *Law of Zakat Committees*, as published by *al-Ra'y* (Amman), 1996.

61. When he made this comment he was implying that government control is desirable because it prevents abuse, but it also points to the state's dominance in *zakat*.

62. This number is agreed upon by members of the Islamic movement, volunteers at *zakat* committees, and Ministry of Awqaf employees.

63. Abdullah El Khatib, "The Impact of the Third Sector," 22.

64. The committees can only absorb a certain number of clients and the waiting lists are often extensive.

65. El-Khatib, "The Impact of the Third Sector," 27.

66. Ibid.

67. For "official" and "unofficial" *zakat* in Egypt, see Sara Ben-Nefissa, "Zakah Officielle et Zakah Non Officielle Aujord'hui en Egypte," *Egypte/Monde Arabe* 7, 3 (1991): 105–20.

68. There are, of course, exceptions, such as Iran and Saudi Arabia. In addition, the trend toward the secularization of the legal system has not been a smooth transition and there have been many instances in which the guiding power of Islamic rules and norms has increased, but the overall trend has been to diminish its role.

69. Richard Antoun, "The Islamic Court, the Islamic Judge and the Accommodation of Traditions: A Jordanian Case Study," *International Journal of Middle East Studies* 12, 4 (December 1980): 455–67.

70. In Islam, there are four schools of jurisprudence: Shafi'i, Hanbali, Hanafi, and Maliki. Jordan is predominantly Hanafi.

71. Ibrahim A. Karawan, "Monarchs, Mullas, and Marshals: Islamic Regimes?" *Annals of the American Academy of Political and Social Science* 524 (November 1992): 108.

72. James P. Piscatori, "Religion and Realpolitik: Islamic Responses to the Gulf War," in Piscatori, *Islamic Fundamentalisms and the Gulf Crisis,* 9–10. There was still opposition from other religious leaders in the country. In particular, Safar al-Hawali, the dean of Islamic studies at Umm al-Qura University, and Sulaiman al-Uwda, a dean at Mohammed Bin Saud University in Qasim, both opposed Western forces on Saudi soil. For a discussion of the various *fatwas* issued for and against the Gulf War, see Yvonne Yazbeck Haddad, "Operation Desert Storm and the War of the Fatwas," in *Islamic Legal Interpretation: Muftis and Their Fatwas,* ed. Khalid M. Masud (Cambridge: Harvard University Press, 1996).

73. Ali E. Hillal Dessouki, "Official Islam and Political Legitimation in the Arab Countries," in *The Islamic Impulse,* ed. Barbara Freyer Stowasser (London: Croom Helm, 1987), 137–38.

74. For a discussion of the principle of *maslaha mursalah,* see Mohammed Hashim Kalami, *Principles of Islamic Jurisprudence,* revised edition (Cambridge: Islamic Text Society, 1991), chapter 13.

75. *Jordan Times,* 26 October 1997.

76. In one *fatwa,* he ruled that all Palestinians should leave the occupied territories because of Israeli control without understanding the complexities or political demographics of the situation. This *fatwa* drew widespread criticism in Jordan. It is unclear why al-Bani, prior to his death in October 1999, continued to issue *fatwas.* In fact, some of his own writings indicate that he understood that scholars such as himself may be more attuned to the intricacies of Islamic law than the complexities of modern circumstances. In one book, al-Bani argued for dialogue between Islamists with an expertise in modern affairs and those with more experience in Islamic law. See Mohammed Nasir al-Din al-Bani, *The Knowledge of Current Affairs,* translated by Abu Talhah Dawud ibn Ronald Burbank (Birmingham, U.K.: Jam'iat Ihyaa' Minhaaj Al-Sunnah, 1994).

77. For a discussion of Ramadan, see Anis Ahmad, "Ramadan," in Esposito, *Oxford Encyclopedia of the Modern Islamic World,* 4:408–10.

78. *Iftar* literally means breaking the fast.

79. There are some groups, however, that are tacitly permitted to collect donations through the mosque. According to many Islamists, the government is selective about which groups it represses, and relatively innocuous groups are allowed to collect donations.

80. Department of Islamic Cultural Centers, Ministry of Awqaf, correspondence to the Lower House of Parliament (in Arabic), January 1996.

81. This is a substantial number of graduates, considering that the total number of female beneficiaries for these kinds of vocational programs among *all* non-state NGOs in the entire country is 6,373 (calculated from General Union of Voluntary Societies, *Profiles,* 4). This includes courses on sewing, tricot, typing, handicrafts, cosmetics, and flower arrangement.

82. Director of the Department of Islamic Centers, interview by author, Amman, 7 November 1996.

83. Prior to the collapse of the Ottoman empire, the Muslim world was guided by a *khalifa,* or religious leader, who was responsible for ruling according to Islam. Turkey abolished the caliphate after World War I.

84. While most observers believe Hizb al-Tahrir is currently marginalized at best, discussions with various Islamic activists indicate that it may not be as

marginalized as many seem to believe. One activist argued that because of its illegal status and objectives, most members will not admit they are from the movement. Others believe in Hizb al-Tahrir's ideas and cause, even if they do not belong as formal members. The influence of Tahrir's ideology among members of the broader Islamic movement, therefore, should not be underestimated. For more on Hizb al-Tahrir, see Amnon Cohen, *Political Parties in the West Bank under the Jordanian Regime, 1949–1967* (Ithaca: Cornell University Press, 1980), 209–29; and Suha Taji-Farouki, "Hizb Al-Tahrir," in Esposito, *Oxford Encyclopedia of the Modern Islamic World*, 2:125–27.

85. *'Umra* is a pilgrimage to Mecca during a period of time other than *hajj*.

86. *Jordan Times*, 20 March 1997.

87. It was registered at the Ministry of Social Development in 1972.

88. Prince Hassan also runs several other NGOs, including the Arab Thought Forum. The sponsorship of NGOs by the royal family is fairly widespread and includes two of the largest NGOs in the country: the Queen Alia Fund for Social Development and the Nur al-Hussein Foundation.

CHAPTER 3. ISLAMIC SOCIAL MOVEMENT ORGANIZATIONS AND THE MUSLIM BROTHERHOOD

1. Berger, *Islam in Egypt Today;* Soheir Morsy, "Islamic Clinics in Egypt: The Cultural Elaboration of Biomedical Hegemony," *Medical Anthropology Quarterly* 2, 4 (December 1988): 355–69; Bianchi, *Unruly Corporatism*, 187–99; Nazih N. Ayubi, *Political Islam: Religion and Politics in the Arab World* (London: Routledge, 1991), 195–99; Iman Roushdy Hammady, "Religious Medical Clinics in Cairo" (master's thesis no. 885, American University in Cairo, 1990); Denis J. Sullivan, *Private Voluntary Organizations in Egypt: Islamic Development, Private Initiative, and State Control* (Gainesville: University Press of Florida, 1994); Janine Astrid Clark, "Democratization and Social Islam: A Case Study of Islamic Clinics in Cairo," in Brynen, Korany, and Noble, *Theoretical Perspectives;* and idem, "Islamic Social Welfare Organizations in Cairo: Islamization from Below?" *Arab Studies Quarterly* 17, 4 (1995): 11–28.

2. This is consistent with Clark's study of Islamic health clinics in Cairo (Clark, "Islamic Social Welfare Organizations in Cairo"). She found that volunteers view their work in terms of services, not as part of a broader religious or political challenge to the state. Her findings are supported by an earlier study by Morsy (Morsy, "Islamic Clinics in Egypt"). The lack of a conscious political objective among volunteers at Islamic NGOs, however, does not mean that there is no political *effect*. Both Denis J. Sullivan (Sullivan, *Private Voluntary Organizations in Egypt*) and Nazih N. Ayubi (Ayubi, *Political Islam*, 195–99) argue that Islamic NGOs in Egypt are challenging the state's achievement-based claim to legitimacy. There is no conscious political strategy to seize power through Islamic NGOs, but the political effect of their work may undermine the regime's socioeconomic development basis of legitimacy. As Diane Singerman has demonstrated, even seemingly self-interested behavior (which is not necessarily apolitical) can have political effects by impacting the effectiveness of the political system (Singerman, *Avenues of Participa-*

tion). A lack of direct political intent does not, therefore, necessarily reflect an apolitical nature.

3. The cultural societies are an exception to this since they are devoted to promoting Islam. To date, however, there are only nine such organizations and they remain limited.

4. Sullivan, *Private Voluntary Organizations,* 69.

5. For the issue of identity in Jordan, see Schirin Fathi, *Jordan—An Invented Nation? Tribe-State Dynamics and the Formation of National Identity* (Hamburg: Deutches Orient-Institut, 1994); and Linda L. Layne, *Home and Homeland: The Dialogics of Tribal and National Identities in Jordan* (Princeton: Princeton University Press, 1994). For the issue of Palestinian identity in particular, see Laurie Brand, "Palestinians and Jordanians: A Crisis of Identity," *Journal of Palestine Studies* 96, 4 (Summer 1995): 46–61.

6. This information was provided informally during a seminar.

7. Some Palestinians with Jordanian citizenship in fact prefer to live in the camps because of community ties.

8. Laurie Brand, for example, notes that the Muslim Brotherhood is generally seen as predominantly Palestinian (Brand, "Palestinians and Jordanians," 55).

9. Calculated using information from Hamed Dabbas, "Islamic Centers, Associations, Societies, Organizations, and Committees in Jordan," in *Islamic Movements in Jordan,* ed. Jillian Schwedler (Amman: al-Urdun al-Jadid Research Center, 1997).

10. Hani Hourani, Taleb Awad, Hamed Dabbas, and Sa'eda Kilani, *Islamic Action Front Party* (Amman: Al-Urdun Al-Jadid Research Center, 1993), 34–37.

11. Ibid., 45.

12. This may be changing in the IAF. There is some preliminary evidence that as the general cultural climate becomes more favorable toward women, the IAF may begin to target female voters and candidates (see Janine A. Clark, "Gender Dynamics of Intra-Party Activism: The Expanding Role of Islamist Women in Jordan's IAF," paper presented at the Middle East Studies Association Annual Conference, Washington, D.C., 20–22 November 1999).

13. This opposition is shared by Jordanian society as a whole. In a survey of 1,419 Jordanians conducted by the Center for Strategic Study (CSS) in 1998, 80 percent indicated that they still believe Israel is an enemy. Around 40 percent attribute this perception to religious reasons, a number that is unquestioningly much higher among Islamists. While a poll conducted by CSS after the signing of the Washington Declaration in 1994 between Israel and Jordan, which is the basis of peace between the two countries, indicated that 80.2 percent of the population favored peace, support seriously dissipated after Netanyahu took office (*Jordan Times,* 14 January 1998). This opposition has manifested itself in parliamentary debates, statements by various professional associations, and grassroots demonstrations against peace with Israel. The attempt on 25 September 1997 by Mossad agents to assassinate a Hamas leader in Amman and the concomitant findings of the Israeli investigative committee, which exonerated Netanyahu and the Mossad, further strained support for peace.

14. *Amman Al-Safir* [Amman], 4 January 1997.

15. Ishaq Farhan, "The Islamic Stand towards Political Involvement (with Reference to the Jordanian Experience)," unpublished paper, 1996. This piece was

written in English and I have quoted Farhan without changing grammar. By "opposite violence," he means government sponsored counterviolence. Farhan was the president of the IAF and a leader in the Muslim Brotherhood, but lost his seat on the Brotherhood's *shura* council, which serves as the decision-making body of the movement, in July 1998 (*Jordan Times,* 14 July 1998).

16. Ibid., 23.

17. *Al-Ra'y* [Amman], 6 November 1996.

18. Thunaybat as quoted in *Federal Broadcast Information Service* [FBIS-NES-94-168], 30 August 1994.

19. This is particularly the case in domestic issues. For the pragmatic view of the Muslim Brotherhood in the domestic arena, see El-Said, *Between Pragmatism and Ideology.*

20. Abdul Latif Arabiyyat, interview by author, Amman, 27 November 1996. Arabiyyat is a leader in the Brotherhood and is currently the president of the Islamic Action Front Party (IAF).

21. *Al-Ra'y,* 12 November 1996. Umoush was a leader in the Muslim Brotherhood and IAF and a member of parliament from 1993 to 1997. In 1997, both Bassam Umoush and Abdullah Akaileh broke with the IAF election boycott and were elected to the Lower House. Prime Minister Majali included Umoush in his cabinet as the minister of administrative development. Akaileh and Umoush were both subsequently expelled from the IAF and the Muslim Brotherhood for breaching the decision to boycott.

22. Abdullah Akaileh, "The Experience of the Jordanian Islamic Movement," in *Power-Sharing Islam?* ed. Azzam Tamimi (London: Liberty for Muslim World Publications, 1993); *Al-Ra'y,* 9 November 1996; and *Al-Ra'y,* 12 November 1996.

23. See for example, the interviews in *al-Ra'y* with Zayd Hamzeh, a progressive liberal (9 November 1996), and Ibrahim 'Izz-al-Din (5 November 1996).

24. I. William Zartman, "Opposition as Support of the State," in *Beyond Coercion: The Durability of the Arab State,* ed. Adeed Dawisha and I. William Zartman (London: Croom Helm, 1988).

25. Ibid., 62. See also Freij and Robinson, "Liberalization, the Islamists, and the Stability of the Arab State," 5.

26. Thomas C. Schelling, *The Strategy of Conflict* (New York: Oxford University Press, 1963).

27. Juan J. Linz, *The Breakdown of Democratic Regimes: Crisis, Breakdown, and Reequilibration* (Baltimore: Johns Hopkins University Press, 1978).

28. Cohen, *Political Parties,* 146–54.

29. Awni Obaidi, as quoted in Hani Hourani, Taleb Awad, Hamed Dabbas, and Sa'eda Kilani, *Islamic Action Front Party* (Amman: Al-Urdun Al-Jadid Research Center, 1993), 9.

30. Hourani et al., *Islamic Action Front Party,* 10–11.

31. Obaidi, as quoted in Hourani et al., *Islamic Action Front Party,* 11.

32. *Al-Ra'y,* 6 November 1996.

33. Mitchell, *Society of the Muslim Brothers,* 151–62.

34. Abdul Latif Arabiyyat, interview by author, Amman, 27 November 1996.

35. As a charitable organization, the Brotherhood could receive foreign funding and donations. Many observers of the movement believe that over the years Saudi Arabia contributed to the Muslim Brotherhood's charitable activities.

36. Robert B. Satloff, *Troubles on the East Bank: Challenges to the Domestic Stability of Jordan,* policy paper number 39 (Washington, D.C.: The Washington Institute for Near East Policy, 1986).

37. Ibid.

38. Hilmi Asmar, interview by author, Amman, 29 October 1996.

39. Layth Shubaylat, interview by author, Amman, 13 March 1997.

40. Leader of the Mu'tazila movement, interview by author, Amman, 19 October 1996.

41. *Amman Al-Safir,* 4 January 1997.

42. For this perspective, see Fahd al-Fanik's statements in *Al-Ra'y* (5 November 1996). Al-Fanik is an Arab nationalist and newspaper columnist who argues that the prospects for violence remain real. He claims that the threat of violence "has been used on more than one occasion." But even al-Fanik admits that while the Brotherhood has expressed opposition to policies, "they have yet to display opposition to the regime."

43. General Union of Voluntary Societies, *Directory of Charitable Societies,* 27.

44. Roald, *Tarbiya,* 172.

45. Zaid Abu Ghamineh, interview by author, Amman, 13 October 1996. Ghamineh is an administrator at the hospital and an important figure in the history of the Muslim Brotherhood. He was expelled from the Brotherhood in 1996 because of outspoken disagreements with the leadership. Despite this expulsion, he still views himself as a member of the movement.

46. Ibid.

47. Roald, *Tarbiya,* 207.

48. Zaid Abu Ghamineh, interview by author, Amman, 13 October 1996.

49. Roald, *Tarbiya,* 208.

50. Zaid Abu Ghamineh, interview by author, Amman, 13 October 1996.

51. Laurie Brand, "'In the Beginning was the State . . .': The Quest for Civil Society in Jordan," in *Civil Society in the Middle East,* vol. 1, ed. Augustus Richard Norton (New York: Brill,1995), 164.

52. Roald, *Tarbiya,* 204–6.

53. Aruri , *Jordan,* 99.

54. IIIT also has a branch in Herdon, Virginia.

55. Omar Subeyhe, director of the Preservation of the Qur'an Society, interview by author, Amman, 16 October 1996.

56. Ibid.

57. Ibid.

58. Other Muslim Brotherhood NGOs include al-Afaf and the Green Crescent Society. Al-Afaf is a marriage society that provides a matchmaking service and helps young couples pay for weddings. Its most prominent work has been a series of small collective weddings (see Quintan Wiktorowicz and Suha Taji-Farouki, "Islamic Non-Governmental Organizations and Muslim Politics: A Case from Jordan," *Third World Quarterly* 21, 4 [Summer 2000]). Abdul Latif Arabiyyat is the president of the organization. The Green Crescent Society provides disaster assistance to Muslims throughout the world. It is run by Muslim Brotherhood hardliner Hamzah Mansour.

59. Omar Subeyhe, director of the Preservation of the Qur'an Society, interview by author, Amman, 16 October 1996.

60. Zaid Abu Ghamineh, interview by author, Amman, 13 October 1996.
61. Ra'if Nijim, interview by author, Amman, 15 October 1996. Although he is not a member, Nijim works extensively with the Muslim Brotherhood on various projects, particularly those that require engineering skills. He was also a founding member of the IAF, though like other independents he resigned because of differences about the distribution of leadership positions and the balance between members of the Brotherhood and independent Islamists. He has also served as the minister of Awqaf.
62. As quoted in Raold, *Tarbiya*, 146.
63. Ra'if Nijim, interview by author, Amman, 15 October 1996.
64. Zaid Abu Ghamineh, interview by author, Amman, 13 October 1996.

CHAPTER 4. THE SALAFI MOVEMENT
AND INFORMAL NETWORKS

1. John O. Voll, "Renewal and Reform in Islamic History: *Tajdid and Islah*," in *Voices of Resurgent Islam*, ed. John L. Esposito (Oxford: Oxford University Press, 1983).
2. Emad Eldin Shahin, "Salafiyyah," in Esposito, *Oxford Encyclopedia of the Modern Islamic World*, 3:463.
3. A good overview of *tawhid* can be found in Tamara Sonn, "Tawhid," in Esposito, *Oxford Encyclopedia of the Modern Islamic World*, 4:190–98.
4. Muhammad Jibali, *Allah's Rights Upon His Servants: Tawhid vs. Shirk* (Cincinnati: Al-Qur'an Was-Sunnah Society of North America, 1995), 5.
5. The Wahhabis are considered a Salafi movement based in Saudi Arabia.
6. Qur'an 39:62. All quotes from the Qur'an are from Mohammed Marmaduke Pickthall, *The Meaning of the Holy Qur'an* (New Delhi: UBS Publishers' Distributors, 1995).
7. Qur'an 64:1.
8. Abdul Aziz Bin Abdullah Bin Baz, "The Beautiful Names and Lofty Attributes," *Al-Ibaanah* 2 (August 1995): 31–33.
9. Qur'an 112:1–4.
10. Qur'an 42:11.
11. For a brief summary of the Salafi *'aqida* written by a Salafi scholar, see Naasir al-'Aql, "Principles and Methodology for the 'Aqeedah of Ahlus-Sunnah wal-Jamaa'ah," *Al-Ibaanah* 2 (August 1995): 25–26.
12. Jibali, *Allah's Rights upon His Servants*, 24.
13. I would like to thank Vincent Cornell for pointing this out.
14. Qur'an 72:18.
15. As cited in Jibali, *Allah's Rights upon His Servants*, 25.
16. *Tawhid al-ilahiya* is also a foundation for Islamic critiques of Christianity and Judaism. One *hadith* states, "The curse of Allah be upon the Jews and the Christians, for they took the graves of their Prophets as places of worship" (as cited in "Mankind's Greatest Need," *Al-Ibaanah* 1,2 [August 1995]: 11). Christians in particular are criticized for worshipping Christ. While Christ is considered an important prophet in Islam, he is not considered God. Muslims believe, therefore, that Christ should not be worshipped.

17. Qur'an 30:31.

18. Qur'an 5:72.

19. Qur'an 4:48.

20. Jibali, *Allah's Rights upon His Servants,* 30–32.

21. For a Salafi explanation of *shirk,* see Ibid. and Mohammed Nasir al-Din al-Bani, "The Origins of Shirk," *Al-Ibaanah* 3 (April 1996): 32–33.

22. *Hadith* cited in Muhammad Ibn Jameel Zaynoo, "Methodology of the Saved Sect," *Al-Ibaanah* 3 (April 1996): 22.

23. Mohammed Abu Shaqra, *The Truth about the Extremists* (in Arabic), sound cassette, n.d.

24. Not every Salafi dresses in this manner, however. In fact, a few of the more radical Salafis I met during this research wore Western-style clothing. Some argued that the evidence pointing to the use of the white robe is weak. Still others reject the use of such apparel as "living in the past" and as irrelevant to the Islamist cause.

25. Muhammad Zubayr Siddiqi, *Hadith Literature: Its Origins, Development, and Special Features* (Cambridge: The Islamic Texts Society, 1993), 31–36.

26. For the methodology of the *hadith* science, see M. M. Azami, *Studies in Hadith Methodology and Literature* (Indianapolis: American Trust Publications, 1992).

27. See Siddiqi, *Hadith Literature,* 76–90.

28. Ibid., 109.

29. Each *mathhab* is named after its founder. For the various sources used in Islamic jurisprudence, see Kalami, *Principles of Islamic Jurisprudence.*

30. Saleem al-Hilali, "Who is the Victorious Group," *Al-Ibaanah* 2 (August 1995): 39–42; and Zaynoo, "Methodology of the Saved Sect."

31. As cited in Jam'iat Ihyaa' Minhaaj Al-Sunnah, *A Brief Introduction to the Salafi Da'wah* (Ipswich, Suffolk, U.K.: Jam'iat Ihyaa' Minhaaj Al-Sunnah, 1993), 5.

32. Ibid., 3.

33. Ibid., 2–3.

34. These new militant groups include Mohammed's Army and the Vanguards of Islamic Youth. For more on militant groups in Jordan, see Beverley Milton-Edwards, "Climate of Change in Jordan's Islamist Movement," in *Islamic Fundamentalism,* ed. Abdel Salam Sidahmed and Anoushiravan Ehteshami (Boulder: Westview Press, 1996).

35. *Jordan Times,* 29 September 1996.

36. Four of the men responsible confessed that their actions were inspired by jihadi writers such as Abu Muhammad al-Maqdisi (*Jordan Times,* 18 August 1997).

37. *Jordan Times,* 11 May 1998; *Jordan Times,* 23 May 1998.

38. For more on *takfir,* see Ibrahim Karawan, "Takfir," in Esposito, *Oxford Encyclopedia of the Modern Islamic World,* 4:178–79.

39. Qur'an 4:17.

40. For the reformist Salafi interpretation of *takfir,* see Ahmad Fareed, *On the Issue of Takfir* (Suffolk, U.K.: Jam'iat Ihyaa' Minhaaj Al-Sunnah, 1997).

41. 'Ali Hasan al-Halabi, "Tarbiyah: The Key to Victory," *Al-Ibaanah* 2 (August 1995): 15–19. The most thorough discussion of *tarbiya* and Islamic movements is Roald, *Tarbiya.*

42. Salim al-Hilali, interview by author, Amman, 2 April 1997.

43. Al-Halabi, "Tarbiyah," 16.

44. As quoted in 'Ali Hasan al-Halabi, *Fundamentals of Commanding Good and Forbidding Evil According to Shayk Ul-Islam Ibn Tamiyya* (Cincinnati: Al-Qur'an Was-Sunnah Society of North America, 1995), 2.

45. Ibid.

46. Ibid., 3–4. For the Khawarij, see John Alden Williams, "Khawarij," in Esposito, *Oxford Encyclopedia of the Modern Islamic World*, 2:419–20.

47. In some cases, radical Salafis from the lower classes are co-opted through material incentives. They receive financial assistance in exchange for a more moderate stance directed toward reform.

48. For Ibn Taymiyya's interpretation of jihad and its effect on contemporary Islamic movements, see John O. Voll, "Fundamentalism in the Sunni Arab World: Egypt and the Sudan," in *Fundamentalisms Observed*, ed. Martin E. Marty and R. Scott Appleby (Chicago: University of Chicago Press, 1991), 353–54; Gilles Kepel, *Muslim Extremism in Egypt: The Prophet and the Pharaoh*, trans. Jon Rothschild (Berkeley: University of California Press, 1986), 191–222; and Emmanuel Sivan, *Radical Islam: Medieval Theology and Modern Politics* (New Haven: Yale University Press), 94–107. For an overview of various interpretations of jihad, including those of Ibn Taymiyya, see Rudolph Peters, *Jihad in Classical and Modern Islam* (Princeton: Markus Wiener Publishers, 1996). For a Salafi perspective on Ibn Taymiyya, see al-Halabi, *Fundamentals of Commanding Good and Forbidding Evil.*

49. These arrests were not publicized by the media but were well known within the Salafi movement. During my research, I spent a great deal of time with a graduate student who was arrested in Salt during one of the crackdowns.

50. A good example is one Salafi who is not involved in militant operations, but published a book entitled *al-Umma wa al-Sulta*, which critiques current Arab systems of power. The book condones the use of force as an acceptable method of change. The book was published in Lebanon and copies were confiscated by Jordanian authorities, although I later found a copy in an Islamic bookstore. This Salafi was detained by the *mukhabarat* for two days and was only released after he used *wasta.*

51. 'Ali Hasan al-Halabi, interview by author, Zarqa, 26 October 1996.

52. Not all Salafis agree that Qutb was a Salafi, and this is a point of current debate.

53. This reading of al-Bani's motives was proposed by several Salafis from the "second wave" that I interviewed during my fieldwork. Despite al-Bani's reputation, there was a group of Salafis who rejected the first *fatwa* and left al-Bani's circle of followers to pursue their own objectives. While al-Bani is a renown scholar of *hadith*, he is not widely respected in *fiqh*, and his *fatwas* have little impact beyond the Salafi movement. His weakness in *fiqh* made it easier for this group to oppose the spirit of the initial *fatwa* against organizations.

54. 'Ali Hasan al-Halabi, interview by author, Zarqa, 26 October 1996.

55. Shaykh Huthayfa, interview by author, Amman, 25 March 1997.

56. Jonathan Berkey, *The Transmission of Knowledge in Medieval Cairo: A Social History of Islamic Education* (Princeton: Princeton University Press, 1992), 20.

57. See the introduction n. 16, above.

58. Bert Klandermans, "The Formation and Mobilization of Consensus," in Klandermans, Kriesi, and Tarrow, *From Structure to Action*, 175.

59. There is a growing, though still limited, trend of family conversions as well, whereby a husband adopts the Salafi approach and passes it to his wife and children. Salafis argue that this is becoming more prevalent because the nuclear family is breaking away from the extended family by moving into separate residences. Cross-cutting familial pressures are thus less severe. Less affected by family pressures in daily existence, members of the nuclear family are more receptive to alternative ideologies. This phenomenon, however, remains limited.

60. Mark S. Granovetter, "The Strength of Weak Ties," *American Journal of Sociology* 78, 6 (May 1973): 1360–80.

61. Adrian F. Aveni, "Organizational Linkages and Resource Mobilization: The Significance of Linkage Strength and Breadth," *Sociological Quarterly* 19 (Spring 1978): 185–202.

62. David A. Snow, E. Burke Rochford Jr., Steven K. Wordon, and Robert D. Benford, "Frame Alignment Processes, Micromobilization, and Movement Participation," *American Sociological Review* 51 (1986): 464–68; and Snow and Benford, "Ideology, Frame Resonance, and Participant Mobilization."

63. *Tabligh* has been translated in various ways, but implies a missionary purpose. For the various definitions, see Muhammad Khalil Masud, "Tabligh," in Esposito, *Oxford Encyclopedia of the Modern Islamic World*, 4:162–65. For the Jama'at Tabligh, see Ahmad Mumtaz, "Tablighi Jama'at," in Esposito, *Oxford Encyclopedia of the Modern Islamic World*, 4:165–69.

64. There is frequent confusion in distinguishing members of Tabligh from Salafis. Not only do members of both movements share similar appearances, but they share many religious perspectives. However, the more active Salafi agenda is distinct from the exclusive *da'wa* orientation of Tabligh. Tabligh is purely a missionary movement, and members are not usually as well educated or involved in the Islamic sciences because they are committed primarily to *da'wa*. In a few instances, both Jordanian academics and non-Salafi Islamists conflated Tabligh with the Salafi movement.

65. A good comparison is the Pentecostal and black power movements discussed in Gerlach and Hine, *People, Power, Change*.

66. The claim that a person is not knowledgeable is used as a pejorative insult within the Salafi movement and as a polemic tool to discredit particular Salafi perspectives.

67. Although al-Bani published through Saudi companies, he was reputedly independent of Saudi influence. This is most likely due to the fact that after al-Bani taught at Medina University, he was banned from the country because some of his former students participated in the 1979 seizure of the Grand Mosque.

68. This group includes jihadi scholars who do not enjoy the financial success of reformists. As a result of scarce resources and their radical message, jihadi scholars maintain small followings.

69. Gerlach and Hine, *People, Power, Change*, 161.

70. Ibid., 46.

71. Doug McAdam, "Micromobilization Contexts and Recruitment to Activism," in Klandermans, Kriesi, and Tarrow, *From Structure to Action*, 134–35.

72. Ibid., 135–36. For the classic treatise on the "free-rider" dilemma, see Mancur Olson, *The Logic of Collective Action* (Cambridge: Harvard University Press, 1965).

73. Melucci, *Nomads of the Present*, and Schneirov and Geczik, "Alternative Health's Submerged Networks."

74. The difficulty of monitoring mosque activities throughout the country on a consistent basis means that many lessons are still given without prior approval. In such cases, the state will not impose sanctions so long as the content of the lesson is not objectionable to the authorities. Logistically, it would be difficult for the state to prevent all unregistered lessons in mosques. But the threat is always present; and since the regime has become more conscious about criticisms of its policies, especially those involving Israel, Salafi lessons in mosques have become less prevalent.

75. There are a number of Salafi conferences held in other countries that serve as opportunities for extending the informal network to the international level.

76. Most of the tapes deal with the basic principles of Salafi thought. For example, see Suleiman al-'Audah, *Hadith about the Salafi Manhaj* (in Arabic) (Amman: Tasjilat Bayt al-Maqdis al-Islamiyya, n.d.).

77. For the concept "imagined community," see Benedict Anderson, *Imagined Communities* (London: Verso, 1991).

78. These Islamic bookshops also sell mass quantities of religious tapes in addition to written materials.

79. Hilmi Asmar, interview by author, Amman, 29 October 1996.

80. Gerlach and Hine, *People, Power, Change*, 33.

81. Joseph R. Gusfield, "Social Movements and Social Change: Perspectives of Linearity and Fluidity," in *Research in Social Movements, Conflict and Change*, vol. 4, ed. Louis Kriesberg (Greenwich, Conn.: JAI Press, 1981).

82. Not all Salafis reject the term "social movement." But they point out that the term *harakat*, or movement, connotes an organized political movement. They generally accept the term "social movement" because they feel it captures the grassroots orientation of the Salafis.

83. Unlike a social movement predicated upon formal organizations, the Salafis do not maintain membership lists or records of participants. While Salafis themselves estimate that the movement is as large as the Jordanian Muslim Brotherhood, usually deemed the largest Islamic group in the kingdom, precise numbers are impossible. However, during my fieldwork, it became readily apparent that they are numerous and ubiquitous throughout Jordan. My primary informant kept a black book with Salafi phone numbers and put me in touch with Salafis all over the kingdom. In virtually every neighborhood in the large cities, there are clusters of Salafis. Interviews with non-Salafi Islamists confirmed this impression.

⟨Conclusion

1. Laurie Brand, "'In the Beginning Was the State,'" 185.

2. Finer, *Comparative Government*; Bennoune, "Algeria's Façade Democracy"; and Milton-Edwards, "Façade Democracy and Jordan."

3. See, for example, Augustus Richard Norton, ed., *Civil Society in the Middle East*, vols. 1 and 2 (Leiden: E. J. Brill, 1995, 1996); and Jillian Schwedler, ed., *Toward a Civil Society in the Middle East? A Primer* (Boulder: Lynne Rienner Publishers, 1995).

4. Rachad Antonius and Qassal Samak, "Civil Society at the Pan-Arab Level? The Role of Non-Governmental Organizations," in *Arab Nationalism and the Future of the Arab World*, ed. Hani A. Faris (Boston: Association of Arab-American University Graduates, 1987); Gharba, "Voluntary Associations in Kuwait"; Mustapha Kamal al-Sayyid, "A Civil Society in Egypt?" *Middle East Journal* 47, 2 (Spring 1993): 228–42; Sullivan, *Private Voluntary Organizations in Egypt;* Amani Kandil, *Defining the Non-Profit Sector in Egypt* (Baltimore: Johns Hopkins University Institute for Policy Studies, 1993); idem, *Civil Society in the Arab World;* Singerman, *Avenues of Participation*, 244–68; Zaki, *Civil Society and Democratization in Egypt,* 56–65; Laurie Brand, *Women, the State, and Political Liberalization: Middle Eastern and North African Experiences* (New York: Columbia University Press, 1998); and Mustapha Hamarneh, *Civil Society in Jordan* (in Arabic) (Amman: Center for Strategic Studies, 1995).

5. For the Salafis in the United States, see Steve Johnson, "Political Activity of Muslims in America," in *The Muslims of America*, ed. Yvonne Yazbeck Haddad (New York: Oxford University Press, 1991).

6. Piven and Cloward, *Poor People's Movements*, 5.

Bibliography

ARABIC SOURCES

Administrative Committee for the Union of Voluntary Societies, Amman Governate. Minutes for Meeting No. 21, 14 December 1996.

al-'Audah, Suleiman. *Hadith about the Salafi Manhaj.* Amman: Tasjilat Bayt al-Maqdis al-Islamiyya, n.d.

Center for Strategic Studies, University of Jordan. *Democracy in Jordan.* Amman: Center for Strategic Studies, 1995.

Department of Islamic Cultural Centers, Ministry of Awqaf. "Correspondence to the Lower House of Parliament," January 1996.

General Union of Voluntary Societies. *Directory of Charitable Societies.* Amman: GUVS, 1995.

———. *Executive Council Report.* Amman: GUVS, 1996.

Hamarneh, Mustapha. *Civil Society in Jordan.* Amman: Center for Strategic Studies, 1995.

Law of Preaching, Guidance, and Teaching in Mosques, Law 7 of the Year 1986. Provided by the Ministry of Awqaf.

Law of Public Meetings, Law 60 of 1953. Published in the *Official Gazette* no. 1139, 1 April 1953, p. 651.

Law of Societies and Social Organizations, Law 33 of 1966. Published in the *Official Gazette* no. 1927, 11 June 1966.

Law of Zakat Committees, as published by *al-Ra'y* (Amman), 1996.

Ministry of Awqaf. *Annual Report.* Amman: Hashemite Kingdom of Jordan, 1996.

Ministry of Culture. *Annual Report.* Amman: Hashemite Kingdom of Jordan, 1995.

Ministry of Social Development. *Annual Report.* Amman: Hashemite Kingdom of Jordan, 1995.

Sanduq al-Zakat. "Report." Amman: Hashemite Kingdom of Jordan, 1995.

Abu Shaqra, Mohammed. *The Truth about the Extremists,* sound cassette, n.d.

ENGLISH AND FRENCH SOURCES

Abun-Nasr, Jamil. "The Salafiyya Movement in Morocco: The Religious Bases of the Moroccan Nationalist Movement." *Middle Eastern Affairs (St. Anthony's Papers)* 16 (1963): 90–105.

Adams, Linda Schull. "Political Liberalization in Jordan: An Analysis of the State's Relationship with the Muslim Brotherhood." *The Journal of Church and State* 38, 3 (Summer 1996): 507–28.

Ahmad, Anis. "Ramadan." In *The Oxford Encyclopedia of the Modern Islamic World,* vol. 3, ed. John Esposito. Oxford: Oxford University Press, 1995.

Ahmed, Akbar S. "Mosque: The Mosque in Politics." In *The Oxford Encyclopedia of the Modern Islamic World,* vol. 3, ed. John Esposito. Oxford: Oxford University Press, 1995.

Ajami, Fouad. "In the Pharaoh's Shadow: Religion and Authority in Egypt." In *Islam in the Political Process,* ed. James P. Piscatori. Cambridge: Cambridge University Press, 1983.

Akaileh, Abdullah. "The Experience of the Jordanian Islamic Movement." In *Power-Sharing Islam?,* ed. Azzam Tamimi. London: Liberty for Muslim World Publications, 1993.

Akhavi, Shahrough. "Shi'ism, Corporatism, and Rentierism in the Iranian Revolution." In *Comparing Muslim Societies: Knowledge and the State in World Civilization,* ed. Juan Cole. Ann Arbor: University of Michigan Press, 1992.

Algar, Hamid. "Imam." In *The Oxford Encyclopedia of the Modern Islamic World,* vol. 2, ed. John Esposito. Oxford: Oxford University Press, 1995.

Anderson, Benedict. *Imagined Communities.* London: Verso, 1991.

Antonius, Rachad, and Qassal Samak. "Civil Society at the Pan-Arab Level? The Role of Non-Governmental Organizations." In *Arab Nationalism and the Future of the Arab World,* ed. Hani A. Faris. Boston: Association of Arab-American University Graduates, 1987.

Antoun, Richard T. "The Islamic Court, the Islamic Judge, and the Accommodation of Traditions: A Jordanian Case Study." *International Journal of Middle East Studies* 12, 4 (December 1980): 455–67.

————. *Muslim Preacher in the Modern World: A Jordanian Case Study in Comparative Perspective.* Princeton: Princeton University Press, 1989.

————. "Themes and Symbols in the Religious Lesson: A Jordanian Case Study." *International Journal of Middle East Studies* 25 (1993): 607–24.

al-'Aql, Naasir. "Principles and Methodology for the 'Aqeedah of Ahlus-Sunnah wal-Jamaa'ah." *Al-Ibaanah* 2 (August 1995): 25–26.

Aruri, Naseer H. *Jordan: A Study in Political Development (1921–1965).* The Hague: Martinus Nijhoff, 1972.

Aveni, Adrian F. "Organizational Linkages and Resource Mobilization: The Significance of Linkage Strength and Breadth." *The Sociological Quarterly* 19 (Spring 1978): 185–202.

Ayubi, Nazih N. *Political Islam: Religion and Politics in the Arab World.* London: Routledge, 1991.

Azami, M. M. *Studies in Hadith Methodology and Literature.* Indianapolis: American Trust Publications, 1992.

Bablawi, Hazem, and Giacomo Luciani, eds. *The Rentier State.* London: Croom Helm, 1987.

Baily, Clinton. *Jordan's Palestinian Challenge, 1948–1983: A Political History.* Boulder: Westview Press, 1984.

al-Bani, Mohammed Nasir al-Din. *The Knowledge of Current Affairs.* Translated by Abu Talhah Dawud ibn Ronald Burbank. Birmingham, U.K.: Jam'iat Ihyaa' Minhaaj Al-Sunnah, 1994.

————. "The Origins of Shirk." *Al-Ibaanah* 3 (April 1996): 32–33.

Bayat, Asef. *Street Politics: Poor People's Movements in Iran, 1977–1990.* New York: Columbia University Press, 1997.

————. "Un-Civil Society: The Politics of the 'Informal People'." *Third World Quarterly* 18, 1 (1997): 53–72.

Bin Baz, Abdul Aziz Bin Abdullah. "The Beautiful Names and Lofty Attributes." *Al-Ibaanah* 2 (August 1995): 31–33.

Benford, Robert D. "Frame Disputes within the Nuclear Disarmament Movement." *Social Forces* 71, 3 (March 1993): 677–701.

Ben-Nefissa, Sara. "Zakah Officielle et Zakah Non Officielle Aujord'hui en Egypte." *Egypte/Monde Arabe* 7, 3 (1991): 105–20.

Bennoune. Mahfound. "Algeria's Façade Democracy." *Middle East Report* (March–April 1990).

Berger, Morroe. *Islam in Egypt Today: Social and Political Aspects of Popular Religion.* Cambridge: Cambridge University Press, 1970.

Berkey, Jonathan. *The Transmission of Knowledge in Medieval Cairo: A Social History of Islamic Education.* Princeton: Princeton University Press, 1992.

Bianchi, Robert. *Interest Groups and Political Development in Turkey.* Princeton: Princeton University Press, 1984.

———. *Unruly Corporatism: Associational Life in Twentieth-Century Egypt.* Oxford: Oxford University Press, 1989.

Bill, James A. "The Plasticity of Informal Politics: The Case of Iran." *The Middle East Journal* 28, 2 (1973): 131–51.

Borthwick, Bruce M. "The Islamic Sermon as a Channel of Political Communication." *Middle East Journal* 21, 3 (1967): 299–313.

Boulby, Marion. *The Muslim Brotherhood and the Kings of Jordan, 1945–1993.* Atlanta: Scholars Press, 1999.

Brand, Laurie A. "Economic and Political Liberalization in a Rentier Economy: The Case of the Hashemite Kingdom of Jordan." In *Privatization and Liberalization in the Middle East,* ed. Iliya Harik and Denis J. Sullivan. Bloomington: Indiana University Press, 1992.

———. "Palestinians and Jordanians: A Crisis of Identity." *Journal of Palestine Studies* 96, 4 (Summer 1995): 46–61.

———. "'In the Beginning was the State . . .': The Quest for Civil Society in Jordan." In vol. 1 of *Civil Society in the Middle East,* ed. Augustus Richard Norton. New York: Brill, 1995.

———. *Women, the State, and Political Liberalization: Middle Eastern and North African Experiences.* New York: Columbia University Press, 1998.

Brockett, Charles D. "The Structure of Political Opportunities and Peasant Mobilization in Central America." *Comparative Politics* 23 (1991): 253–74.

Brown, Leon Carl. "The Islamic Reformist Movement in North Africa." *The Journal of Modern African Studies* 2, 1 (1964): 55–63.

Brumberg, Daniel. "Survival Strategies vs. Democratic Bargains: The Politics of Economic Reform in Contemporary Egypt." In *The Politics of Economic Reform in the Middle East,* edited by Henri Barkey. New York: St. Martin's Press, 1992.

———. "Authoritarian Legacies and Reform Strategies in the Arab World." In *Theoretical Perspectives,* ed. Rex Brynen, Bahgat Korany, and Paul Noble. Vol. 1 of *Political Liberalization and Democratization in the Arab World.* Boulder: Lynne Rienner, 1995.

Brynen, Rex. "Economic Crisis and Post-Rentier Democratization in the Arab World: The Case of Jordan." *Canadian Journal of Political Science* 25, 1 (March 1992): 69–97.

Brynen, Rex, Bahgat Korany, and Paul Noble, eds. *Theoretical Perspectives.* Vol. 1 of *Political Liberalization and Democratization in the Arab World.* Boulder: Lynne Rienner, 1995.

Buechler, Steven M. *Women's Movements in the United States.* New Brunswick, N.J.: Rutgers University Press, 1990.

Burstein, Paul, Rachael L. Einwohner, and Jocelyn A. Hollander. "The Success of Political Movements: A Bargaining Perspective." In *The Politics of Social Movement Protest: Comparative Perspectives on States and Social Movements*, ed. Craig Jenkins and Bert Klandermans. Minneapolis: University of Minnesota Press, 1995.

Campo, Juan Eduardo. "Mosque: Historical Development." In *The Oxford Encyclopedia of the Modern Islamic World*, vol. 3, ed. John Esposito. Oxford: Oxford University Press, 1995.

Clark, Janine Astrid. "Democratization and Social Islam: A Case Study of Islamic Clinics in Cairo." In *Theoretical Perspectives*, ed. Rex Brynen, Bahgat Korany, and Paul Noble. Vol. 1 of *Political Liberalization and Democratization in the Arab World*. Boulder: Lynne Rienner, 1995.

————. "Islamic Social Welfare Organizations in Cairo: Islamization from Below?" *Arab Studies Quarterly* 17, 4 (1995): 11–28.

————. "Gender Dynamics of Intra-Party Activism: The Expanding Role of Islamist Women in Jordan's IAF." Paper presented at the Middle East Studies Association Annual Conference, Washington, D.C., 20–22 November 1999.

Clemens, Elisabeth S. "Organizational Repertoires and Institutional Change: Women's Groups and the Transformation of U.S. Politics, 1890–1920." *American Journal of Sociology* 98, 4 (January 1993): 755–98.

Cohen, Amnon. *Political Parties in the West Bank under the Jordanian Regime, 1949–1967*. Ithaca: Cornell University Press, 1980.

Cohen, Stanley. *Visions of Social Control: Crime, Punishment, and Classification*. Cambridge: Polity Press, 1985.

Curtis, Russell L., Jr., and Louis A. Zurcher. "Stable Resources of Protest Movements: The Multiorganizational Field." *Social Forces* 52 (September 1973): 53–61.

Dabbas, Hamed. "Islamic Centers, Associations, Societies, Organizations, and Committees in Jordan." In *Islamic Movements in Jordan*, ed. Jillian Schwedler. Amman: al-Urdun al-Jadid Research Center, 1997.

Dann, Uriel. *King Hussein and the Challenge of Arab Radicalism: Jordan, 1955–1967*. Oxford: Oxford University Press, 1989.

Denoeux, Guilain. *Urban Unrest in the Middle East: A Comparative Study of Informal Networks in Egypt, Iran, and Lebanon*. Albany: State University of New York Press, 1993.

Dessouki, Ali E. Hillal. "Official Islam and Political Legitimation in the Arab Countries." In *The Islamic Impulse*, ed. Barbara Freyer Stowasser. London: Croom Helm, 1987.

Donahue, John J., and John Esposito, eds. *Islam in Transition: Muslim Perspectives*. New York: Oxford University Press, 1982.

Eickelman, Dale F., and James Piscatori. *Muslim Politics*. Princeton: Princeton University Press, 1996.

Ericson, R. V., and P. M. Baranek. *The Ordering of Justice: A Study of Accused Persons as Dependents in the Criminal Process*. Vancouver: University of British Columbia Press, 1982.

Fareed, Shaikh Ahmad. *On the Issue of Takfir*. Suffolk, U.K.: Jani'iat Ihyaa' Minhaaj Al-Sunnah, 1997.

Farhan, Ishaq. "The Islamic Stand towards Political Involvement (with Reference to the Jordanian Experience)." Unpublished paper, 1996.

Farsoun, Samih K. "Family Structure and Society in Modern Lebanon." In *Peoples and Cultures of the Middle East*, ed. Lousie Sweet. Garden City, N.Y.: National History Press, 1970.

Farsoun, Samih K., and Lucia P. Fort. "The Problematics of Civil Society: Intellectual Discourse and Arab Intellectuals." Unpublished paper, 1992.

Fathi, Asghar. "Preachers as Substitutes for Mass Media: The Case of Iran, 1905–1909." In *Towards a Modern Iran*, ed. Elie Kedourie and Sylvia G. Haim. London: Cass, 1980.

———. "The Islamic Pulpit as a Medium of Political Communication." *Journal for the Scientific Study of Religion* 20, 2 (1981): 163–72.

———. "Khutba." In *The Oxford Encyclopedia of the Modern Islamic World*, vol. 2, ed. John Esposito. Oxford: Oxford University Press, 1995.

Fathi, Schirin. *Jordan—An Invented Nation? Tribe-State Dynamics and the Formation of National Identity*. Hamburg: Deutches Orient-Institut, 1994.

Finer, S. E. *Comparative Government*. London: Pelican, 1970.

Foran, John, ed. *A Century of Revolution: Social Movements in Iran*. Minneapolis: University of Minnesota Press, 1994.

Foucault, Michel. *Discipline and Punish*. New York: Vintage Books, 1979.

Freeman, Jo. "The Origins of the Women's Liberation Movement." *American Journal of Sociology* 78 (1973): 792–811.

Freij, Hanna Y., and Leonard C. Robinson. "Liberalization, the Islamists, and the Stability of the Arab State: Jordan as a Case Study." *The Muslim World* 86, 1 (January 1996): 1–32.

Gaffney, Patrick D. "The Changing Voice of Islam: The Emergence of Professional Preachers in Contemporary Egypt." *The Muslim World* 81, 1 (January 1991): 27–47.

———. *The Prophet's Pulpit: Islamic Preaching in Contemporary Egypt*. Berkeley: University of California Press, 1994.

———. "Mosque: The Mosque in Society." In *The Oxford Encyclopedia of the Modern Islamic World*, vol. 3, ed. John Esposito. Oxford: Oxford University Press, 1995.

Gamson, William A. *The Strategy of Social Protest.* Homewood, Ill.: Dorsey Press, 1975.

Gellner, Ernest, and John Waterbury, eds. *Patrons and Clients in Mediterranean Societies.* London: Duckworth, 1977.

General Union of Voluntary Societies. *GUVS, An Overview.* Amman: GUVS, 1995.

———. *Profiles, Programs, Projects.* Amman: GUVS, 1996.

Gerlach, Luther P., and Virginia H. Hine. *People, Power, Change: Movements of Social Transformation.* Indianapolis: Bobbs-Merrill, 1970.

Ghadbian, Najib. *Democratization and the Islamist Challenge in the Arab World.* Boulder: Westview Press, 1997.

Gharba, Shafeeq. "Voluntary Associations in Kuwait: The Foundation of a New System." *Middle East Journal* 45, 2 (Spring 1991): 199–215.

Gould, Roger V. "Multiple Networks and Mobilization in the Paris Commune, 1871." *American Sociological Review* 56, 6 (December 1991): 716–29.

———. *Insurgent Identities: Class, Community, and Protest in Paris from 1848 to the Commune.* Chicago: University of Chicago Press, 1995.

Granovetter, Mark S. "The Strength of Weak Ties." *American Journal of Sociology* 78, 6 (May 1973): 1360–80.

Gusfield, Joseph R. "Social Movements and Social Change: Perspectives of Linearity and Fluidity." In *Research in Social Movements, Conflict, and Change*, vol. 4, ed. Louis Kriesberg. Greenwich, Conn.: JAI Press, 1981.

Haddad, Yvonne Yazbeck. "Operation Desert Storm and the War of the Fatwas." In *Islamic Legal Interpretation: Muftis and Their Fatwas*, ed. Khalid M. Masud. Cambridge: Harvard University Press, 1996.

al-Halabi, 'Ali Hasan. *Fundamentals of Commanding Good and Forbidding Evil According to Shaykh Ul-Islam Ibn Taymiyya.* Cincinnati, Ohio: Al-Quran Was-Sunnah Society of North America, 1995.

———. "Tarbiyah: The Key to Victory." *Al-Ibaanah* 2 (August 1995): 15–19.

Hammady, Iman Roushdy. "Religious Medical Clinics in Cairo." Master's thesis no. 885, American University in Cairo, 1990.

Hannigan, John A. "Social Movement Theory and the Sociology of Religion: Toward a New Synthesis." *Sociological Analysis* 52, 4 (1991): 311–31.

Hermassi, Abdelbaki. "The Political and Religious in the Modern History of the Maghrib." In *Islamism and Secularism in North Africa*, ed. John Reudy. New York: St. Martin's Press, 1994.

al-Hilali, Saleem. "Who is the Victorious Group." *Al-Ibaanah* 2 (August 1995): 39–42.

Hirschman, Albert O. *Exit, Voice, and Loyalty.* Cambridge: Harvard University Press, 1970.

Hourani, Hani, Taleb Awad, Hamed Dabbas, and Sa'eda Kilani. *Islamic Action Front Party.* Amman: Al-Urdun Al-Jadid Research Center, 1993.

Hourani, Hani, Hamed Dabbas, Taleb Awad, and Omar Shnikat. *Jordanian Politics Parties.* Amman: Al-Urdun Al-Jadid Research Center, 1993.

Hudson, Michael C. *Arab Politics: The Search for Legitimacy.* New Haven: Yale University Press, 1977.

Human Rights Watch. *Jordan: Clamping Down on Critics: Human Rights Violations in Advance of the Parliamentary Elections,* vol. 9, no. 12 (October). New York: Human Rights Watch, 1997.

Ibn Khaldoun Center for Development Studies. *An Assessment of Grass-Roots Participation in Egypt's Development.* Unpublished study, 1993.

International Press Office, Royal Hashemite Court. *Selected Speeches by His Majesty King Hussein, The Hashemite Kingdom of Jordan, 1988–1994,* 2d ed. Amman: International Press Office, Royal Hashemite Court, 1995.

Jam'iat Ihyaa' Minhaaj Al-Sunnah. *A Brief Introduction to the Salafi Da'wah.* Ipswich, Suffolk, U.K.: Jam'iat Ihyaa' Minhaaj Al-Sunnah, 1993.

al-Jibali, Muhammad. *Allah's Rights upon His Servants: Tawhid vs. Shirk.* Cincinnati, Ohio: Al-Quran Was-Sunnah Society of North America, 1995.

Johnson, Steve. "Political Activity of Muslims in America." In *The Muslims of America,* ed. Yvonne Yazbeck Haddad. New York: Oxford University Press, 1991.

Kahf, Monzer. "Waqf." In *The Oxford Encyclopedia of the Modern Islamic World,* vol. 4, ed. John Esposito. Oxford: Oxford University Press, 1995.

Kalami, Mohammad Hashim. *Principles of Islamic Jurisprudence,* revised edition. Cambridge: Islamic Text Society, 1991.

Kandil, Amani. *Defining the Non-Profit Sector in Egypt.* Baltimore: Johns Hopkins University Institute for Policy Studies, 1993.

———. *Civil Society in the Arab World: Private Voluntary Organizations.* Washington, D.C.: Civicus, 1995.

Karawan, Ibrahim A. "Monarchs, Mullas, and Marshals: Islamic Regimes?" *The Annals of the American Academy of Political and Social Science* 524 (November 1992): 103–19.

———. "Takfir." In *Oxford Encyclopedia of the Modern Islamic World,* vol. 4, ed. John Esposito. New York: Oxford University Press, 1995.

Kepel, Gilles. *Muslim Extremism in Egypt: The Prophet and the Pharaoh.* Berkeley: University of California Press, 1986.

El Khatib, Abdullah. "The Experience of NGOs in Jordan (A Brief Description)." Paper presented at the Experts Meeting on Strategies for Strengthening NGO Networking and Research in the Middle East, Arab Thought Forum, Amman, 26 March 1994.

———. "The Impact of the Third Sector in Economic Development of Jordan." Paper presented at the ISTR Second International Conference, Mexico City, 18–21 July 1996.

Kitschelt, Herbert P. "Political Opportunity Structures and Political Protest: Anti-Nuclear Movements in Four Democracies." *British Journal of Political Science* 16 (1986): 57–85.

Klandermans, Bert. "The Formation and Mobilization of Consensus." In *From Structure to Action: Comparing Movement Participation across Cultures*, ed. Bert Klandermans, Hanspeter Kriesi, and Sydney Tarrow. Vol. 1 of *International Social Movement Research*. Greenwich, Conn.: JAI Press, 1988.

———. "Introduction: Interorganizational Networks." In *Organizing for Change: Social Movement Organizations in Europe and the United States*, ed. Bert Klandermans. Vol. 2 of *International Social Movement Research*. Greenwich, Conn.: JAI Press, 1989.

———. "Linking the 'Old' and the 'New': Movement Networks in the Netherlands." In *Challenging the Political Order: New Social and Political Movements in Western Democracies*, ed. Russell J. Dalton. New York: Oxford University Press, 1990.

Korany, Bahgat, Rex Brynen, and Paul Noble, eds. *Comparative Experiences*. Vol. 2. of *Political Liberalization and Democratization in the Arab World*. Boulder: Lynne Rienner, 1998.

Kriesi, Hanspeter, Ruud Koopmans, Jan Willem Duyvendak, and Marco G. Giugni. *New Social Movements in Western Europe: A Comparative Analysis*. Minneapolis: University of Minnesota Press, 1995.

Kurzman, Charles. "Structural Opportunity and Perceived Opportunity in Social Movement Theory: The Iranian Revolution of 1979." *American Sociological Review* 61 (February 1996): 153–70.

Lapidus, Ira M. *Muslim Cities in the Late Middle Ages*. Cambridge: Cambridge University Press, 1967.

———. "Hierarchies and Social Networks: A Comparison of Chinese and Islamic Societies." In *Conflict and Control in Late Imperial China*, ed. F. J. Wakemann. Berkeley: University of California Press, 1975.

Layne, Linda L. *Home and Homeland: The Dialogics of Tribal and National Identities in Jordan*. Princeton: Princeton University Press, 1994.

Linz, Juan J. *The Breakdown of Democratic Regimes: Crisis, Breakdown, and Reequilibration*. Baltimore: Johns Hopkins University Press, 1978.

Loveman, Mara. "High-Risk Collective Action: Defending Human Rights in Chile, Uruguay, and Argentina," *American Journal of Sociology* 104, 2 (September 1998): 477–525.

Luciani, Giacomo. "Economic Foundations of Democracy and Authoritarianism: The Arab World in Comparative Perspective." *Arab Studies Quarterly* 10, 4 (Fall 1988): 457–75.

"Mankind's Greatest Need." *Al-Ibaanah* 1, 2 (August 1995): 9–12.

El Mansour, Mohamed. "Salafis and Modernists in the Moroccan Nationalist Movement." In *Islamism and Secularism in North Africa*, ed. John Reudy. New York: St. Martin's Press, 1994.

Masud, Muhammad Khalil. "Tabligh." In *Oxford Encyclopedia of the Modern Islamic World*, vol. 4, ed. John Esposito. New York: Oxford University Press, 1994.

McAdam, Doug. *Political Process and the Development of Black Insurgency, 1930–1970*. Chicago: University of Chicago Press, 1982.

———. "Tactical Innovation and the Pace of Insurgency." *American Sociological Review* 48, 6 (December 1983): 735–54.

———. "Recruitment to High-Risk Activism: The Case of Freedom Summer." *American Journal of Sociology* 92 (1986): 64–90.

———. "Micromobilization Contexts and Recruitment to Activism." In *From Structure to Action: Comparing Movement Participation across Cultures*, ed. Bert Klandermans, Hanspeter Kriesi, and Sydney Tarrow. Vol. 1 of *International Social Movement Research*. Greenwich, Conn.: JAI Press, 1988.

McAdam, Doug, and Ronnelle Paulsen. "Specifying the Relationship between Social Ties and Activism." *American Journal of Sociology* 98 (1993): 640–67.

McCarthy, John D., David W. Britt, and Mark Wolfson. "The Institutional Channeling of Social Movements by the State in the United States." In *Research in Social Movements, Conflict, and Change*, vol. 13, ed. Louis Kriesberg. Greenwich, Conn.: JAI Press, 1991.

Melucci, Alberto. *Nomads of the Present: Social Movements and Individual Needs in Contemporary Society*. Edited by John Keane and Paul Mier. Philadelphia: Temple University Press, 1989.

———. *Challenging Codes: Collective Action in the Information Age*. Cambridge: Cambridge University Press, 1996.

Milton-Edwards, Beverley. "A Temporary Alliance with the Crown: The Islamic Response in Jordan." In *Islamic Fundamentalisms and the Gulf Crisis*, ed. James Piscatori. Chicago: Fundamentalism Project of the American Academy of Arts and Sciences, 1991.

————. "Façade Democracy and Jordan." *The British Journal of Middle East Studies* 20, 2 (1993): 191–203.

————. "Climate of Change in Jordan's Islamist Movement." In *Islamic Fundamentalisms*, ed. Abdel Salam Sidahmed and Anoushiravan Ehteshami. Boulder: Westview Press, 1996.

Mishal, Shaul. *West Bank/East Bank: The Palestinians in Jordan, 1948–1967.* New Haven: Yale University Press, 1978.

Mitchell, Richard P. *The Society of the Muslim Brothers.* London: Oxford University Press, 1969.

Mitchell, Timothy. *Colonising Egypt.* Berkeley: University of California Press, 1988.

Morris, Aldon D. *The Origins of the Civil Rights Movement: Black Communities Organizing for Change.* New York: Free Press, 1984.

Morsy, Soheir. "Islamic Clinics in Egypt: The Cultural Elaboration of Biomedical Hegemony." *Medical Anthropology Quarterly* 2, 4 (December 1988): 355–69.

Mufti, Malik. "Elite Bargains and the Onset of Political Liberalization in Jordan." *Comparative Political Studies* 32, 1 (February 1999): 100–129.

Mumtaz, Ahmad. "Tablighi Jama'at." In *Oxford Encyclopedia of the Modern Islamic World*, vol. 4, ed. John Esposito. New York: Oxford University Press, 1995.

Norton, Augustus Richard. *Civil Society in the Middle East.* Vol 1. Leiden: E. J. Brill, 1995.

————. *Civil Society in the Middle East.* Vol. 2. Leiden: E. J. Brill, 1996.

Oberschall, Anthony. *Social Conflict and Social Movements.* Engelwood Cliffs, N.J.: Prentice-Hall, 1973.

Oliver, Pamela E. "Bringing the Crowd Back in: The Nonorganizational Elements of Social Movements." In *Research in Social Movements, Conflict and Change*, vol. 11, ed. Louis Kriesberg. Greenwich, Conn.: JAI Press, 1989.

Olson, Mancur. *The Logic of Collective Action.* Cambridge: Harvard University Press, 1965.

Opp, Karl-Dieter, and Christiane Gern. "Dissident Groups, Personal Networks and Spontaneous Cooperation: The East German Revolution of 1989." *American Sociological Review* 58 (1993): 659–80.

Parsa, Misagh. *Social Origins of the Iranian Revolution.* New Brunswick, N.J.: Rutgers University Press, 1989.

Peters, Rudolph. *Jihad in Classical and Modern Islam.* Princeton: Markus Wiener Publishers, 1996.

Pfaff, Steven. "Collective Identity and Informal Groups in Revolutionary Mobilization: East Germany in 1989." *Social Forces* 75, 1 (September 1996): 91–118.

Phillips, Susan D. "Meaning and Structure in Social Movements: Mapping the Network of National Canadian Women's Organizations." *Canadian Journal of Political Science* 24, 4 (December 1991): 755–82.

Pickthall, Mohammed Marmaduke. *The Meaning of the Holy Quran*. New Delhi: UBS Publishers' Distributors, 1995.

Piscatori, James P. "Ideological Politics in Sa'udi Arabia." In *Islam in the Political Process*, ed. James P. Piscatori. Cambridge: Cambridge University Press, 1983.

———. "Religion and Realpolitik: Islamic Responses to the Gulf War." In *Islamic Fundamentalisms and the Gulf Crisis*, ed. James Piscatori. Chicago: Fundamentalism Project of the American Academy of Arts and Sciences, 1991.

Piven, Frances Fox, and Richard A. Cloward. *Poor People's Movements: Why They Succeed, How They Fail*. New York: Vintage Books, 1979.

———. "Normalizing Collective Protest." In *Frontiers in Social Movement Theory*, ed. Aldon D. Morris and Carol McClurg Mueller. New Haven: Yale University Press, 1992.

Political Party Law, Law 32 of 1992. Published in the *Official Gazette* no. 3851, 1 September 1992, p. 1670.

Porter, Sam. "Contra-Foucault: Soldiers, Nurses, and Power." *Sociology* 30, 1 (February 1996): 59–79.

Provisional Law 5 of 1993, Amendment to the Law of Election to the House of Deputies, Law 22 of 1986. Amman: Press and Publications Department, 1993.

Rath, Katherine. "The Process of Democratization in Jordan." *Middle Eastern Studies* 30, 3 (July 1994): 530–57.

Roald, Anne Sofie. *Tarbiya: Education and Politics in Islamic Movements in Jordan and Malaysia*. Stockholm, Sweden: Almqvist and Wiksell, 1994.

Roberts, Hugh. "From Radical Mission to Equivocal Ambition: The Expansion and Manipulation of Algerian Islamism, 1979–1992." In *Accounting for Fundamentalisms: The Dynamic Character of Movements*, ed. Martin E. Marty and R. Scott Appleby. Chicago: University of Chicago, 1994.

Robinson, Glenn E. "Can Islamists Be Democrats? The Case of Jordan." *The Middle East Journal* 51, 3 (Summer 1997): 373–88.

———. "Defensive Democratization in Jordan." *International Journal of Middle East Studies* 30 (1998): 387–410.

Rucht, Dieter. "Environmental Movement Organizations in West Germany and France: Structure and Interorganizational Relations." In *Organizing for Change: Social Movement Organizations in Europe and the United States*. Vol. 2 of *International Social Movement Research*, Greenwich, Conn.: JAI Press, 1989.

———. "The Impact of National Contexts on Social Movement Structures: A Cross-Movement and Cross-National Comparison." In *Comparative Perspectives on Social Movements: Political Opportunities, Mobilizing Structures, and Cultural Framings*, ed. Doug McAdam, John D. McCarthy, and Mayer N. Zald. Cambridge: Cambridge University Press, 1996.

El-Said, Sabah. *Between Pragmatism and Ideology: The Muslim Brotherhood in Jordan*. Policy Paper no. 39. Washington, D.C.: The Washington Institute for Near East Policy, 1995.

Salibi, Kamal. *The Modern History of Jordan*. London: I. B. Tauris, 1993.

Satloff, Robert B. *Troubles on the East Bank: Challenges to the Domestic Stability of Jordan*. Policy Paper no. 39. Washington, D.C.: The Washington Institute for Near East Policy, 1986.

———. "Jordan's Great Gamble: Economic Crisis and Political Reform." In *The Politics of Economic Reform in the Middle East*, ed. Henri Barkey. New York: St. Martin's Press, 1992.

———. *From Abdullah to Hussein: Jordan in Transition*. Oxford: Oxford University Press, 1994.

al-Sayyid, Mustapha Kamel. "A Civil Society in Egypt?" *Middle East Journal* 47, 2 (Spring 1993): 228–42.

Schattschneider, E. E. *The Semi-Sovereign People*. New York: Holt, Rinehart, & Winston, 1960.

Schelling, Thomas C. *The Strategy of Conflict*. New York: Oxford University Press, 1963.

Schimmel, Annemarie. *And Muhammad is His Messenger: The Veneration of the Prophet in Islamic Piety*. Chapel Hill: University of North Carolina Press, 1985.

Schneider, Cathy Lisa. *Shantytown Protest in Pinochet's Chile*. Philadelphia: Temple University Press, 1995.

Schneirov, Matthew, and Jonathan David Geczik. "Alternative Health's Submerged Networks and the Transformation of Identity." *The Sociological Quarterly* 37, 4 (1996): 627–44.

Schwedler, Jillian, ed. *Toward a Civil Society in the Middle East? A Primer*. Boulder: Lynne Rienner, 1995.

Scott, James. *Weapons of the Weak: Everyday Forms of Peasant Resistance*. New Haven: Yale University Press, 1985.

————. *Domination and the Arts of Resistance: Hidden Transcripts.* New Haven: Yale University Press, 1990.

Sewell, Graham, and Barry Wilkinson. "'Someone to Watch over Me': Surveillance, Discipline, and the Just-in-Time Labour Process." *Sociology* 26, 2 (May 1992): 271–90.

Shahin, Emad Eldin. "Salafiyyah." In *Oxford Encyclopedia of the Modern Islamic World*, vol. 3, ed. John Esposito. New York: Oxford University Press, 1995.

al-Sheikh, Abdullah. "Zakat." In *Oxford Encyclopedia of the Modern Islamic World*, vol. 4, ed. John Esposito. New York Oxford University Press, 1995.

Siddiqi, Muhammad Zubayr. *Hadith Literature: Its Origins, Development, and Special Features.* Cambridge: The Islamic Texts Society, 1993.

Singerman, Diane. *Avenues of Participation: Family, Politics, and Networks in Urban Quarters of Cairo.* Princeton: Princeton University Press, 1995.

Sivan, Emmanuel. *Radical Islam: Medieval Theology and Modern Politics.* New Haven: Yale University Press, 1991.

Snow, David A., and Robert D. Benford. "Ideology, Frame Resonance, and Participant Mobilization." In *From Structure to Action: Comparing Movement Participation across Cultures,* ed. Bert Klandermans, Hanspeter Kriesi, and Sidney Tarrow. Vol. 1 of *International Social Movement Research.* Greenwich, Conn.: JAI Press, 1988.

Snow, David A., E. Burke Rochford Jr., Steven K. Wordon, and Robert D. Benford. "Frame Alignment Processes, Micromobilization, and Movement Participation." *American Sociological Review* 51 (1986): 464–81.

Snow, David A., Louis A Zurcher, Jr., and Dheldon Ekland-Olson. "Social Networks and Social Movements: A Microstructural Approach to Differential Recruitment." *American Sociological Review* 45, 5 (October 1980): 787–801.

Sonn, Tamara. "Tawhid." In *Oxford Encyclopedia of the Modern Islamic World,* vol. 4, ed. John Esposito. New York: Oxford University Press, 1995.

Stark, Rodney, and William Sims Bainbridge. "Networks of Faith: Interpersonal Bonds and Recruitment to Cults and Sects." *American Journal of Sociology* 85, 6 (May 1980): 1376–95.

Stoecker, Randy. "Community, Movement, Organization: The Problem of Identity Convergence in Collective Action." *The Sociological Quarterly* 36, 1 (1995): 111–30.

Sullivan, Denis J. *Private Voluntary Organizations in Egypt: Islamic Development, Private Initiative, and State Control.* Gainesville: University of Florida Press, 1994.

Taji-Farouki, Suha. "Hizb Al-Tahrir." In *Oxford Encyclopedia of the Modern Islamic World*, vol. 2, ed. John Esposito. New York: Oxford University Press, 1995.

Tal, Lawrence. "Dealing with Radical Islam: The Case of Jordan." *Survival* 37, 3 (Autumn 1995): 139–56.

Taraki, Lisa. "Islam is the Solution: Jordanian Islamists and the Dilemma of the 'Modern Woman'." *British Journal of Sociology* 46, 4 (December 1995): 643–61.

———. "Jordanian Islamists and the Agenda for Women: Between Discourse and Practice." *Middle Eastern Studies* 32, 1 (January 1996): 140–58.

Tarrow, Sidney. *Power in Movement: Social Movements, Collective Action and Politics*. Cambridge: Cambridge University Press, 1994.

Taylor, Verta, and Nancy E. Whittier. "Collective Identity in Social Movement Communities: Lesbian Feminist Mobilization." In *Frontiers in Social Movement Theory*, ed. Aldon D. Morris and Carol McClurg Mueller. New Haven: Yale University Press, 1992.

Tilly, Charles. *From Mobilization to Revolution*. Reading, Mass.: Addison-Wesley, 1978.

Tozy, Mohammed. "Islam and the State." In *Polity and Society in Contemporary North Africa*, ed. I. W. Zartman and W. M. Habeeb. Boulder: Westview Press, 1993.

Tripp, Charles. "Islam and the Secular Logic of the State in the Middle East." In *Islamic Fundamentalism*, ed. Abdel Salam Sidahmed and Anoushiravan Ehteshami. Boulder: Westview Press, 1996.

Tsugitaka, Sato, ed. *Islamic Urbanism in Human History: Political Power and Social Networks*. London: Kegan Paul International, 1997.

United States Department of State. *Jordan Human Rights Report*. Amman: United States Embassy, 1996.

Vatin, Jean-Claude. "Popular Puritanism versus State Reformism: Islam in Algeria." In *Islam in the Political Process*, ed. James P. Piscatori. Cambridge: Cambridge University Press, 1983.

Voll, John O. "Renewal and Reform in Islamic History: *Tajdid and Islah*." In *Voices of Resurgent Islam*, ed. John Esposito. Oxford: Oxford University Press, 1983.

———. "Fundamentalism in the Sunni Arab World: Egypt and the Sudan." In *Fundamentalisms Observed*, ed. Martin E. Marty and R. Scott Appleby. Chicago: University of Chicago Press, 1991.

Wagner, Peter. *A Sociology of Modernity: Liberty and Discipline*. London: Routledge, 1994.

Wiktorowicz, Quintan, and Suha Taji-Farouki. "Islamic Non-Governmental Organizations and Muslim Politics: A Case from Jordan." *Third World Quarterly* 21, 4 (Summer 2000).

Williams, John Alden. "Khawarij." In *Oxford Encyclopedia of the Modern Islamic World*, vol. 2, ed. John Esposito. New York: Oxford University Press, 1995.

Wilson, Mary. *King Abdullah, Britain, and the Making of Jordan.* Cambridge: Cambridge University Press, 1987.

al-Yassini, Ayman. *Religion and State in the Kingdom of Saudi Arabia.* Boulder: Westview Press, 1985.

Zaki, Moheb. *Civil Society and Democratization in Egypt, 1981–1994.* Cairo: Konrad Adenauer Foundation, 1995.

Zald, Mayer N., and John D. McCarthy, eds. *Social Movements in an Organizational Society.* New Brunswick, N.J.: Transaction Books, 1987.

Zartman, I. William. "Opposition as Support of the State." In *Beyond Coercion: The Durability of the Arab State*, ed. Adeed Dawisha and I. William Zartman. London: Croom Helm, 1988.

Zaynoo, Muhammad Ibn Jameel. "Methodology of the Saved Sect." *Al-Ibaanah* 3 (April 1996): 22–26.

Zhao, Dingxin. "Ecologies of Social Movements: Student Mobilization during the 1989 Prodemocracy Movement in Beijing." *American Journal of Sociology* 103, 6 (May 1998): 1493–1529.

Zuo, Jiping, and Robert D. Benford. "Mobilization Processes and the 1989 Chinese Democracy Movement." *The Sociological Quarterly* 36, 1 (1995): 131–56.

NEWSPAPERS CITED

Amman Al-Safir (Amman)
Jordan Times (Amman)
The Star (Amman)
al-Destour (Amman)
al-Ra'y (Amman)

INTERVIEWS CITED

Mifli Adabas, Director of Preaching and Guidance, Ministry of Awqaf, Amman, 5 October 1996

Director of Cultural Exchange, Ministry of Culture, Amman, 8 October 1996

Zaid Abu Ghamineh, Islamic Hospital administrator, Amman, 13 October 1996

Ra'if Nijim, Independent Islamist, Amman, 15 October 1996

Omar Subeyhe, Director of the Preservation of the Qur'an Society, Amman, 16 October 1996

Leader of the Jordanian Mu'tazila Movement, Amman, 19 October 1996.

'Ali Hasan al-Halabi, Salafi Zarqa, 26 October 1996

GUVS official, Amman, 28 October 1996

Hilmi Asmar, Muslim Brother, Amman, 29 October 1996

Founder of the Coalition for Jordanian Women, Amman, 5 November 1996

Leader in the Center for Women's Studies, Amman, 5 November 1996

Director of the Department of Islamic Centers, Ministry of Awqaf, 7 November 1996

Abdul Latif Arabiyyat, Muslim Brother, Amman, 27 November 1996

Leader of an informal women's group, Amman, 14 December 1996

Hashem Azzan, Independent Islamist, Amman, 17 February 1997

Layth Shubaylat, Independent Islamist, Amman, 13 March 1997

President of Islamic Charitable Organization, Zarqa, 18 March 1997

Women's movement activist, Amman, 20 March 1997

Shaykh Huthayfa, Salafi, Amman, 25 March 1997

Mahmoud Kafawee, Director of Chartiable Organizations, Ministry of Social Development, Amman, 28 March 1997

Mohammed Raoud, Salafi, Amman, 1 April 1997

Salim al-Hilali, Salafi, Amman, 2 April 1997

Index